Hype&Sou!

Behind the scenes at Motown
The official archives of the legendary
Hitsville spin doctor

AL ABRAMS

temple Street

DEDICATION

As the Five Royales sang so well in the unfortunately non-Motown song,
"(This is) Dedicated to the One I Love."
Simply put, there is only one reason you are even holding this book in your hand today. And that is because my wife, Nancy Cecilia, has devoted much of her life during these past few years into making my book become a first-person integrated history lesson in pop culture.
This is a story that goes far beyond just changing the music world. It is one in which the musical score of Motown became the soundtrack to the unfolding Civil Rights movement in the United States, and thus intertwined the two as intricately as black and white.
Had my wife chosen to devote all her time and efforts into her personal legacy, she would today be dedicating a book of her creation hopefully to me. Instead, she opted to put aside her own ambitions to concentrate on my Motown legacy and on raising our family,
and I will forever be grateful.
She made *Hype & Soul* a reality through her dedication and diligence so as to insure that every last and minor detail of my Motown memoir would be accurate and heartfelt -
even without my "Hype." And for this I will only say that
"I Love The Way You Love."
I would be remiss if I didn't mention the other members of our little family: My daughter and namesake, Alannah Rose, whose interest in music rivals my own at the same age, and whose insight into the current music scene makes me feel well … rather old. Thank you for being my daughter. I hope to see you take center stage in whatever you endeavor to do and wherever life takes you.
And there are those who contributed merely with their presence: our long-time loyal family dog, N.D. Irish Rose, an oddly-named black wrinkled Chinese Sharpei who loved us and snow in equal measures. She was seventeen-plus when she left us.
Plus our two rescue cats, a friendly inquisitive torty named Misty (who is the song's namesake because as a kitten she was found helpless, up a tree) and a grey and white tabby named Hunnee Adelaide; as well as Dudes Black Mist (Emmy), my daughter's beautiful black American Quarter Horse.
This is also dedicated to the abandoned stray feral kittens and cat we came to love:
Chanukah, Christmas and Dreamsicle.

The receipt book opposite is the original cash disbursement book beginning with the company's move to the Hitsville USA studio on West Grand Boulevard in 1959. The receipts, which originally bore the rubber stamp ownership of Berry Gordy, Jr. Enterprises, covered cash advances to artists, royalties received and even receipts for the rental of the studio for sessions by other Detroit indie record producers. They are signed by Raynoma Liles (Gordy), Esther Edwards, Janie Bradford and even Berry himself, among others. The June 30, 1960 receipt for my return of $146.98 (overleaf) is the aftermath of my short stint as the road manager for the Satintones and followed our big show in Cincinnati.

BERRY GORDY JR. ENTERPRISES INC.
2648 W. GRAND BLVD.
DETROIT 8, MICHIGAN
TR. 1-3340

BERRY GORDY JR. ENTERPRISES INC.
2648 W. GRAND BLVD.
DETROIT 8, MICHIGAN
TR. 1-3340

Fidelity Music Co
Since 11/20/61

TEMPLESTREET PUBLISHING

temple Street

Lilleshall, Shropshire, TF10 9EQ
templestreet@btinternet.com

3-2101

DATE June 23 19 60

RECEIVED OF Shaw Artist Corp.

Eight hundred Eighty nine and 28/100 DOLLARS

For Bal. Due Month of April
Barrett Strong.

$889 28

By R. L.

50

3-2101

DATE June 21 19 60

RECEIVED OF Shaw Artists Corp

Eight hundred Eighty Nine and 28/100 DOLLARS

For Bal. due Month of May
Barrett Strong

$889 28

By R. L.

2727

DATE June 30 19 60

RECEIVED OF Al Abrams

One hundred forty Six and 98/100 DOLLARS

For repayment of Advance to
Statentons for Cincinate trip

146.98/

By

3-2101

DATE June 30 19 60

RECEIVED OF Bengal Music Co.

One hundred thirty five and 02/100 DOLLARS

For Writer's Royalties period
End Mar 1960 "I love your Baby"

135 02

By

tv
magazine

The Sunday Star
WASHINGTON, D. C.
PROGRAM LISTINGS MAY 30-JUNE 5

THE SUPREMES

Foreword by MARY WILSON

WITH SO MUCH excitement over Motown's 50th Anniversary, it is only fitting that Al Abrams, the young Jewish public relations guy who helped sell the music of the Motown acts, should now release a book about those early publicity endeavors. There are so many stories from many of us who were all a part of that phenomenal entity called Motown, but few can give you a look to see how publicity played a key role in exposing the talent to a new public, in the turbulent social condition of America, and the world.

In 1961 when we as the 'Primettes' came to Motown, we were surprised to see that even though the word on the streets was that it was a black owned company, there were quite a few other ethnic groups working there. The great thing about this was no one seemed to make a big deal about it. Berry Gordy had a knack of garnering around him the right person for the job. If you could do it, he gave you that shot. It did not matter what color you were, and believe me in the early 1960's civil rights did not always allow blacks and whites to intermingle, as we all found out on some of those early Motown Revue tours in the south. It was there we found that we could not drink out of public water fountains, unless it said for colored only. But in the north, in Detroit, Michigan in the 1960's, we worked side by side.

Al Abrams was the PR department, and was a great guy with lots of ideas as well as fun to work with. He was young and got along with every one. It did not matter that he was not black in a virtually all black company. Al Abrams was with us, The Supremes, on some of our biggest achievements. To see a black face on the cover of a TV guide in the sixties was unheard of. This and many other firsts were a part of the many accomplishments that Al Abrams spearheaded.

All of you Motown buffs who think you know everything about Motown will love this book, which is filled with so much history and is documented proof that will help fill in the gaps, just when you thought you knew it all. Read'em and weep.

Mary Wilson

opposite: The Supremes grace the cover of the syndicated TV magazine produced in 1965 by and for The Detroit News. The photograph and inside article with additional photos also appeared in that weekend's Washington, D.C. Sunday Star, The New York Journal American and The Houston Chronicle. This was the first time African-American artists were pictured on the weekly magazine's cover.

Al AGRAMS I Just can't say
Al AGRAMS without saying
writer, creater, P.R and promoter.
Honest ~~and~~ giver and FRIEND

Al AGRAMS I can't just say Al AGRAMS
without ~~say ing~~ Thinking Motown 50yr.
Devotion, promotion, simplicity
a part of the family
That's why I am Mickly ste~~
can say Al AGRAMS

William "Mickey" Stevenson,
Motown songwriter and record producer

ESTREL
HOTEL

*TÄGLICH LIVE-SHOW „STARS IN CONCERT" TELEFON +49/(0)30/6831-0 · FAX +49/(0)30/6831-2345
ESTREL HOTEL-BETRIEBS-GMBH · SONNENALLEE 225 · 12057 BERLIN · TELEFON +49/(0)30/6831-0 · FAX +49/(0)30/6831-2345
WWW.ESTREL.COM · E-MAIL: HOTEL@ESTREL.COM

LAMONT DOZIER
LAS VEGAS, NEVADA 89104

Dear Alan,

I am so excited to be writing this Introduction to your book, *HYPE&SOUL* ! I have thoroughly enjoyed reading it over and over again. It's almost as if I have relived the experiences by reading your press releases of a very hectic time in my life, during those MOTOWN years when I, along with the Holland Brothers, wrote and produced so many hits for the Supremes, The Four Tops, Marvin Gaye, Martha & The Vandellas, The Marvelettes, Smokey Robinson, The Isley Brothers and so many more talented artists signed to the label.

We were very fortunate to make Musical History, but what is History without the Chronicles that you have maintained? I didn't keep copies of any press releases, so for me this was reading them for the first time!

I believe that everyone who loves MOTOWN and the sixties music, will enjoy owning and reading your book over and over again.

I wish you the best of luck with it, and I endorse it completely. Alan Abrams was the best PR man the label ever had, he was and still is my friend , and he still is doing his thing with this book!

Very best always,

LAMONT DOZIER

LD/bu

Foreword by MORT PERSKY

JUST MY LUCK! It was just my incredibly good luck, way back in 1964, that I picked the year of "Where Did Our Love Go?" to join the *Detroit Free Press* as its 32-year-old Sunday editor. Do you remember 1964? The little record I just mentioned turned it not only into the year when the Supremes "made it," but the year when, because of the Supremes, Motown really made it.

No doubt about it. Motown really made it that year...because of the Supremes, because of Berry Gordy Jr., because of Motown's musicians, who wouldn't catch the spotlight until somebody made a movie about them 38 years later. Because of all those other Tamla-Motown musical acts (to name a few: Smokey Robinson and the Miracles; Marvin Gaye: the Temptations; the Marvelettes; Mary Wells, Brenda Holloway; Martha and the Vandellas; Stevie Wonder). Because of Holland-Dozier-Holland, the gang of three who wrote the really big hits. And yes, because of Al Abrams, the tirelessly clever, innovative, persistent and self-effacing public-relations guy who, before Berry Gordy got around to it, invented his own job - that of letting the great public know all this was happening, that Motown's burgeoning list of artists was making news which ought to be reported - which, in fact, just had to be reported.

But nobody loomed larger as newsmakers or hitmakers in 1964, and for a handful of years after that, than the Supremes, the no-need-to mention-their-names Diana, Florence and Mary. How did I find out about them? Like this. One of the first presents I got from Al when I arrived in Detroit, mid-1964, was *Where Did Our Love Go* the album, which of course contained the single of the same name, along with nine or 10 other pieces of ear candy from this group of girl singers I'd never heard of.

But Al had already shown me the latest issue of Billboard, where the album and the single were both climbing to the top of the charts (of course, the same information was available in his press releases). Anyway, I took the LP home and put it on my turntable - where the Supremes made Al's point for him. They completely turned my head around. They were terrific! The record was terrific! I loved them, and I was deeply in love with their renditions of the three songs I still identify as their signature recordings - "Baby Love" being song No. 2, and "Come See About Me" No 3.

You might wonder why I was so excited when I made my Abrams-sponsored discovery that an actual group of three Detroit girls was about to become THE big news in popular music. Let me explain. My job at the *Free Press* included editing a brand-new Sunday

magazine called *Detroit*, and that magazine was conceived as a showcase for everything glamorous and exciting in that gray and, even then, widely dilapidated old city. I was new in town and had yet to learn what those glamorous things were. Eventually we editors found many things to excite our imaginations, but it's only fair to say that Al pointed me straight at the first and perhaps-most-important glittering phenomenon - Motown. Not just the Supremes, though Lord knows they were glittery enough, but that whole glamorous, history-making enterprise up on West Grand Boulevard, the musical laboratory of the mad scientist - Berry Gordy, master entrepreneur, talent-spotter, mixologist and, of course, musician of a very special kind.

Which reminds me that, months later, Al decided to bring my wife and me up to the Gordy house - that's what Motown's "office" was, an old house - to meet Berry Gordy himself. He couldn't have been nicer, but he did not share the modesty of his chief public-relations officer. For one thing, he told Yolanda and me that he could make us - yes, even us - into stars. Credit us, please, with not believing his magic extended that far - but we did get what he was trying to tell us: that much of what went into successful record-making took place in Berry's lab. It was in his hands, and in the hands of his musicians, his arrangers, and the men who turned knobs and watched dials on the control panels where the final product was produced.

That was the first time I met Berry Gordy. I remember the last time I met him as well. I was working for *Playboy* in the very late '70s, and was roaming the grounds at Hugh Hefner's Holmby Hills mansion in Los Angeles, where I'd come, believe it or not, for a business meeting. Berry, by then an Angeleno and a registered Friend of Hefner, was sitting at a patio table. I sat down too and asked, "How are things back in Detroit?" (It had been some years since I'd lived there.)

"Detroit?" answered Berry Gordy. "Where's that?"
He didn't make it seem like a light-hearted response.
Hmmm...Yes, well...go figure.

But back in 1964, at the dawn of Motown's glory years, we newspaper folk did write, often and sometimes at length, about the Supremes. And we wrote about the other Gordy acts as Al Abrams shoved them into our consciousness, one or two or three at a time. Here's one of the most lovable dirty P.R. tricks Al had up his sleeve - one that I'd be sure to remember: When we editors produced a *Sunday* magazine that spotlighted Detroit's entertainment world, Al (in concert with Berry Gordy? I doubt it) decided to make the cover into an engraved plate mounted on a rich slab of dark wood - a plaque from all of Motown to the

Sunday editor. So as I returned from lunch one day, Al and the beautiful Brenda Holloway - then a budding Motown star - presented me with the plaque "in honor of what I'd done for Detroit entertainment" or something. The plaque was a thing of beauty, and there was MY cover, reproduced in gold (well, it looked like gold)! And I, ever a sucker for flattery, accepted it with a big smile. Treasured it for years, in fact..

One more memory of Al Abrams and mid-'60s Detroit: Occasionally Al invited me to come see Motown acts doing their showbiz stuff at a Detroit night club that served as Motown's home away from home. The club was called the 20 Grand, and it was in the heart of a dirt-poor black neighborhood, where it stuck out like a sore thumb. But the shows Motown put on there were rich and dazzling. Acts like the Temptations and the Four Tops not only sang - they were colorfully, royally outfitted, and choreographed to a fare-thee-well. It must have been a wonderful ego feast for master showman Berry Gordy, back in the days before he forgot where Detroit was. And it couldn't have been too shabby for Al Abrams, that extra-special P. R. guy, either.

Mort Persky, *Detroit Free Press*

Mort Persky has been an editor at several big American newspapers including *The Miami Herald*, *The New York Herald Tribune*, *New York Newsday* and the *Philadelphia Inquirer*. He was Sunday editor and assistant managing editor of the *Detroit Free Press*, and co-edited the paper's Pulitzer-winning coverage of Detroit's 1967 riots. In the magazine world, he was editor and vice-president of *Family Weekly* and editorial director for new publications at *Playboy*. He started his career as a sports writer for the *Atlanta Constitution*.

Foreword by MARK CLAGUE

AS PART OF the celebration for the fiftieth anniversary of Berry Gordy's record company (what began on January 12, 1959 as Tamla Records and would soon become the Motown Record Corporation), publicist Al Abrams began putting together the project that evolved into *Hype & Soul* and offers a fresh view of the day-to-day work that transformed popular music, not only in the United States but across the globe. Abrams gives due deference to Gordy's mantra that "If It Ain't In The Grooves, It Ain't Got It." As immortalized in Gordy's eponymous label slogan "It's What's In The Grooves That Count," it is equally true that if the songs don't get airplay and if the artists don't get press coverage, then "It Don't Matter What The Grooves Got!"

Serving as Motown's first employee (originally as record promotion director and later as publicist) from May 1959 through 1966, Abrams amplified the artistry of Motown, along the way helping to expand and shape popular culture. Abrams was just a kid when he began working for Gordy. He was scrappy and determined - important characteristics as his training for the job involved only some fledgling reporting about his high school (Detroit Central) and a passion for rhythm and blues music. That Abrams got the now forgotten song "Teenage Sweetheart" by an artist known as Mike Powers onto the airwaves of WCHB radio on Memorial Day in 1959 won him the job. At that point, Motown Records was still a dream. Gordy ran what was little more than a series of vanity labels out of his home, and for $100 he would record anyone in his makeshift studio and 'guarantee' radio play. As Abrams tells the tale, Gordy challenged an upstart Jewish kid (Abrams) who came knocking at his door to get Powers' record on the air, knowing that he'd likely "never see that white boy again." When the song came through his car's speakers as Gordy visited Detroit's Belle Isle in celebration of the holiday, he nearly crashed his car.

The spirit that propelled Abrams' career - a belief that with gumption and a bit of guile, a press agent could make any dream come true, was distilled from watching Alexander Mackendrick's 1957 film *The Sweet Smell of Success*. When Abrams accepted Gordy's job (at a salary of $15 a week plus all the chili he could eat,) everything he knew about what a press agent did he had learned from actor Tony Curtis. In the movie, Curtis plays a young, ambitious press agent, named Sidney Falco, who is fascinated by the media's power to make or break careers, as depicted in the form of gossip columnist J.J. Hunsecker (played by Burt Lancaster but based on famed New York columnist Walter Winchell.) Although cast in a dark tale of nefarious intrigue, Curtis' portrayal of the press agent as media magician captured Abrams' imagination. It is a romanticized fantasy, but one in which anything is possible if only the aspiring promoter has both the creativity and chutzpah to see things through. This is the spirit that inspired a young Jewish kid to take on Gordy's dare to promote one of the least likely of hits. Abrams' gift was that he lacked the experience to know what was impossible.

The documents here offer insight into how Abrams' energy and imagination combined with the work of Hitsville USA's talented array of recording artists, songwriters, producers and musicians to help reshape popular music as we know it today. Yesterday's publicity stunts have become today's expectations. We want our stars to be larger than life and we insist that the media offer intimate views into our idols' most personal thoughts. With an instinct for what motivates our emotions, attachments, and actions, Abrams helped create these expectations. In the pages reprinted here for the first time, we get a sense of the intensity of Motown's day-to-day operations; we observe pivotal breakthrough moments from the early careers of The Supremes, the Temptations, Marvin Gaye, the Four Tops, Stevie Wonder, and Martha and the Vandellas; and we catch fleeting images of early Motown acts not often remembered by history.

We see how a pioneering record company – black owned but with a strategically assembled mixed race staff – navigated hypercharged issues of race relations in the United States, just as the tide of American Civil Rights was finally shifting. Motown not only helped inspire this change but also extended the political progress of Martin Luther King, Jr.'s activism and the 1964 Civil Rights Act further into the social realm by harnessing the power of radio, television, and print. When Abrams in 1965 deftly engineered the appearance of The Supremes on the cover of a weekly television magazine – distributed to readers in Houston, New York, Detroit and our then-still segregated nation's capital along with their Sunday newspapers – it marked a watershed change in American life. (Previously, only white performers had been depicted on the cover of these weekly guides, as these booklets were intended to remain face-up in the living rooms of subscribers for a full seven days.)

Reproduced here without alteration from the archives at the University of Michigan, Abrams' selections represent an invaluable and long-overdue resource. Nevertheless, they remain only the tip of the iceberg in a larger project of re-examining Motown – its mechanisms and impact – with the benefit of five decades of historical perspective. Readers inspired by this treasury should view the complete Al Abrams Papers, a collection that includes correspondence, scrapbooks, promotional materials, and additional press releases, at the Bentley Historical Library in Ann Arbor, Michigan. These documents chronicle not only the early history of Motown, but little known tales from the annals of Stax-Volt Records (1967–69), and other publicity work by Al Abrams Associates. Enjoy this tour through the annals of Motown; it is a journey that transformed a nation and one whose legacy continues to influence the way we hear America.

Mark Clague, Ph.D.
Associate Professor of Musicology, American Culture and AfroAmerican Studies
University of Michigan-School of Music, Theatre & Dance

Foreword by NEIL RUSHTON

AT ONE POINT, while working on this book I got upset. But happy at the same time.

While swapping emails with Al, I thought for the first time in many years how my Mum used to love the records by The Four Tops and The Isley Brothers that I brought home as a teenager. She died in 1981, aged just 49, when I was 27, and her passing traumatised me. I have never been able to face going to the cemetery where her ashes are buried, and always just shut down when thinking or talking about her.

The process of explaining to Al how much Motown means to so many Brits was inspired with a call from an old mate (and music industry legend) Tilly Rutherford getting in touch to say he had become a proud granddad. Tilly's daughter had grown up listening to Tamla Motown records thanks to her Dad, and as a result the new arrival, a baby girl, had been named Tamla. A few weeks earlier I had run in to another old mate, Phil Dick, who reminded me how he and Kim, as good Yorkshire based Soul fans, had got married at the Motown Museum in Detroit! Somehow the idea of British people connecting so deeply to Motown even though it is music from another continent and another culture got me thinking of my mother and how much she loved "This Old Heart Of Mine" and "Reach Out I'll Be There" even though she was not a big follower of music. And for the first time for many years I was able to think about her and not cut off my emotions. I cried a little. And I smiled remembering her.

I should not have been surprised. After all, Soul music specialises in making you upset and happy at the same time. And Motown's magic was that it took the music from the Detroit Projects and made it captivating for people from another world...like my Mum.

Berry Gordy's remorseless production line ethos of "funk at the bottom, pop at the top" meant Motown crossed over in a way other Soul labels could only dream about. They sold millions and millions of records, and despite the pop gloss still told breathless love stories full of angst and raw emotion. How on earth could one (originally very tiny) record label even dream of doing that, never mind achieve it? Al's "I was there" book delves into the background scenes at Motown to answer those questions. Gordy's genius was that he surrounded himself with other geniuses. Enthusiastic, purposeful, workaholic and multi-talented they were imbued with Berry's single-minded ambition to take the sound of West Grand Boulevard far behind the confines of Michigan. Everyone knows about Hitsville's legendary producers, musicians and arrangers. Inevitably there is little information about the background people like Al who did so much behind the scenes. This book sets right that injustice. When you are talking to Berry Gordy's first employee it is hard not to get educated while he entertains you. There is no greater, enthusiastic, keeper of the Motown flame than Al, genial, funny and always with yet another spellbinding "I was there" anecdote not far away.

The book started off as a vague idea of showcasing unreleased Motown photos from Al's private archives. Very soon afterwards his press releases were added into the mix, then newspaper and magazine cuttings from a collection so large that a print shop spent seven hours reproducing just some of them! Priceless documents were followed by essays about Al's pioneering days at the label – and I instantly became addicted to them, desperate for Al to finish the next one and send it over for me to devour and marvel. Before reading them I thought I knew quite a lot about 60's Soul music. Afterwards I realised I am simply a consumer.

The fascinating essays, the original press releases, the many previously unpublished photographs, and the documents and newspaper/magazine clippings are spellbinding. If you want to learn about the evolution and revolution – musical and social – that forged Soul music, and Motown's central role in it you need go no further. Of course, there have been other Motown books. But up till now none from the black music loving hyperactive and proudly Jewish kid who lived his dream promoting what the whole world got to know as the "The Detroit Sound." Al came up with that trademark name – after meeting him I would be astonished if he had not. This is the story of Motown, quite simply the world's greatest ever record label. And the story of (and tales from) Al Abrams, one of the extraordinary people who helped Berry Gordy create the legend, Al Abrams was quite simply the Motown messenger. His incredible book shows why Al Abrams is a Motown legend. Believe the *Hype & Soul.*

Neil Rushton
Author of *Northern Soul Stories*

My favourite photo of Berry

Chapter 1

AIN'T THAT PECULIAR

opposite: It's true! It's true! Berry Gordy DID have horns. Well, that's the impression you get from this light-hearted photo shot in Japan during the Supremes tour in 1966.

Al Abrams
PUBLIC RELATIONS

DETROIT'S TWO-BIT LABELS

Detroit was a melting pot of tiny labels vying for a piece of the Motown action. At first I used to offer encouragement, but soon that bordered on contempt if I thought they might be stealing our thunder.

I was very possessive, if not obsessive, about what we had created from scratch. Certainly they would all look to Motown for divine guidance. However, they needed more than that to make it in a competitive world where Motown had just raised the ante.

"It's What's In The Words That Count"

I still believe I was the luckiest kid in all of Detroit that May of 1959.

THAT'S HOW IT felt to me walking into a virtual wonderland of music at Berry Gordy's flat at 1719 Gladstone in Detroit's inner city.

When Berry hired me I was an 18-year-old white Jewish kid in an all-black company where people my age were making music and history. He put me in charge of record promotion for the songs published by his Jobete Music Company and I thought I was in heaven.

My primary job was to get the records played on the radio, especially by white disk jockeys on mainstream radio stations. I certainly wasn't going to ignore the black DJs, some of whom - like Larry Dean and Bill Williams - quickly became my closest friends.

Berry had given me the job because I was able to get Larry Dixon, a DJ on Detroit's WCHB, to play a god-awful record by Mike Powers called "Teenage Sweetheart" that Berry's Rayber Music Writing Company had produced and recorded for a $100 fee. I still think it is the absolute worst record Berry has ever produced.

When I applied for a promotion job with Berry, he had given me the virtually impossible task of getting that record played on the radio before he would consider hiring me. Eager to get rid of me, he was convinced he would never see me again once I left his flat with the Powers disk in hand. But it was my good luck that after four hours of begging and pleading in the hot sun, Dixon gave it a spin on the Memorial Day holiday at the very time that Berry was listening to the station in his car. That was also the only time that record was ever played on the radio.

That accomplishment was enough to get me hired the very next day for $15 a week and all the chilli I could eat - cooked and served by Miss Lillie Hart.

BERRY HAS ALWAYS had a reputation for being a tough negotiator, but I got the best of him that day. I worked for Jobete, Rayber, the fledgling five-month-old Tamla Record Company, and the then-personal management entity of Berry Gordy Jr. Enterprises. Motown was still more than a year in the future.

It didn't take me long to realize that I was surrounded by geniuses in that cramped little flat. In addition to Berry and his future wife, Raynoma Liles, there was Bill "Smokey" Robinson and the Miracles, Eddie Holland, Marv Johnson, Barrett Strong, Robert Bateman and a house-full of now-legendary talented songwriters, performers and musicians, all of whom welcomed me as a member of the family.

I was often a source of great amusement to my new co-workers. Robert Bateman still remembers my refusal to ride in the company's old Volkswagen bus because it was German and still associated in my mind with Nazis. But political correctness didn't stop me from showing up at work wearing one of my mother's white sheets to promote a record, totally oblivious to the image of the white sheet-wearing Ku Klux Klan who were still terrorizing American blacks in that pre-Civil Rights era.

Berry and the others quickly became my surrogate family with Berry assuming the role of my knowing older brother. I will be eternally indebted to him for some of the truly valuable knowledge he imparted that summer.

My responsibilities soon expanded to include writing the first Jobete and Tamla advertisements for Billboard, Cashbox, and the other music trade publications, writing artist biographies and liner notes and getting favorable mentions and stories about us into print. That quickly became my favorite endeavor and eventually I gladly abdicated my record promotion responsibilities to others so that I could fully concentrate upon publicity and press relations.

I traveled with the Miracles, Barrett Strong, and even did a short stint as road manager of the legendary Satintones. Returning from a road trip to Cleveland where we had gone to see Jackie Wilson perform, I co-wrote the lyrics with Berry and two of my colleagues for "I Love The Way You Love" which became a hit record for Marv Johnson.

I also did my share of mischief, once convincing Janie Bradford to answer phone calls for our Miracle subsidiary label with the greeting, "Good morning! If it's a hit, it's a Miracle." Berry was not amused.

Somewhat later, I guaranteed that I would never again be invited to attend a Quality Control meeting by suggesting that we re-record Marvin Gaye's "Ain't That Peculiar" as "Isn't That Peculiar" in order not to offend English teachers across America. Well, at least I never forgot the words to our Smokey Robinson-penned company song whenever Berry called upon me to do a solo before the meeting began. Who can ever forget those immortal lyrics, "Oh we have a very swinging company…"

But my ultimate goal was to tell the world through newspapers and magazines about the real 'Miracle' on Detroit's West Grand Boulevard…and that's what I was happiest doing.

That is what this book is all about.

above: L-R Billy Johnson, Al Abrams, Johnny "JJ" Jones, Berry Gordy, Jr., Jackie Wilson, Robert Bateman (backstage - Cleveland, circa 1960)

BANK of the C

PROMISSORY NOTE AN

On or before **thirty six**

the BANK of the COMMON

y One Hundred Eight

d in successive monthly instal

DOLLARS ($**88.53**

on the **16** day of **Au**

obligation and any and all

or) to BANK of the COM

a security interest in the f

Year	
1965	I

d accessories now or he

l agrees with Secured

greement evidences a pu

used primarily:

ousehold purposes,

rming or a profession).

of the Collateral and

d repair, free of misu

dispose of the Collate

suffered by Debtor

Secured Party any

he security interest

misstatement in this

of Debtor's oblig

ll be in default

nefit of cre

rcise i

see

Al Abrams

RECORD PROMOTION
1719 GLADSTONE AVENUE
DETROIT 6, MICHIGAN

TRinity 1-3340

Al Abrams
Promotions
JOBETE MUSIC COMPA

MEDIA DIRECTORS
Detroit Advertising Agencies

ng a former ad man myself, I realize the tremendous care that

st be taken in preparing a package for a client. Naturally, you

nt them to have the very best at the least nominal cost.

When it comes to radio and T.V. spots; a medium in high

by your clients, I believe I have the answer for you.

We now have available some of the nation's top rec

and groups, who are at your service to fill any ne

We also have a skilled team of some of the top so

country, with a list of proven hits behind them, pr

you and work with you on your campaigns.

n't you please give me a ring at TRinity 1-3340 a

Jobete can benefit both

MARV JOHNSON
UA 208
Time: 2:32

FREEBIE

PROMOTION COPY

UNITED

ARTL

Al Abrams

"I LOVE THE WAY YOU LOVE"
(Gordy-Mikaljon)
Jobete Music Co., Inc.-BMI
PRODUCED BY BERRY GORDY, JR.
WITH THE RAYBER VOICES
ZTSP 62164

UNITED ARTISTS RECORDS, INC. MADE IN U.S.A.

I love the way you l

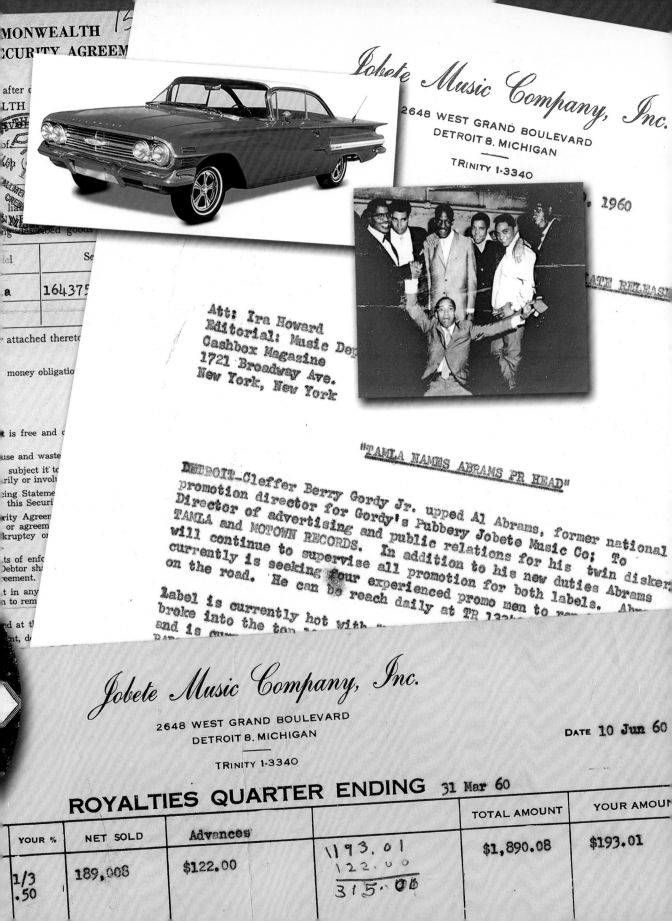

MONWEALTH
CURITY AGREEM

after

LTH

of

ch (5)

liab

NWF

g described goods

el   Se

a   164375

attached thereto

money obligatio

it is free and c

use and waste

subject it to

rily or invol

eing Statement

this Securi

rity Agreem

or agreem

kruptcy or

ts of enf

Debtor sha

ement.

t in any

n to rem

ed at th

ent, de

Jobete Music Company, Inc.

2648 WEST GRAND BOULEVARD

DETROIT 8, MICHIGAN

TRINITY 1-3340

1960

ATE RELEAS

Att: Ira Howard
Editorial: Music Dep
Cashbox Magazine
1721 Broadway Ave.
New York, New York

"TAMLA NAMES ABRAMS PR HEAD"

DETROIT—Cleffer Berry Gordy Jr. upped Al Abrams, former national
promotion director for Gordy's Pubbery Jobete Music Co; To
Director of advertising and public relations for his twin disker
TAMLA and MOTOWN RECORDS. In addition to his new duties Abrams
will continue to supervise all promotion for both labels. Ab
currently is seeking four experienced promo men to rep
on the road. He can be reach daily at TR 13
label is currently hot with "
broke into the top
and is

Jobete Music Company, Inc.

2648 WEST GRAND BOULEVARD

DETROIT 8, MICHIGAN

TRINITY 1-3340

DATE 10 Jun 60

ROYALTIES QUARTER ENDING 31 Mar 60

YOUR %	NET SOLD	Advances		TOTAL AMOUNT	YOUR AMOUN
1/3 .50	189,008	$122.00	1193.01 122.00 ——— 315.00	$1,890.08	$193.01

Best Wishes to "Cal." Marv Johnson

MoRE MARV JOHNSON

Produced by BERRY GORDY, Jr.

United Artist
Record Star

MARV JOHNSON

Personal Management
Berry Gordy, Jr.

BERRY GORDY, JR. ENTERPRISES

2648 WEST GRAND BOULEVARD
DETROIT 8, MICHIGAN

TRINITY 1-3340

MARV JOHNSON, who already has proven his tremendous versatility when it comes to selling a song — be it a soft, warm ballad or a house rocker belted out in his inimitable fashion — with a string of hits and a first successful album entitled "Marvelous Marv Johnson" again comes through with flying colors on this his second album for U.A. aptly entitled "More Marv Johnson." Not only does this album fill the demands of many fans for more recordings with the Marvelous Johnson sound; but it will no doubt attract many more admirers to the ranks of Johnson devotees; giving both the opportunity to again hear more different sounds from the tremendous Johnson range, all octaves of which are covered in this collection; which includes some songs heard here for the very first time, along with more of Johnson's fabulous successes. Again, these songs are contributed - some by MARV himself and others in collorobation with his manager, "MR. HITSVILLE", Berry Gordy, Jr.

Especially outstanding in this great collection are the cute uptempo "Baby Baby"; and the lush, feelingful, "When You've Lost Your Love" - both of which give MARV the chance to use to his utmost his unrestrained capacity for delivering a song with "SOUL" — a commodity

27

My hands are chock full of these very photos

L-R Al Abrams, Brian Holland, Eddie Holland and Michaela Williams of the Chicago Daily News

Can a Woman Find Happiness After 35?

Text by Marjory Jackson, Photographs by Sue Marx

ESTHER EDWARDS

Record company executive

"Ever since we've been old enough to work," says Esther Edwards, vice president in charge of talent for the Motown Records Corp. and sister of Berry Gordy Jr., president of Motown, "we've had to put $10 a month in the family kitty. That's where Berry got the $700 he needed to start Hitsville, USA. Berry has always been a creative, 'I'd-rather-do-it-myself' type and he wanted me on hand as his business adviser."

The rest is musical history.

"The novelty for me is not that I began working later in my life, but that I moved into an entirely new industry," says Mrs. Edwards, who in private life is the wife of State Representative George G. Edwards and the mother of a 21-year-old son serving in the Army.

Six years ago Mrs. Edwards was chairman of the Recorder's Court Jury Commission, a bookkeeper in another brother's printing company and Berry's assistant. Her day went something like this: 8 a.m. to 2 p.m., Recorder's Court, 2 to 4 p.m., printing company; 4 p.m. to midnight, working with Berry . . . besides running her own home.

But Motown and the Detroit Sound mushroomed into a multi-faceted enterprise and Mrs. Edwards gave up her other commitments to work there full time. Today 36 of the top 100 record hits in the country bear the Motown label.

A serene, capable woman, she handles all bookings and merchandising for the Supremes and Marvin Gaye. She also oversees the internal organization of the corporation.

Mrs. Edwards, who attended both Howard and Wayne State Universities, thinks the most important factor in the success of her brothers and sisters was the confidence, encouragement and example of hard-work given them by their parents, Mr. and Mrs. Berry Gordy Sr.

Eddie Holland whose record of "Merry-Go-Round" firmly entrenched him as one of todays top new singing stars was born in Detroit Michigan twenty-one years ago.

Having always had a talent for music, Eddie began singing around his neighborhood while still in grade school. After graduation from high school he found a job with a local music publishing house. His duties there included singing all the company's songs to interested buyers and singers on demonstration discs of these songs which were sent to various recording companies. Among the songs that Eddie recorded on these "dubs" (as they are called in the trade) were three songs destined later to make a star out of the young man who sang them -- the songs were "To Be Loved", "Lonely Teardrops" and "I'll Be Satisfied", and the singer -- of course; Jackie Wilson. It was one of these demonstration discs that brought his qualifications to the attention of Berry Gordy, Jr. Berry "flipped" over Eddie's voice and asked Eddie to record for him. Eddie accepted and shortly afterward he recorded "Merry-Go-Round".

Among the Detroit teenage set Eddie is looked upon as somewhat of an idol. He usually has to have a police escort to and from his many record hops. Recently he has been forced to do less of these hops because of the avid reactions of his many fans. One experience in particular found Eddie in the uncomfortable position of having the clothes torn off his back by a pack of screaming teenage girls.

31

Al Abrams

HOLLAND-DOZIER-HOLLAND THE ARISTOCRATS

I was close enough to H-D-H that they would select me as their PR director for Invictus/Hot Wax.

I always tried to work them into major media stories, as you can see from that photo with Michaela Williams of the Chicago Daily News.

The best H-D-H story, about our moving crew, appears elsewhere in this book. But I also remember a strange phase Brian and Eddie were going through maybe in 1959-1960 when they decided to add an aristocratic German "von" to their names as in Brian von Holland.

Fortunately, it didn't last long.

United Artist Recording Star   EDDIE HOLLAND   Personal Management
BERRY GORDY JR.

"It's What's In The Words That Count"

opposite: prankster Al shows a rubber snake to a shocked Berry Gordy, Marv Johnson and Eddie Holland while promoting "Snake Walk" by the Swinging Tigers

33

WHO ARE THE WORLD'S MOST SUCCESSFUL SONGWRITERS?

BRIAN HOLLAND

EDDIE HOLLAND

LAMONT DOZIER

Are they Lerner & Loewe, Rodgers & Hart, McCartney & Lennon or — the writers of:

"Leaving Here"
"Just Ain't Enough Love"
"Where Did Our Love Go?"
"I Can't Help Myself"
"It's The Same Old Song"
"Baby Love"
"Come See About Me"
"Baby, I Need Your Lovin'"
"Stop, In The Name Of Love"
"Back In My Arms Again"
"Without The One You Love"
"Nothing But Heartaches"
"There's Something About You"
"Can I Get A Witness?"
"How Sweet It Is To Be Loved By You"
"Live Wire"
"Quick Sand"
"Wonderful One"
"Heat Wave"
"Baby, Don't Go"
"Come And Get These Memories"
"Mickey's Monkey"
"I Hear A Symphony"
"Take Me In Your Arms"

Of the above titles, eleven have been number one in the Top 40, and six have sold over a million copies, with the seventh presently nearing the mark ■ From the pen, piano and producing techniques of this writing team comes the most remarkable achievements in the pop field to date — the team very inconspicuously known as:

HOLLAND-DOZIER-HOLLAND

These three young men, 24-year-old Lamont Dozier, 24-year-old Brian Holland and his 25-year-old brother Eddie, form a behind the scenes force that has helped to skyrocket the Supremes, Four Tops, Mar-

tha and The Vandellas, Marvin Gaye and Kim Weston to their positions as top talents in the world today □ They are the people who not only write their material but are responsible for producing their own sessions, thus gaining them the incomparable title of "Hit-Makers" □ They are the "in crowd" of their own, being amongst the select few who have discovered that hard to come by formula for success □ Brian and Lamont got together through Motown president Berry Gordy, and Eddie joined them as lyricist when he abandoned a recording career of his own □ Three years ago it all started with their first joint effort, "Come And Get These Memories" by Martha and The Vandellas □ It was a hit □ The hits have been coming ever since ■ The talents of the three are varied □ All have been featured artists with hits of their own, but in working together they perform specific functions □ Brian is responsible primarily for the production end, Lamont writes the music and Eddie supplies the lyrics □ In doing so, Eddie always assumes the feminine approach, which he obtains from his tight daily schedule of watching soap-operas and reading Love-Romance Magazines ■ They admire and respect the

trend offered by the British, the Protesters, etc., due to their stimulating effect on record sales □ However, they are constantly writing in order to remain topical and current with the present day trend, which they within themselves are □ This is evidenced by the fact that they have written and produced five consecutive million sellers with the Supremes alone (the sixth well on its way) □ Presently they have four songs on the charts □ Nearly three complete albums, as well as the above hits are products of Holland-Dozier-Holland and the team appears far from slowing down □ "We've had about eight big ones this year," said Eddie to T40R in a recent interview, "and I'm sure we'll have quite a few more" □ Added to these credits you can now include two motion picture scores, "Nothing But A Man" for Cinema IV and the recently released Paramount Picture "Beach Ball," starring the Supremes ■ The Top 40 Reviewer and the music industry THANK YOU . . .

HOLLAND-DOZIER-HOLLAND

for your continued fantastic "sound" and good taste in music ■

FROM: Hitsville, U.S.A.
2648 West Grand Blvd.
Detroit, Michigan 48208
871-3340 (Al Abrams)

December 21, 1965

FOR IMMEDIATE RELEASE

BRIAN HOLLAND APPOINTED
VICE-PRESIDENT OF MOTOWN RECORD CORPORATION

Berry Gordy Jr., President of Motown Record
Corporation, announced on Friday, December 17th, the appointment of Brian Holland as Vice-President in charge of
Creative Evaluation of Motown Record Corporation. Holland,
who has been associated with the company since its early
days, assumed the directorship of this department last
August. Holland is well known in association with Lamont
Dozier as one of the country's leading record producers;
and as a songwriter with his brother, Eddie Holland, as well
as with Dozier.

His creative work in connection with such leading
Motown Artists as The Supremes, Four Tops, Martha and The
Vandellas, and others, has contributed to the establishment
of Motown's leading position in the record business and
the world-wide acceptance of "The Detroit Sound."

Saturday magazine

Saturday, July 31, 1965

tv and radio
features
pictures

16 M

Detroit Is Also The Hub Of The U. S. Rock Sound

By PETER HOFFMAN
Associated Press Writer

DETROIT (AP) — Until recently, this motor town's chief contributions to the American culture might be rated as dual headlights, the tailfin and the throb and rumble of hot V-8s.

But for the last year or so, the hot, hard-driving rhythms of Motown, a record company, have put Detroit on the music map.

The Supremes, three Negro girls who are Motown's star performers, recently picked up a cool $100,000 in royalties — each—from record sales in the previous six months.

The Supremes dash round the country making personal appearances and taping TV shows, as well as recording. This summer they will play for one month at New York's Copacabana.

In April they and other Motown artists made a three-week tour of England, France and Germany.

The Liverpool Daily Post, the Beatles' hometown paper, called the show "electric."

The paper said, "so far as rhythm and blues is concerned, these Detroit people most certainly have a superb stage act.'

"By comparison, Britain's pop singers look like garden party amateurs."

In Hamburg, Germany, where the Supremes appeared on television, the "Hamburger Abendecho" gushed that they are "America's sweetest girls," with "voices clear as bells" and who are "slim and supple like pussy willows."

Diana Ross, lead singer, said, "We almost got thrown in jail in Paris.

"We were taping a show for French television where we were supposed to sort of dance down the Champs Elysee, weaving in and out of traffic while

TOP GIRL ROCK GROUP — The Supremes, from left, Florence Ballard, Mary Wilson and Diana Ross, stand in front of recording company Motown's main display window in Detroit.

we were lipsyncing." (synchronizing the movement of their lips to the sound of one of their recordings.

"They wanted to arrest us for obstructing traffic," she said.

No charges were filed.

The European reviewers loved Motown's brand of bluesy pop singing with its faint gospel overtones, but the concert halls were only half filled part of the time.

"When I'm traveling with my girls, I lose a lot of money," boss Berry Gordy Jr. told the Hamburger Abendblatt reporter.

But Gordy, 36-year-old former assembly line worker who is now one of America's top pop record producers, was publicizing the fact that Motown is starting to distribute records in Europe.

In the United States, the Cashbox Magazine chart of best-selling singles for June 19 showed the Four Tops with the No. 1 song in the country, "I Can't Help Myself," the Supremes with No. 7, "Back in my Arms Again," and Junior Walker and All Stars, the Marvelettes and Brenda Holloway all in the top 100.

A recent week in which company artists occupied eight of the top 55 spots in the best-selling 100 was described by a company spokesman as typical.

Motown Record Corporation is currently the second largest producer of singles. It ranks right behind Capitol Records—which holds the U.S. distribution rights for the Beatles.

Last year Motown grossed

about $10 million. In addition to its seven record labels—Tamla, Motown, Gordy, VIP, Soul, Melody and Jazz Workshop, it includes a talent management office, a sales corporation and a music publishing firm.

Motown owner Gordy, who once was a Golden Gloves boxer, built his company in little over five years.

After borrowing some $700 from his family, he quit his $85-a-week job installing upholstery trim at the Lincoln-Mercury Division of the Ford Motor Co. and produced his first master recording, "Come To Me," sung by Marvin Johnson.

The disc did well in the Detroit area. Gordy sold it to United Artists for national distribution.

A few hits later, singer Smokey Robinson, now at 25 the firm's youngest vice president, urged Gordy to go it nationally on his own.

Gordy is reluctant to hang labels of "rock 'n' roll" or "rhythm and blues" labels on Motown's sounds. "It's simply popular music," he said.

over dinner with Smokey and Diana Ross. We were trying to figure out what makes the sound different. We thought back, about the neighborhoods we were in, the struggles, the rats, and we came up with a six-word definition, 'Rats, roaches, struggle, talent, guts, love.' "

Gordy could have added electronics.

Unlike most companies which record on three-track tape, Motown uses custom-built machinery that records eight separate tracks at each session.

Producers and sound engineers can mix the eight in any proportion they want, creating special effects, overdubbing, distorting, emphasizing, for example, the insistent thump of the rhythm section, or suppressing the background strings, usually hired from the Detroit Symphony Orchestra.

Practically all of Motown's some 100 performers were born and reared in and around Detroit. Exceptions are singer Tony Martin who joined Motown last fall and Billy Eckstine, who after years of occasional recordings with different firms recently signed an exclusive three-year contract.

Gordy commented that while he likes "to build talent," it would be "uneconomical to turn down top talent that could benefit the company."

Motown still is largely a Gordy family enterprise. Members of the family hold most of the stock and two of Gordy's sisters are vice presidents.

The administrative staff is about half white and half Negro. Almost all artists are Negro.

GORDY

HERE'S AN EXTREME RARITY for any Motown historian. I'm sure this ephemeral article has not been published anywhere in the 51 years since it first saw print.

When columnist Jerry Kabel of the *Detroit Times*, then one of Detroit's three daily newspapers, came to the Hitsville, USA studios on West Grand Boulevard during the week in February 1960 in which Smokey Robinson, Bobby Rogers and I celebrated our birthdays (they turned 20, I became 19), Motown didn't exist other than perhaps as an idea in the minds of Berry and Raynoma. As you can see from the story, the thrust of the article was the Rayber Music Writing Company and our "$100 fee" for our "coaching and music course."

You'll notice there's no mention of the existence of Tamla. Fortunately, Kabel didn't mention the Ping-Pong table in the studio, which I think we hid before he arrived. This may be the only contemporary newspaper account of the Rayber Music Writing Company ever published. You'll note that I'm described by Kabel as being "the studio's promotion man."

However, this was the first mainstream newspaper article ever to mention Berry, Smokey (even though Kabel spelled his name as "Smoky"), Marv Johnson or any of us. Up to this time, with the exception of the June 1959 *Windsor Star* story on their hometown hero Mike Powers which you'll also find in this book, all our print media coverage appeared in what was then called Negro newspapers and magazines: *The Michigan Chronicle*; *The Pittsburgh Courier* (Detroit edition); *Jet* magazine and the weekly music trades: *Billboard*; *Cashbox*; *Music Vendor* (later *Record World*) and *Variety*.

How much of a role this *Detroit Times* story played in propelling Berry to move forward and incorporate the Motown Record Corporation six weeks later on April 14, 1960 can only be pure speculation on my part. But I like to think that it may have been a catalyst.

Unfortunately, Jerry Kabel omitted the word "Boulevard" from our address, and I've always wondered how many eager young would-be performers descended upon the residence at 2648 West Grand Avenue - ironically a street on which I used to live and on which I had a newspaper route delivering the *Detroit Times* in 1952 when I was eleven.

But this article will always remain frozen in time as a forerunner of the success and the glory that was awaiting Motown. Within one year, on February 12, 1961, we had our first million seller with "Shop Around" by Smokey Robinson and the Miracles.

The rest, as the phrase goes, is history.

Detroit Times

60TH YEAR, No. 148   3   **THURSDAY, FEBRUARY 25, 1960**   **8 CENTS**

DETROIT

Three Million Stories

By Jerry Kabel

THE TRICK of producing a successful hit record, Mr. Berry Gordy explained, is to compose a song with a complete and meaningful message.

Gordy is the president of a recording studio at 2648 W. Grand that he believes is the only one in Detroit devoted to popular music rather than singing commercials.

"Songs are composed, arranged and master-recorded right in this building," said Gordy, leading me to the studio control room. "We don't go for 'Dilly-dilly-gum-gum' type lyrics. We want songs that can be understood, that people can relate to themselves."

A large picture window afforded an excellent view of the studio where a young man identified as "Smoky" Robinson was seated at a piano, crooning into a microphone.

"Babee-ee-ee, you've taken my lo-ove and makin' me blue," Robinson trilled.

AL ABRAMS, the studio's promotion man, explained that Smoky was composing and simultaneously recording his ideas

JERRY KABEL

on tape so that they might not be forgotten in the welter of musical notes that might crowd his mind a few hours later.

"You are keepin' us apaa-ah-ah-rt," Robinson sang with appropriate thumps on the piano. Gordy nodded approvingly, the lyrics seeming to meet his criteria of complete meaning.

Hundreds of aspiring artists crowd Gordy's studio every month, certain that they have the necessary voice talent for overnight. Rather than turn them rudely away, the studio has arranged a coaching and music course that may be undertaken for a $100 fee.

However, Gordy has a select few of the more promising singers under contract.

"THE BEST THING we've got going right now is 'You Got What It Takes' by Marv Johnson," said Mr. Abrams, searching my face for some sign of recognition.

Disappointed, he pointed out reprovingly, "It reached fifth place in the national popularity ratings."

He searched out a recording of the song, put it on a turntable and Johnson's voice throbbed:

"You don't drive a big, fat car,

"You can't be a movie star.

"On your money we won't go far,

"But, baby, you've got what it takes."

The record is distributed by the United Artists label, Abrams said, and has faded to No. 16 in the nation, but has nevertheless sold 650,000 copies.

"You can hear how the song tells a complete story," said Gordy. "It's the story of a man who loves a girl even though she's unattractive in some ways."

I ASKED Gordy how he picks the artists he puts under contract and he said that talent was necessary, but secondary. "The first thing I look for is personality and character," he said.

He explained further: "Sometimes you will get a man who has talent but nothing else and you will nurse him along to the big-time. Then he goes, say, to New York and other agencies promise him movies and TV and all.

"Next thing you know he's got another manager. No loyalty, no character. It can be very serious."

Gordy listed other hits as "Lonely Tear Drops," "I'm Comin' Home" and "River of Tears."

Another was "Money, That's All I Want." It didn't make No. 1 but Gordy is proud of it. Because there is, after all, no more complete and meaningful message than that.

below: The Supremes with then-Detroit mayor Jerome P. Cavanagh; page 42: on stage with the Cavanagh family.
Cavanagh was on a fast track for the Democratic 1968 presidential nomination until he had the misfortune of being mayor when the
1967 riots erupted. Career-killer!
opposite: my ambitious plans to promote the 1964 Motortown Revue

Sounds very good!

NOVEMBER 17, 1964

TO: MR. BERRY GORDY JR.
    MRS. ESTHER EDWARDS

HERE, BRIEFLY STATED, ARE MY PLANS
TO PUBLICIZE THE 1964 MOTORTOWN REVUE:

(A) I WOULD GET MAYOR CAVANAUGH
OF DETROIT, TO ISSUE AN OFFICIAL
PROCLAMATION RENAMING DETROIT AS
"MOTOWN" (OR "MOTORTOWN") FOR THE DAY
OF DECEMBER 25, 1964 IN HONOR OF
MOTOWN / MOTORTOWN'S SIGNIFICANT CONTRIBUTION
TO DETROIT.

(B) I WOULD ALSO HAVE GOVERNOR RUMNEY ISSUE A PROCLAMATION. IF NASHVILLE CAN DO IT, WE CERTAINLY CAN!

(C) AS GUESTS OF HONOR TO OPEN THE FIRST DAY'S SHOW, I WOULD INVITE LUCI BAINES AND LYNDA BIRD JOHNSON, THE PRESIDENT'S TEEN DAUGHTERS.

(D) IMMEDIATELY PRECEDING THE FIRST PERFORMANCE, I WOULD STAGE A FULL SCALE PARADE FROM THE FOOT OF WOODWARD AVENUE TO THE FOX THEATRE, WITH EACH ARTIST ARRIVING IN AN EXPERIMENTAL AUTOMOBILE TO BE FURNISHED BY FORD, CHRYSLER, AND G.M.

(E) I WOULD ERECT A FULL SCALE NEON

SIGN AT THE FOOT OF WINDSOR ONTARIO
(CANADA — AND FACING (AND VISIBLE
TO) THE DETROIT CIVIC CENTER, WITH
30 FOOT LETTERS READING:

       MOTORTOWN REVUE
       FOX   THEATRE

(F) I WOULD INVITE THE TOP LEADERS
IN SOCIETY, THE AUTOMOTIVE WORLD,
CIVIC LEADERS, CONSULS, ETC TO A
GALA FIRST-NIGHT BLACK-TIE PERFORMANCE
COMPLETE WITH KLEIG LIGHTS, RED
CARPETS AND AN M.C. THEIR KIDS WILL
ATTEND, WHY SHOULDN'T THEY? THIS
WILL MAKE THEM AWARE OF OUR
"DETROIT" PRODUCT, AND THE IMPORTANT
PART IT PLAYS.

Know why ?

(G) WITH ALL THIS, WE WOULDN'T NEED
NEWSPAPER ADS.!

LET'S THINK BIG.!
LET'S LET EVERYONE KNOW
WHO MOTOWN IS !

          Respectfully SUBMITTED,
          Al Abrams
          Special Projects

Berry and his longtime personal secretary Rebecca Jiles

The Detroit News

SECTION G

Entertainment • Stage
Movies • TV-Radio
Music • Records

Books • Columns • Art
Medicine • Features
Fraternal • Gardens

The Passing Show

SUNDAY, JULY 25, 1965

Something for Everyone in the Family

Berry Gordy Jr., in front of "Hitsville, U.S.A.," headquarters of the Motown complex that had estimated gross sales of $10 million last year, is aiming at $15 million in '65   —News Photo by Charles T. Martin

THE AMAZING EMPIRE ON WEST GRAND BOULEVARD

Six years ago an $85-a-week auto worker quit his job, borrowed $700 and started making records for teen-agers. Today, his Motown Record Corp. is the home of the unique "Detroit Sound" that echoes in waves of rocking rhythm heard around the world.

By EARL B. DOWDY
Of the Detroit News Staff

A thin, baby-faced little man named Berry Gordy Jr. recently appeared in Mayor Cavanagh's office to be cited as Detroit's "Small Businessman of the Year."

To most of the mayor's staff and newsmen who cover hundreds of such ceremonies, the exceedingly shy visitor seemed "just some fellow who makes records for teen-agers."

But to millions of teen-agers around the world, this recognition for the former automobile assembly line worker from his native community was long overdue. They don't understand why Detroit has taken so long to discover it has, in Berry Gordy's "Detroit Sound," one of the hottest-selling properties since Henry Ford developed the "Tin Lizzy."

Incredible as it may seem to adults, what used to be known as the Motor City now is more often referred to — from Stockholm to Singapore as "Motown" (from Motor Town), which happens to be the parent company of Gordy's mushrooming empire.

What is happening here is difficult for "senior citizens" of the Glenn Miller-Artie Shaw Age to comprehend. The rocking, rocking sounds must seem to many of them an orgy in cacophony.

$15 Million Sales Forecast

But to Gordy, the multilingual demands pouring into Detroit from every point of the huge globe are a symphonic concerto scored for the cash register.

And even a tone-deaf bookkeeper could hardly be blamed for humming a happy tune after listening to the crescendo build up from $4.5 million gross sales in 1963 to an estimated $10 million last year — with $15 million-plus predicted by some industry sources in 1965.

This spiral has pushed Motown Record Corp. to second place in total U.S. single record sales — behind Capitol Records, which holds U.S. rights to the output of England's priceless Beatles. It has made Motown the world's largest independently owned producer.

Frontline troops in Gordy's personal war on poverty ("Yes, I guess I can call myself a millionaire now.") are the Supremes, three Detroit girls who until recently were better known in Berlin than Bloomfield Hills.

Having won the adulation of Europe,

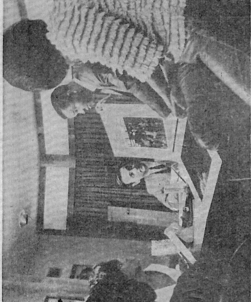

RECORD TALK — Berry Gordy (seated), single sales director; and the Supremes, the three Detroit girls who are Motown's world-famous stars. Berry Gordy discusses plans with Irv Biegel.

Copacabana nightclub as the most sought-after female act on Broadway since Barbra Streisand.

Somehow, despite reassuring receipts estimated at more than $300,000 for their records and personal appearances last year, this engagement seems to stamp their success as official at last, lifting them far above scores of other entertainers in Gordy's stable.

Staked by His Father

Motown is housed in a labyrinth of four converted, interconnecting flats on West Grand Boulevard, known to occupants and pilgrims as "Hitsville, U.S.A.," — and to some nearby residents as "Din Pan Alley."

Gordy began with a rented bedroom of the first flat, at 2648, six years ago. He had $700, borrowed from his father, a grocer and plastering contractor.

Several weeks ago the Motown organization began spilling over into the fourth flat and Gordy Jr. jokingly said that Gordy Sr. would get the plastering contract "for remodeling "if the price is right."

Scattered through the Motown maze are an estimated 100 officers and employees (no one is quite sure from day to day), and some of the 175 artists who perform as individuals, duos, trios and quartets.

Bedrooms, kitchens, closets, cellars and attics are packed with people, plucking at guitars or pianos, banging on drums pecking at typewriters, all seeking peace where there is no peace.

One of the most popular pursuits seems to be a daily game of "musical offices." The composer who may be sweltering in a garret today may find himself sniffling in the damp of a basement broom locker tomorrow; the vice-president who has an outside view may end up in an airless powder room.

Sisters Are Vice-Presidents

And there are vice-presidents aplenty. In keeping with a recording industry characteristic, two of them are Berry's sisters: Mrs. Esther Edwards, in charge of the international division and talent management and Mrs. Loucye Wakefield in charge of credit billings and collection.

Another sister, Mrs. Gwen Fuqua, is publicity director while a fourth, Anna, is married to Marvin Gaye, a Motown

are assistants to the president and brother Robert is quality control director. Inlaws' and cousins fill other key posts.

A Negro, Berry Gordy draws no color line in choosing aides, employes or artists. His vice-president for sales, Barney Ales, is white, as are Irv Biegel single sales director; Ralph Seltzer, administration director; Edward Yeszin, art director; and Michael McLean, engineering chief.

The Supremes and Marvin Gaye are perhaps the best known among the veteran Negro artists, but Gordy recently signed longtime Hollywood and nightclub star Tony Martin. Vocalist Connie Haines was put under contract last Thursday.

And the newest name being planned for promotion to possible stardom is that of an eight-year-old white girl from Los Angeles, "Little Lise" Lewis. Her voice reminded some audition listeners of the now almost matronly (21) Brenda Lee.

Lise's mother, Kay, and aunt, Helen, are known in the music trade as the singing Lewis Sisters.

The sisters sat beaming beside her recently as Lise cut her first tape in a makeshift studio cluttered with band instruments, cables and old coffee containers. It was the drab, unglamorous source of a thousand brightly colored phonograph albums and might have stilled a less precocious voice.

Gordy sat high above her head in a plate glass window in a booth filled with knobs, buttons and spools that he played like a cathedral organ, pouring out pre-

one hand while weaving the strong young voice onto the tape with his other.

The result was good. A lot better than most girls could do. But not good enough yet, Gordy explained to his new find, but the voice must have Motown quality to be best among countless competitors.

'It's Love, And Character'

Later, in the dark-paneled privacy of his office, insulated against the conflicting sounds all around, Gordy tried to explain for the umpteenth time how the Motown quality comes about.

"It's love," he declared. "And character.

"We love what we are doing and we try to bring that through every recording. And the artists we work with show their character by giving everything they've got to make each number better.

"We get hundreds of applicants for our auditions (held the first Saturday of each month), and feelers from established acts with other companies. But we don't take them on unless they've got character.

"The Supremes, for example. They were just high school kids when they came in for an audition and their first few numbers didn't move at all.

"When they finally did make it big, they could just about write their own ticket with anybody else.

"But they've got character," Gordy asserted.

"A lot of kids who come in here, and some big names, too, have got the talent but that's about all.

dio, undependable on the road, and disloyal the first time somebody offered them a little more money.

"A lot of these one-hit wonders fade out as fast as they come in, then have to go back to washing cars and waiting on tables. We don't take anybody on unless we are convinced they've got both talent and character, then we help them along between hits no matter how many months it might take."

Many young entertainers mistake their first hit recording as an open door to lasting stardome, Gordy explained, but for many it is merely a fork in the road — and for some it is a dead end.

"They buy flashy cars and clothes, living it up on royalties they expect to get," Gordy said. "But they learn that taxes, promotion costs and road expenses gobble up most of the money until an artist is really established. There isn't anything left for luxuries until then.

"At Motown, we try to help our people with financial advice on taxes and other overhead items, and how to save some of what's left to carry them in slow times..."

Golden Gloves, Then Korea

Gordy knows something about slow times.

Born on the lower east side 35 years ago as one of eight children, he came out of Northeastern High School in 1948 to try for success the way Joe Louis did, with his fists. He had 15 fights as a Golden Gloves featherweight. Then the Army sent him to another form of fighting, in Korea.

Afterward he worked with his father as a plasterer, ran a record shop and plugged other composers' songs while writing his own largely unproductive numbers with a friend, "Smokey" Robinson. (William Robinson is now Motown's youngest vice-president, at 25.)

Gordy finally gave up the security of an $85-a-week upholstery-trimmer's job on the Ford Lincoln-Mercury line to take a chance on his bedroom-studio recording business.

With another young friend, Motown publicist Al Abrams, he once went to promote a record in New York City, then the acknowledged center of the industry. They found themselves with just enough money for one bedroom at a hotel posh enough to make them appear more successful than fate was ready to grant at the time.

"We flipped a coin and Berry got the bed while I settled for the floor," Abrams recalled. "I guess I had a hunch he would be my boss. I only told him recently that I actually won the bed."

Gordy now resides in a Lafayette Park townhouse. He probably could retire to the Caribbean or Riviera if desired, having been offered "let's say more than $5 million" for the Motown complex. Last year it put out more than 12 million single

VICE-PRESIDENT — Mrs. Esther Edwards, Gordy's sister, is vice-president in charge of the international division and talent management.

BROTHER-IN-LAW AND STAR—Gordy tries out the motorcycle that Marvin Gaye (right), one of his top performers, rides to "Hitsville, U.S.A." Gaye's married to Gordy's sister, Anna.

★ ★ ★   ★ ★ ★   ★ ★ ★   ★ ★ ★   ★ ★ ★

Million Dollar Music in Four Flats

(Continued from Page 1-G)

records under various labels. These include Motown itself, with Tamla, Gordy and V.I.P. for popular music; Soul, for blues; Mel-O-Dy, for country and Western, and Workshop for jazz.

Its corporate subsidiaries include Hitsville, U.S.A. (properties); Motown Sales; International Talent Management; Jobete Music Publishing, and Stein & VanStock (publishing), with branches in New York, Los Angeles and Dallas.

Its major artists, aside from the Supremes and Marvin Gaye, are Tony Martin, Billy Eckstine, "Smokey" Robinson and the Miracles, Martha and the Vandellas, Little Stevie Wonder, the Velvelettes, Junior Walker, the Four Tops the Marvelettes and Brenda Holloway.

Fan clubs for the "Detroit Sound" and its oracles number up to 5,000 members in some European cities.

It Takes Youth to Understand

Most of the Motown star galaxy may be less familiar to parents than a roster of Vietnamese army generals, but they convey a magical, meaningful message to boys and girls 8 to 18 — who buy more of their records than earlier generations did for Toscanini, or Stan Kenton, either.

Gordy calls it love and character. Psychologists, sociologists and other learned men, who fear that the conveyor-belt which carries adolescents toward cultural

maturity has developed some strange new clanking, are not all ready to agree, however.

They observe the passion to picket for a cause, any cause from civil rights to California's "Filthy Speech Movement"; the fashion trend toward "unfashion" — beards, Beatle-cuts and baggy clothes; the apathy toward, and even attacks upon, policemen, and the almost disdainful separation of sexes while dancing.

Every adult who dwells on the subject of "What's the matter with kids today? winds up with a different answer and a headache.

The kids meanwhile, keep on jerking, swimming and frugging (these are dances, Dad) to the Motown sound.

What makes Motown go? "It's simply popular music," Gordy told a recent interviewer who sought the secret. "It's the music of today. Anything that sells a million records is pop.

"We have a sound that's a little different from anybody else's. We have that sincere feeling.

"I talked about this one night over dinner with Smokey (Robinson) and Diana Ross (of the Supremes). We were trying to figure out what makes the sound different.

"We thought back, about the neighborhoods we were raised in, the struggles, the rats, and we came up with a six-word definition: Rats roaches, struggle, talent, guts, love . . .''

Lots of love, with some electronic assistance from Chief Engineer Mike McLean, a bearded youth who built much of Motown's recording devices such as the eight-track taping system which allows sound mixers to blend almost any combination of instruments and voices over and over. Most companies use three tracks.

Dub, Distort, Emphasize

This custom-built equipment thus enables Gordy, the final arbiter of Motown's output, to dub sounds in or out, distort, emphasize, tone down or up, and otherwise manipulate the stockpile of prerecorded effects without recalling artists and technicians.

When necessity requires, he can call in a flock of string players from the Detroit Symphony Orchestra to tape a lush background in the afternoon, then record a hot rhythm section in the wee hours after a nightclub date, and a week later dub in the singers' voices — twirling dials until it comes out in a well-doctored blend.

The master disc is then made at Motown. Most companies send tapes out to be filtered through the not always loving care of a commercial processing laboratory.

The final stop is one or more of six "pressing" plants for copying, depending on the demand. Right now Motown is keeping most of them busy with assembly-line methods and quotas which would have amazed Henry Ford himself.

July 26, 1965

Mr. Robert Lubeck
Associate Editor
The Detroit News
615 West Lafayette Avenue
Detroit, Michigan 48231

Dear Bob:

   Berry wanted me to let you know how much he liked and appreciated
the Motown story in Sundays Passing Show section.

   As you may know, Mrs. Loucye Wakefield, Berry's sister, and one
of Motown's Vice Presidents passed away Saturday morning.

   All of us wish that Loucye could have seen Earl's story. She
had been greatly upset when her name had inadvertently been omitted
from a story on Motown which recently appeared locally. She had
been looking forward to seeing Earl's story on Saturday morning.
(As you may recall, I even asked you when the earliest copies of the
Passing Show section would be available.) She would have been very
happy seeing the story. You probably are aware of the fact that she
suffered her first stroke just three hours after Earl had interviewed
her two weeks ago today.

   I am sorry that the story appeared at a time of such great sorrow
for the Motown family. I did want you to know that the story shall
always be warmly regarded and considered by all of us to be an apropos
monument to Loucye Wakefield, her memory, and the legacy that she has
left to all of us.

                                    Cordially,
                                    MOTOWN RECORD CORPORATION

                                    By_____
                                       Al Abrams
                                       Press Relations

AA:met

Al Abrams
PUBLIC RELATIONS

THE GOSPEL TRUTH

Many people think that Berry regularly cruised the local active nightclub scene in Detroit looking for talent to sign. Sure, that happened, but there was also another way we scouted for talent. And this IS the Gospel Truth.

Even before we moved into the Hitsville studio building in 1959, every Sunday evening Berry and Raynoma would tell me to get into the car with them and we'd start driving almost aimlessly around Detroit's inner city. Berry would have the radio turned to WJLB which on Sunday night would carry live broadcasts from various African-American churches around the city. Berry and Ray would listen carefully to the choir when it sang. If they heard what they'd agree upon was a potentially interesting singing voice, we'd figure out what church the broadcast was emanating from and head over there. We'd go into the church and take a seat and Berry and Ray would check out a choir singer who had no idea they were actually auditioning for Motown.

If Berry and Ray liked what they heard, they'd give the singer one of their Rayber Music business cards. And what about me? Besides being literally blessed with an opportunity to see and hear some powerful gospel music close up and personal, I was along for the ride.

More than once after hearing a great gospel song performed on the radio, I'd tell Berry "You know all you have to do is take out the name of Jesus and replace it with Baby and you'd have a smash. You wouldn't even have to change the music." Berry would just smile at me knowingly probably thinking "Only a white Jewish kid would think of that."

So that might also explain why so many of those iconic early Tamla recordings have such a great Gospel sound. Divine Providence? Perhaps that too. You just gotta' believe.

"It's What's In The Words That Count"

Mr. Joe X. Price
Daily Variety
6404 Sunset Boulevard
Hollywood, California

Dear Mr. Price:

Thank you very much for the item in the August 9th issue regarding the signing of Barbara McNair to a Motown contract.

Actually, Miss McNair is not the latest Los Angeles performer to sign with us. That honor belongs to an eight year old girl known as Little Lisa whose first Motown recording, "HANG ON BILL" (on the V.I.P. label) will be released this week and should be on your desk shortly thereafter.

Berry Gordy, Jr., Motown's President is personally excited over Lisa's record, a feeling which is shared by everyone who has heard the dub of the record around the office. The comments about Lisa in the enclosed article from the Detroit News may be of interest.

Incidentally, your list of recent L.A. pactees to Motown omitted Brenda Holloway, who is currently touring the U.S. with the Beatles.

As regards Tony Martin, you should have a copy of his new Motown release "THE BIGGER YOUR HEART IS (The Harder You'll Fall)" in front of you by the time you read this letter.

Babbara McNair's first Motown release, which is coming up shortly, will be quite a departure from her usual style. I hope that it meets with your approval. Miss McNair will be appearing at one of Detroit's top clubs, The Act IV October 18th through 31st.

Chapter 2

GOING TO A GO-GO

opposite: Bon Voyage at Detroit's Metro Airport as Berry poses with the Miracles before they board a flight to carry them to the UK. This was the journey that culminated with the Miracles' historic appearance on Ready, Steady, Go on December 4, 1964 and helped set the stage for the 1965 UK Tamla Motown Tour

BOB DYLAN SAYS THAT SMOKEY ROBINSON IS AMERICA'S GREATEST LIVING POET

One morning I received a memo from Berry reminding me that Smokey Robinson is one of our nation's greatest songwriters and I should really do something in a hurry to promote him as such in the media because he wasn't getting all the recognition he really deserved.

Until this time, my emphasis was to place the primary spotlight upon the Holland-Dozier-Holland songwriting team. But, I realized Berry was probably right. Smokey needed to be individually recognized for his songwriting capabilities.

I mentioned it to Al Aronowitz, a music writer, who was also Bob Dylan's biographer and very close friend. Al said he had heard Dylan praise some of Smokey's lyrics once as being poetical. So I asked Al if he would let me get a quote from Dylan about Smokey. Al asked me what I had in mind and I suggested Smokey Robinson Is America's Greatest Living Poet.

Al thought about it for a minute and then said, "Why bother even telling Bob? That sounds just like something he'd say anyway. Go ahead and do it. If Bob sees it in print, he'll think he said it. He's certainly never going to deny it."

So I went back to Berry with the quote. I will admit that I lived in fear every time I heard Dylan was doing a major interview and might say "What the fuck? I never said that."

The fact that Dylan may never have actually said it - but probably thought it more than once - should not take anything away from the legacy of Smokey's lyrical compositions. It is just as true in 2011 as it was 46 years ago when Dylan 'said' it, Smokey Robinson IS America's greatest living poet. And maybe some day the Nobel Literature Prize committee will wake up and recognize that fact too.

"It's What's In The Words That Count"

FROM
OUT OF THE
MIDWEST COMES
A NEW LABEL DESTINED
TO TAKE ITS PLACE AMONG
THE LEADERS IN THE INDUSTRY
TAMLA, PREXIED BY ONE OF THE
YOUNG, DRIVING GENIUSES OF THE MUSIC
BUSINESS TODAY: BERRY GORDY, JR., A MAN
WHO HAS GIVEN YOU SUCH GREAT HITS AS "YOU'V
GOT WHAT IT TAKES," "MONEY (THAT'S ALL I WAN
"I LOVE THE WAY YOU LOVE" & "ALL THE LOVE I'VE
AND WHO NOW BRINGS TO YOU A RECORD SOON TO BE N
AMONG HIS GREATEST SUCCESSES . . . .

**BERRY GORDY, JR.
(MR. HITSVILLE)**

"WAY OVER THE
BY THE ("BAD GIRL") MIRA
TAMLA 54028 A PRODUCT OF MOTOWN RECOR
2648 W. Grand Blvd., Detroit 8, Mic

OUT 2 WEEKS: ALREADY A HIT IN WASHINGTON, ST. LOUIS, CINC

TAMLA

2648 W. Grand
Boulevard

Jobete Music
Company, Inc.
BMI

D. J. Copies

Chuck D.

Time 2:48
H-55518-A2

SHOP AROUND
(Gordy - Robinson)
THE MIRACLES
(featuring Bill "Smokey" Robinson)
Produced By
BERRY GORDY JR.
T 54034

From: Al Abrams
         Office of the President

Date: October 27, 1965

Re: Promotion - Smokey Robinson

Now that Smokey Robinson is one of the greates
of our time, I would like to start a promotion ca
him. When writers such as Bob Dylan have a f
they are tremendously publicized.

Smokey has had many great records, such as "S
Around," "My Guy," "Ain't That Peculiar," "I'll
Doggoned," "My Girl" etc. There are even mor
important songs than those I've mentioned.

I would like for you to work out some kind of plan
his promotion and discuss your ideas with me.

Berry Gord
Berry Gordy, Jr./gb

ury Park Astoria.

Ooo Baby Ba
by WILLIAM ROBINSON, Jr. and WARREN MOOR
Recorded by THE MIRACLES
on TAMLA RECORDS

MY GIRL HAS GONE
WORDS and MUSIC by
WILLIAM ROBINSON, MARV TARPLIN, WARREN MOORE and RONALD WHITE

THE MIRACLES—first of the Tamla-Motown artists have a r
lease in "Ooo Baby Baby." Perhaps this could be the disc to cha
British release—the fabul

MIRACLES
Vocal Group

Personal Management
BERRY GORDY, JR.

BIOGRAPHY

"THE MIRACLES", the group who stirred up national attention with "Bad Girl", can give the credit for their success to a man who has helped many other singers on their road to fame, Berry Gordy, Jr.

Four members of the group, all of whom were born in Detroit, Michigan had been singing together with another quintette when it was split up by one of the members joining the army. It was right after he left that an important break came. A friend had heard the group sing and made an appointment for them to see Berry Gordy, Jr. They had no first tenor, and the appointment was just an hour away. The four remaining members of the group remembered that their former member had a sister with a very quick musical ear, and with an hour to go they met with her and the rest is history. For as a result of that meeting a new group, "The Miracles" and a new record, "Got A Job" were born. They soon followed with the equally successful "Money".

The individual members of the group are: BILL "Smokey" ROBINSON, CLAUDETTE ROGERS (who in real life is Mrs. Bill "Smokey" Robinson). RONALD WHITE, ROBERT ROGERS, and WARREN MOORE. Their average age is only 19, but they are widely known to audiences everywhere. Bill, the lead and Ron, the baritone, also comprise the well known Ron and Bill recording duo.

The Miracles have traveled over much of the country with different tours, and have appeared with many well known entertainers on their travels, including: Marv Johnson, Jackie Wilson, Sam Cooke and others, but the tour probably never to be forgotten by the Miracles was the well publicized incident in St. Louis, Mo., where their appearance at a local one caused a near riot when their fans learned that all seats had already been sold out. The crowd was of such proportion that the police had to summon police dogs to quiet them.

Once I got over my Nazi-phobia about Motown's Volkswagen bus, I became an eager driver, even piloting Smokey Robinson and the Miracles to a show in St. Louis, Missouri.

ALTHOUGH THEY ARE both one year older than me, I share the same birthday – February 19 – with Smokey Robinson and Bobby Rogers of the Miracles.

Early on, I discovered that I could bring Smokey to hysterical laughter with the right joke or even a strange-sounding name such as that of one of my former Central High School classmates, Hosea Hornbuckle. Thus, on this trip, Smokey became my captive audience. As we drove through Terre Haute, Indiana I hit a treasure trove of names on rural mailboxes that I could point out to Smokey and bring him to tears of laughter. When we got to St. Louis, I noticed a used book shop along one of the main streets. I parked the bus and leaving everyone inside despite their protestations about the time, told them I'd be right back. I had managed to find a parking space right in front of the bookstore's picture window.

At that time, I was collecting old *National Geographic* magazines (not for the wrong reasons that you may be thinking) but for the vintage automobile ads. As I browsed the store's selection, I noticed the owner and his clerk nervously glancing out the window. Finally, the owner approached me and asked "Are you with that bus out there?" I replied that I was and looked out the window. I realized then what the owner was looking at - a bus load full of five young black males (guitarist Marv Tarplin was with us) - all wearing doo rags on their heads and anxiously staring at the bookstore door waiting for me to exit. (You couldn't see Claudette Rogers from that vantage point.) I looked back over at the owner who now asked, "Okay kid, what exactly do you want from me?" When I told him old National Geographics, he gestured to the pile and said. "Just take them all and get the hell out of here." I protested about needing time to look at the issues and pay for them but he just grabbed the stack, thrust them into my arms, and opened the door for me to leave practically shoving me out. I heard the click of the door being locked behind me.

As I got into the bus, I saw that the owner and his clerk were still staring at me through the window. I told Smokey what had happened and he said "We better get out of here quick." So I drove off.

The show was at a large auditorium and was hosted by Dave Dixon, a popular black St. Louis DJ. So many people had shown up to see the Miracles that crowds were milling about in the street hoping to get tickets. I found a payphone and called Berry in Detroit. I told him that I could quickly turn this into a national publicity coup to promote the Miracles. I asked Berry if he knew anyone at *Jet* magazine, the popular black weekly magazine, and he told me to call Chester Higgins. When I reached Higgins, I told him that there were so many fans of the Miracles out in the street that there was almost a riot. He was excited and asked me to take a photo. I had Berry's Leicaflex with me and shot some photos of the black crowd, making sure to include the groups of white menacing-looking police who were standing guard.

When we got back to Detroit, I wrote a story about the near-riot and sent the photos to Jet. And that's exactly how the magazine played up the story in their next issue. We had succeeded in cracking yet another barrier - entry into the world of the black entertainment weeklies.

A few weeks later, I went to Chicago to do advance promotion for an appearance the Miracles were making on the popular *Bandstand Matinee* TV show. Hosted by Jim Lounsbury, whose wife Debbie Dean wound up with a Motown contract (she was our first white female artist), the show also featured an appearance by Paul Anka.

I arrived in Chicago a few days early to visit the DJs and checked into a hotel in the Hyde Park area. When Smokey arrived, he came to the hotel to pick me up. He had just come to my room when there was a loud knock on the door.

It was the white manager of the hotel. "I'm sorry, Mr. Abrams, but you'll have to leave this hotel immediately," he told me. I asked him why and he responded "You are not allowed to have Negroes in your room," as he pointed to Smokey who was standing there in shock.

This is no Negro, I quickly responded. This is Smokey Robinson of the Miracles!

BUT THE MANAGER was not impressed and told me I had to leave immediately or he was calling the police. Smokey looked at me and told me not to argue as he started gathering and packing my belongings. As we left, the hotel manager told me I was not getting a refund for the room.

When we got to the bus where the other Miracles were waiting, I asked Smokey where they were staying. "With some folks on the South Side," he replied. "Is there any room for me?" I asked. Smokey laughed. "Of course there is."

I never stayed in another 'white' hotel again when I was on the road for Motown.

Did the Hyde Park area sound familiar to you? Fifty years later, that's the still-swanky area of Chicago in which president-elect Barack Obama and his family lived before they moved to the White House.

MIRACLES
Vocal Group

Personal Management
BERRY GORDY, JR.

FROM: Hitsville, U.S.A.
       2648 West Grand Boulevard
       Detroit, Michigan 48208
       871-3340 (Al Abrams)

October 12, 1965

FOR IMMEDIATE RELEASE

"SMOKEY" ROBINSON AND THE MIRACLES, MOTOWN Recording Artists, will be headlining a Revue at Detroit's Club
20 Grand beginning Friday, October 29th and running through
November 7th. Bill "Smokey" Robinson, leader of the group,
is a triple threat man. In addition to being a popular
recording artist, he is a songwriter and producer (with
three Gold Records to his credit), as well as a Vice-
President of Detroit's MOTOWN RECORD CORPORATION. THE
MIRACLES will be following their MOTOWN stable-mate,
MARVIN GAYE into the 20 Grand. MARVIN takes the Club's
stage October 15th through the 24th.

On the college circuit, JR. WALKER AND HIS ALL STARS
will be appearing at Notre Dame University in South Bend,
Indiana on November 24th.

THE MOTORTOWN REVUE will return to Detroit's Fox
Theatre with another all-star lineup this year. The annual
"live" Christmas Holiday stage show will present MARVIN
GAYE, THE FOUR TOPS, MARTHA AND THE VANDELLAS, THE TEMP-
TATIONS, SMOKEY ROBINSON AND THE MIRACLES, JR. WALKER AND
HIS ALL STARS and many others. THE MOTORTOWN REVUE will
open Christmas Day, December 25th and run through December
31st.

Luci Johnson Offered Contract

LUCI BAINES JOHNSON, 17-year-old daughter of President Lyndon B. Johnson, has been offered a MOTOWN RECORD-ING CONTRACT to record the song of her choice with proceeds from the record to be donated to the Democratic National Campaign Fund.

Miss Johnson was recently offered a motion picture contract during her appearance at a California Rally of the young Democrats for Johnson, at which she was pictured in a national magazine doing the "Watusi," the West Coast dance rage.

LIFE

LUCI BAINES JOHNSON

QUICKI-NOTE® DATE 10/2 1964

TO MR. RALPH SELTZER

① WOULD YOU HAVE ANY OBJECTION TO MY ORGANIZING AN UNOFFICIAL MOTOWN FOR JOHNSON COMMITTEE — AND/OR PASSING OUT JOHNSON CAMPAIGN MATERIAL OFFICE (UNOFFICIALY)

FROM AL ABRAMS

SEPTEMBER 8, 1964

NEWS RELEASE

LUCI BAINES JOHNSON, 16 YEAR OLD DAUGHTER OF PRESIDENT LYNDON B. JOHNSON, HAS BEEN OFFERED A MOTOWN RECORDING CONTRACT — TO RECORD THE SONG OF HER CHOICE — WITH

① PROCEEDS FROM THE RECORD TO BE DONATED TO THE DEMOCRATIC NATIONAL CAMPAIGN FUND.

③ MISS. JOHNSON WAS RECENTLY FILM CONTRACT DURING HER CALIFORNIA JOHNSON

② KAY BJORK THE A REPLY

Luci Declines Record Offer

The White House announced today that Luci Baines Johnson, President Lyndon B. Johnson's 17-year-old daughter, will be unable to record for Detroit's Motown Recording Company.

In a letter to Motown, Liz Carpenter, Press Secretary to

Recorded By THE TEMPTATIONS

MY GIRL

By WILLIAM ROBINSON and RONALD WHITE

Last minute preparations are made by girls before performance. Here, Mary "zips up" Florence, as Diana primps before dressing room mirror. Many of their gowns are from famed Saks Fifth Avenue.

Lead singer Diana Ross gesticulates frantically while caught up in magic of song at "Eli" prom. Most of Supremes' hits are written by Holland-Dozier-Holland and arranged by veteran bandleader Maurice King.

THE TRACKS OF
MY TEARS
THE MIRACLES
Tamla 54118
June 23, 1965

Al Abrams
PICKS

TAMLA RECORDS, DETROIT, MICHIGAN

AUDITION COPY   NOT FOR SALE

TAMLA 54118
© 1965
Jobete (BMI)
DM WLL-140311
S4KM-7754

Produced By
Smokey
Time 2:53
45 R PM

THE TRACKS OF MY TEARS
(Robinson, Moore, Tarplin)
THE MIRACLES

A TRADEMARK   CORP. © 1965

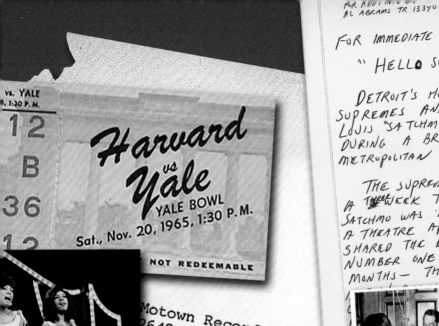

Harvard *vs* **Yale**

YALE BOWL

Sat., Nov. 20, 1965, 1:30 P.M.

NOT REDEEMABLE

vs. YALE
1:30 P.M.

12
B
36
12

FOR ADDITING ...
AL ABRAMS TR 13340   OCTOBER 6, 1964

FOR IMMEDIATE RELEASE

"HELLO SUPREMES — THIS IS LOUIS"

DETROIT'S HOT VOCAL GROUP THE
SUPREMES AND PERENNIAL FAVORITE
LOUIS "SATCHMO" ARMSTRONG WERE PHOTOGRAPHED
DURING A BRIEF ENCOUNTER IN DETROIT'S
METROPOLITAN AIRPORT.

THE SUPREMES WERE EMBARKING ON
A THREE WEEK TOUR OF EUROPE WHILE
SATCHMO WAS ARRIVING IN DETROIT FOR
A THEATRE APPEARANCE. BOTH HAVE
SHARED THE DISTINCTION OF HAVING A
NUMBER ONE RECORD IN THE LAST FEW
MONTHS — THE SUPREMES...

Motown Record Corpor...
2648 West Grand Boule...
Detroit, Michigan 48...

...tional information
...l Abrams (TR 1-3340)

EBONY

HOW TWO "JANITORS"
BOUGHT WHITE BA...
IN TEXAS

...LE BACHELORS 1965
...for Single Girls

...MEN CRY?

JUNE 1965 50¢

The
Supremes

Girl singers t...
rock 'n' roll fa...

Maestro Duke Ellington congratulates Supremes for fine
performance at Yale University where more than 2,000
"swingers" turned out to witness show which he led.

FOR IMMEDIATE REL...

...REMES WENT TO YALE: SO HARVARD WANTS MIRACLES

Smokey Robinson and the Miracles, popular Detroit
recording artists, are following in the footsteps of the
Supremes, by entering the new frontier of personal appearances
at the nations leading college campuses.

The Miracles will perform at Harvard University in Cambridge, Massachusetts on May 14th. The Supremes recently
appeared at Yale University and at Colby College in Waterville,
Maine.

The Miracles are currently touring England as part
of the TAMLA-MOTOWN REVUE. Their new Tamla single "OOO
BABY BABY" is quickly moving up the nation's best selling
record lists.

Bill "Smokey" Robinson, lead singer of the Miracles is
...o a well known songwriter; having written the recent Number
...record "MY GIRL" for the Temptations. In addition, he is
...ce President of Motown Record Corporation.

⌐ Apr. 12, 1966 ⌐

Dear Mr. Abrams,

Here's what the U.S. Information Agency is specifically
interested in with regard to the Supremes! They want the story
developed along these lines:

"The experience of The Supremes as young Negro
entertainers who have hit the top reflects the progress that has
been made in the entertainment world as far as Negroes are
concerned. Many of the problems faced by Negro entertainers
in the U.S. in the past no longer exist thanks to the efforts
of pioneers in securing equal rights. For example, the refusal
to sing before segregated audiences on the part of such white
entertainers as Frank Sinatra and such Negro entertainers as
Lena Horne accounts for the fact that today the Supremes would
not even be asked to perform before segregated groups.
The same applies in the matter of public accommodations and
other situations that have been changed by the improvement
in the Negro rights picture generally. Because of the progress
made over the years, these young girls and other talented
young Negroes find greater opportunities and happier circum-
stances than existed even a decade ago."

The story is for audiences in Africa who are specially
̶ ̶ ̶ ̶ ̶ ̶ ̶ ̶oes in the U.S. I will deeply

Sincerely,

Neal Shine
City Desk
Detroit Free Press

PEOPLE
you'll meet in Sunday's
Free Press

THE SUPREMES:
three Detroiters

DETROIT FREE PRESS
Friday, January 22, '65 9-D

ary swing

1144A EST

8 PD
TRI 1 3340

BERRY GORDY JR

SEASIDE HOTEL
ON THE BOARDWALK

ATLANTIC CITY NJER

PLEASE UTILIZE HOLIDAY TO WRITE POVERTY PROGRAM

SONG

AL
ABRAMS

CFM FORN
MOTOWN RECORDS CORP

AL ABRAMS

2648 WEST GRAND BLVD DETROIT MICHIGAN   R

THE SUPREMES
Motown Recording Artists

Personal Management
BERRY GORDY, JR. ENTERPRISES, INC.
2648 W. Grand Blvd.
Detroit 8, Mich.

a street in Brew

THE SUP

T

CONTIN

BUT THE "Detr
of records comin
outfit. The girls
over-all "sound,"   prefer their own name for their
blend. "We call it 'sweet music,'" says Diana Ross.
Though the records that have brought the S——

— ——— back to see me."
The girls stayed in school — Florence at North-
western, Mary at Northeastern and Diana at Cass
Tech. To help ——

Two events occurred which didn't help my situation with Berry and Esther.

ONE DAY, A YOUNG DETROIT SINGER named Della Reese told me she was having trouble getting on Bud Davies' daily live music television show broadcast over CKLW-TV in Windsor, Ontario, Canada - across the Detroit River.

I told Della I knew Bud. I phoned him and he said sure, bring her over. We were in my convertible with its top down coming out of the Detroit-Windsor Tunnel which connects the US and Canada, and had just turned onto busy Jefferson Avenue when a white Detroit motorcycle cop motioned me to pull over.

The cop walked over to me, pointed to Della (who back then was quite svelte) and asked, "Where did you pick up the n----r whore?" I was incensed. I copied the cop's badge number and after taking a tearful Della back home, informed Berry about the incident. Although he was angry that I was once again moonlighting with a non-Motown artist, he was supportive.

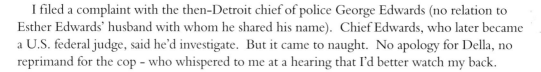

I filed a complaint with the then-Detroit chief of police George Edwards (no relation to Esther Edwards' husband with whom he shared his name). Chief Edwards, who later became a U.S. federal judge, said he'd investigate. But it came to naught. No apology for Della, no reprimand for the cop - who whispered to me at a hearing that I'd better watch my back.

The other incident happened after I intercepted a racist petition designed to bar African-American students from a high school in a then-white Detroit suburb. It happened outside the home of Judy Robinson Berger, the woman I was then dating. I had hired her as my secretary and she became Motown's first white female employee, but Berry refused to pay her salary when he learned that she couldn't type or take dictation.

The police were called after I took the petition with the intention of giving it to the editors of the Michigan Chronicle. In fact, I ate it. But that didn't stop an angry mob from following the police car and demanding I be turned over to them for 'justice.'

above: Della Reese

Once again, Berry was angry at first. His reason was that the reportage of the arrest would reveal that I was only 19, and thus too young to be frequenting bars and clubs like the Twenty Grand.

So we decided we'd tell the *Chronicle* that I was actually 22 and we wouldn't identify Motown as my employer. And that's what the front page headlines reflected. I was just a "record promoter."

The other promotion men in town were jealous and accused me of orchestrating the arrest just to further solidify my relationships with the black DJs to play my records.

On the day of my trial, Berry, Raynoma, Smokey Robinson and other Motowners showed up in the courtroom. The judge fined me $110 for disrupting the peace and Berry immediately stepped forward and paid my fine.

No record exists today of my arrest other than the headlined story in the *Michigan Chronicle*. The high school was successfully integrated without incident.

March 18, 1965

FROM: Motown Record Corporation
      2648 West Grand Boulevard
      Detroit, Michigan 48208

For additional information
contact Al Abrams (TR 1-3340)

FOR IMMEDIATE RELEASE

MARTHA AND THE VANDELLAS
TO MAKE NATIONAL TELEVISION DEBUT

Martha and The Vandellas, Gordy recording artists, whose record of "NOWHERE TO RUN" becomes the nation's number 12 best selling record according to Billboard Magazine,(as of Monday March 22nd) will make their national television debut on ABC-TV's "Shindig" on Wednesday, April 7th at 8:30 P.M. E.S.T.

"Shindig" is televised locally over WXYZ-TV (channel seven) in Detroit.

Martha (Reeves) and The Vandellas; Betty Kelly and Rosiland Ashford are currently touring England as part of the Tamla-Motown Revue. Last year the trio received a "GRAMMY" award, the recording industry's highest tribute, in recognition of the nomination of their recording of "HEAT WAVE" as one of 1963's best recordings.

Originally the background group on recordings by vocalist Marvin Gaye, the girls began recording on their own while Martha was employed as a secretary in the Detroit offices of Motown Recording Corporation. All three of the girls are native Detroiters.

opposite: Martha Reeves

THE DETROIT NEWS PICTORIAL MAGAZINE   JUNE 27, 1965

'Detroit Sound' Goes Network

THE "DETROIT SOUND" again will be heard throughout the land at 9:30 Monday night when Detroit-based entertainers are among those featured on a 90-minute television special.

The show is an unusual merger of the U.S. Office of Economic Opportunity (OEO) and teen-age appeal entertainers. Segments of the program—called "It's What's Happening, Baby!"—were filmed at Dearborn's Greenfield Village, the Mustang assembly line at the Ford Rouge plant and the Detroit offices of Motown Records.

Al Abrams
PICKS

AUDITION COPY

NOT FOR SALE

THAT COUNT

G-7056
© 1966
Jobete (BMI)
HQV-251M08
TK4M-6855

Produced by
Holland, Dozier
2:52

"I'M READY FOR LOVE"
(Holland, Dozier, Holland)
MARTHA & THE
VANDELLAS
In album "Watch Out" G 920

A TRADEMARK

RECEIVE AWARD — Martha and The Vandellas, Gordy Recording Artists, were presented with the recording industry's highest tribute, the "Grammy" award, by comedian Phil Silvers during his appearance in Windsor. The Grammy Award was made to Martha and The Vandellas in recognition of the nomination of their recording of "Heat Wave" as one of 1963's best recordings.

...NDELLAS RECEIVE "GRAMMY" AWARD

Martha and The Vandellas, Gordy Recording Artists, were ...sented with the recording industry's highest tribute, ... "Grammy" award, by comedian Phil Silvers during his ...arance at Windsor Ontario's Elmwood Casino. The Grammy ... was made to Martha and The Vandellas in recognition of ...omination of their recording of "Heat Wave" as one of ... best recordings.

...e "Grammy" Award is presented yearly by the National ... of Recording Arts and Sciences to honor significant ...ent in various categories of recorded music. The ...are selected by a vote of the entire Academy mem-... The "Grammy" Award is equivalent to the motion ...'Oscar" or televisions "Emmy".

...rtha and the Vandellas current record, "Dancing In The Streets" is now the number two record in the nation. They have just completed a night club engagement in Bermuda, and are preparing for an upcoming schedule of personal appearances in England and Europe. In addition to Martha Reeves, lead singer, the other members of the group are Rosalind Ashford and Betty Kelley. All are native Detroiters.

MARTHA
AND THE
VANDELLAS
HEAT
WAVE

MY BOY FRIENDS BACK
IF I HAD A HAMMER
WAIT TILL MY BOBBY
GETS HOME
THEN HE KISSED ME
MORE
HEY THERE LONELY BOY
DANKE SCHOEN
MOCKING-BIRD
HELLO STRANGER
JUST ONE LOOK

73

and copies to Ralph Seltzer.
other people listed

MEMORANDUM

TO: Mr. Berry Gordy, Jr.
           Mrs. Esther Edwards
           Mr. Ronald Wakefield

cc: Mrs. Rebecca Jiles
           Mr. Don Foster

FROM: Al Abrams

DATE: August 18, 1965

RE: The Chicago Daily News (story on Motown)

[handwritten marginal notes:] why between 1st & 2nd shows — more time between 2nd & 3rd — not necessary to send to Rebecca & Don — ~~Anything~~ a copy — anything having to do with studio or co. as a whole must go thru Ralph Seltzer for security purposes — (it will be available any time for interview) but it must be limited.

      The Chicago Daily News is interested in doing a story on Motown and the Motown Sound for their weekend supplement, "Panorama". This story would be similiar to the story which appeared on the first page of the Detroit News Passing Show.

      The Chicago Daily News will fly *Miss Rickella Williams* ~~a man~~ in for one day in order to look over the studioes, interview some of our key people, and if possible talk with the Supremes.

      In checking with Ronald Wakefield, I have determined the best time for this paper to talk with and photograph the Supremes would be during the break between their first and second shows at the State Fair. The Fair schedule is as follows:

best day 1st or 2nd

Thursday, September 1   2:30, 4:30, 9:00
Friday-Sunday, September 2-5 2:30, 5:00, 9:00
Monday, September 6   3:00, 5:30, 9:00

[handwritten:] Holland & Dozier should be included in overall story & not singled out

      Does this meet with your approval?

      Also, I would like to schedule appointments for whatever day is decided upon with both Mr. Gordy and Mrs. Edwards for one half hour each.

      The rest of the time will be occupied by a tour, etc.

      Please advise me of your comments as soon as possible.

      I would also like to schedule appointments with Holland-Dozier, etc.

                        By *Al Abrams*
                                 Al Abrams

74

AA:met

CHICAGO DAILY NEWS

panorama

SEPTEMBER 25, 1965

... IN INDIANAPOLIS
The Metropolitan Opera National Company Is Born

... IN DETROIT
The Supremes Swing to the Big Beat in Hitsville, U.S.A.

THE SOUNDS OF MUSIC...

... AT THE UNIVERSITY OF CHICAGO
Two Composers Discuss the Avant-Garde in Practice and Performance

... IN MONTEREY
A Tribute to the Trumpet from the Best in Jazz

BOB SMITH LOOKS BACK ON ALL THE NEW TV SHOWS • SAM LESNER LOOKS AHEAD TO A BIG WEEK AT THE MOVIES AND ON THE NIGHT BEAT • PAUL ENGLE REVIEWS FREDERICK MANFRED'S NOVEL

Berry and Michaela Williams

Berry is being interviewed by Michaela Williams of the Chicago Daily News for the Panorama Motown feature (see page 78)

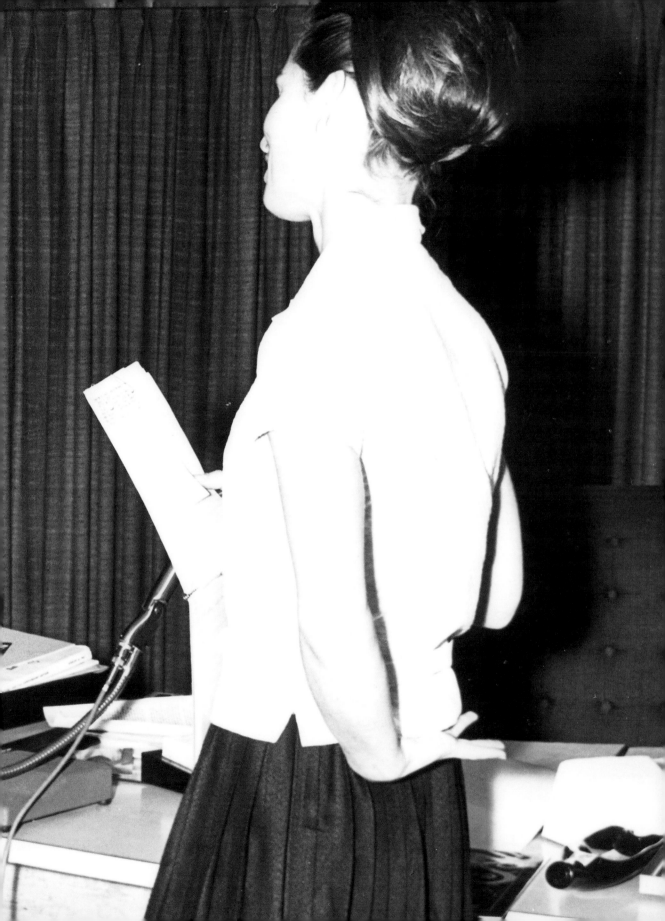

IN THIS OLD HOUSE THE BEAT IS BOOMING

That Motown Sound

By Michaela Williams

THEY LIKE to talk about culture in Detroit. They have seminars there about the arts, and they say things like, "Take away New York's million tourists, take away Las Vegas' gambling, and Detroit is going to be the entertainment capital of the United States." They say this because they are worried about luring conventions and visitors, and they fear they do not have enough to attract the world's spendthrift travelers.

But even while the burghers are developing their own Apologia Detroitorum, millions of people around the world actually are discover-

Berry Gordy Jr.: The soul, the spirit, the matrix of Motown.

ing, relating to and trying to get to Detroit. Because for these millions of people, this city is Hitsville, U.S.A. They know it from a sound, the "Detroit Sound," born in four houses in a shifting residential area on West Grand Blvd., houses that for years have been as unobtrusive as their Monopoly game neighbors, but which are now the home of a multimillion dollar anomaly also known as Motown.

Hitsville is Detroit is Motor Town is Motown. An American Liverpool, an industrial city expressed in music whose roots and appeal are as vague as sentiment and as sure as a heartbeat, whose style is as much a product of this city as Vernor's Ginger Ale.

Motown the company is the largest independent producer of records in America, the second largest producer behind Capitol, which has the Beatles. It has grown from a 1963 gross of $4,500,000 to $10,000,000 in 1964 to an anticipated $15,000,000 in 1965. Last year, of the 60 single records released, 42 made the lists of industry magazines like Billboard and Cash Box. An album, "Where Did Our Love Go," has just begun its second year on the charts. In August the Supremes' single of "Where Did Our Love Go" made it to outer space as a Cooper-Conrad request in Gemini V.

FROM A stable of little known Negroes—The Temptations, The Four Tops, The Supremes, The Marvelettes, Martha and the Vandellas, Marvin Gaye, Smokey Robinson and the Miracles, The Velvelettes, Brenda Holloway—Motown has grown to attract established stars such as Tony Martin, Connie Haines, Billy Eckstine and Barbara McNair. They record under seven labels: Motown, Tamla, Gordy and VIP for pop music; Soul for blues; Mel-O-Dy for country and Western; Workshop for jazz. European distribution is handled by Tamla-Motown. The International Talent Management Inc. (ITMI) and Jobete Music Publishing Co. are corporate subsidiaries.

Activity in front of Hitsville's houses spills over in both directions onto the lawns of a funeral home and doctor's office/home. There are whites in Sporting Life tee shirts with orange and black stripes, Negroes in continental cut sports jackets, girls in color coordinated pants and hair. The curious, the famous, the ambitious, the scared, the satisfied.

The whole operation from conception to master disk comes out of the four houses (except the art department, which recently moved to the Graystone Ballroom). Inside there are people—working, waiting, looking—and constant noise, not remotely musical—like construction. The buildings are in a permanent state of remodeling, expansion, modernization. Phones don't ring. But they flash perpetually and a girl who operates a mystifying switchboard is on the inter-com paging someone about every two minutes. Piles of 45's, tapes, lp's, correspondence and clippings fight to stay shelved as people breeze through two- or three-man offices that were once a sixteenth of a bedroom, or a broom closet. Long lists of TV airing dates flutter from the walls: Hullabaloo, The Red Skelton Show, Ed Sullivan, Dean Martin, Shindig.

The current debate is whether or not they should all move downtown to the Graystone Ballroom. Feelings are strong on this point. Most of the personnel have been with Motown since the beginning — some having been fired and re-hired a couple times. They feel the houses out on West Grand Blvd. have been lucky.

THE SOUL, the spirit, the matrix of it all is Berry Gordy Jr. The 36-year-old Negro sits upstairs behind an advance guard of aides, secretaries and closed doors in a big comfortable teak and leather office equipped with remote control TV, console with two turntables and a tape recorder. He is amiable if reserved, brightly level-headed with honest enthusiasms that flow into catch-me-if-you-can hyperbole ("Can I sing? I'm just the best, I'm the greatest guy around for singing, except carrying a tune.").

"Detroit is a warm, sensible town," he says, trying to isolate what his "Detroit Sound" is. "There are factories, a sort of warm-type working man. It's not coldly commercial as, say, Chicago, but people in Chicago and other big cities can understand the music." The early Detroit Sound (they also do Broadway hits, Liverpool, Sam Cooke) is about love, heartbreak, emotion. Typical titles: "Baby Love," "Back In Your Arms Again," "When the Lovelight Starts Shining Through His Eyes," "Stop! In the Name of Love."

On one paneled wall of the office, between a gold record for "Shop Around," a map of the world, photos and citations (including Detroit Small Businessman of the Year in 1965), is a picture of Gordy's parents. Across from it hangs a gold plaque: A Special Tribute To Our Son. The Gordy seniors still live in the old neighborhood on Detroit's tough East Side. It is a rambling, ramshackle frame house on St. Antoine (pronounced Antwyne in Detroit) St., in a neighborhood of rundown bars, marginal groceries, deserted houses, gobs of kids and empty lots cleared by the city, one of which once contained the Flame Show Bar, where Berry Gordy used to listen to music.

Gordy, his wife and three children now live in Lafayette Park, a new central downtown development. But emotionally the East Side is still important and the experience of it is part of the Detroit Sound.

Next to the plaque in Gordy's office is a portrait of "Smokey" Robinson and his wife Claudette. "He's a genius," says Gordy, "he's the most talented person in the world." It was Smokey who convinced Gordy to start making his own records when Gordy quit nailing upholstery in Lincolns at the Ford plant around 1958. Gordy had tried featherweight boxing, the retail record business, the Army; had sold a few of his own songs to distributors. Smokey kept auditioning for him and being rejected. Finally they decided neither could be less successful and they teamed up with a $700 loan from Gordy's father, each with a messianic sense of his potential.

Smokey's vice-president's office is a windowless square downstairs just big enough for a desk, settee and piano. He is headliner for The Miracles and one of Motown's main songwriters, along with Eddie Holland.

Perhaps because of the silky, gospel, church-meeting rhythms of the music, and the large Negro population of Detroit, Motown has been called the Brown Sound. The moniker is unpopular. "That's ridiculous," says one of the Supremes. "Colored people don't have 'A Sound' any more than white people."

FROM A WALL that is half speakers comes the familiar blend of the world's most popular female vocal group — The Supremes. These three girls are prototypes of what Gordy expects from his young stars. When they first came to him they hadn't finished high school. "They were skinny little girls in dirty sneakers." They came back after school, and the skinny girls are now being booked in the Copacabana, Sybil Burton's Arthur, El San Juan Hotel in Puerto Rico, Philharmonic Hall in Lincoln Center and in capitals all over the world.

"I want to develop a new breed of entertainer . . . clean cut, no temperament, lots of character. Kids have to be convinced to respect Uncle Sam. They have to learn to deal with money, pay their taxes, cooperate with the government."

Last year the Supremes made $300,000; they will surely be richer at the end of this year. They have all recently bought homes on the same street near the Russell Woods section for themselves and their families (Florence Ballard, 22, has 11 brothers and sisters, Diana Ross, 5, Mary Wilson, 2). All

Diana Ross records her segment of the big Motown sound.

three were raised in the East Side Brewster Project where, according to a Detroiter, "you have to prove you are poor to get in."

The Supremes act is straight: audible lyrics, subtle choreography, great-looking clothes. (What do they do when they aren't traveling, taping for TV shows, making movies or recording? Shop.)

Diana, the supple-voiced lead singer, has just finished dubbing in her parts for a Christmas album of 10 favorites and 10 originals. With a head-set clapped over one of the black wigs that has become standard equipment for all of them, she can purr along with a background of counterpoint, harm[ony] and accompaniment that has already b[een] taped.

THIS RECORDING technique is ano[ther] part of the Motown success guarantee. [With] a specially constructed eight-track tape [re]corder the major parts of the sound can [be] taped at different times — strings from [the] Detroit Symphony Orchestra, tambourin[es,] saxophones, whatever, and mixed mecha[ni]cally and scientifically until just the ri[ght] blend is achieved.

The result is then checked in a tiny ro[om] called Quality Control where a young la[dy]

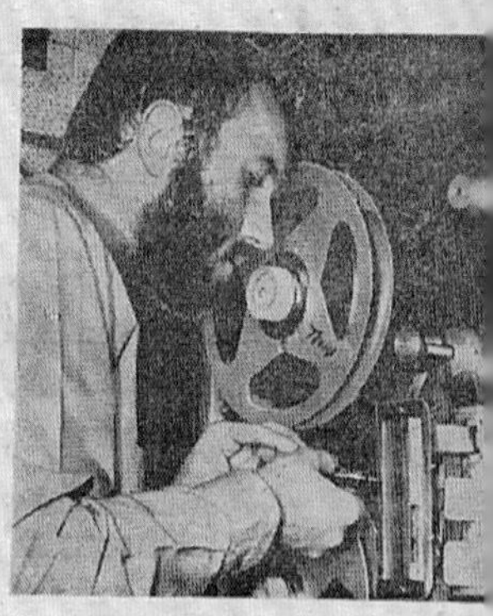

Michael McLean checks on the marvels of his multi-track tape.

and two producers listen to songs. All da[y.] Maybe one song 500 times a day and [at] maximum strength. They listen for discre[p]ancies in the mix — is the lead voice o[ut] far enough, is there enough or too mu[ch] echo, how is the bass feeling?

To reach the red-bearded genius who h[as] developed the electronic system you go ou[t]side and down some dingy backstairs, pa[st] little kids who hover around all day. "Where[']s the Supremes at?" "Got any pictures today[?"]

Downstairs in a workshop hung with ele[c]tronic blueprints, tubes, spools of red and ye[l]low wire, chief engineer Michael McLea[n] explains his eight-track system by drawi[ng] little guitar-playing people with earphon[es] on. He developed an Ampex three-track r[e]corder in the Les Paul manner. Mainly, [he] says, he built it himself for financial reason[s] and saved Gordy $8,000. "The point is [to] get the exact sound balance you want, th[e] proper light on the music."

He started with the company in 1961 b[y] answering an ad for an electronic repai[r]man. He is a music nut. He can almost te[ll] you who's playing what by the pattern th[e] notes make on an Oscilloscope (electrocard[i]ograph?).

But McLean affirms what everyone the[re] understands. "The success of it all revolve[s] around the uncanny ability of the boss. [It] mystifies me but he's never wrong."

UPSTAIRS, the boss is talking about tw[o] white kids they just signed from Alma, Mic[h.] "They're just sensational. His songs are to[o] controversial, Viet Nam, the bomb, Bob Dy[l]lan protest-type stuff. We'll try to tone hi[m] down a bit. But this girl, she's so beautiful. . ."

Chunks of diamonds that mark the hour[s] on his watch say almost seven o'clock. H[e] moves outside where people are still swir[l]ing around. An impromptu executive sessio[n] is held on the lawn with the financial, leg[al] and creative departments and a vice-presi[]dent just returned from Europe. A paper [is] brought outside for him to sign. His pea[rl] grey custom Cadillac with phonograph, tap[e] recorder and phones pulls up. The jovia[l] young man floats away.

It has been a day like any other day: A license for yellow sweatshirts with Mary, Di[]ana and Florence sketched on them has bee[n] okayed; negative to someone who wants hi[m] to sponsor eyeglasses with transistor radio[s] in the frames, to backing Supreme Bread to Motown book covers.

Bigger things are coming to Berry Gordy Jr. Rather, he is going to find them.

September 28, 1965

Miss Michaela Williams
Panorama
The Chicago Daily News
401 North Wabash Avenue
Chicago, Illinois 60611

Dear Michaela:

You were right.

You said that your story about Motown would be the
best yet.

And it is.

You have written _the_ definitive Motown story.

For the last few years, whenever someone (including
yourself) has asked me to explain what makes Motown tick,
I couldn't find the words to fit the answer.

From now on, I am just going to hand them a copy of
your story.

Congratulations on truly capturing the spirit of Motown,
and presenting it to your readers in an most interesting
manner.

                              Best regards,
                              MOTOWN RECORD CORPORATION

                              BY_____
                                 Al Abrams
                                 Publicity Director

AA:met
P.S. Lest I forget, I have finally been moved from my attic.
Part of my promotion entailed my relocation to a new office,
in the basement. But There is one consolation-the basement
occasionally floods. This is a promotion?
~~occasionally file~~

BOOKER BRADSHAW
Guitarist & Folk Singer

Direction
INTERNATIONAL TALENT MANAGEMENT, INC.
2652 W. Grand Boulevard
Detroit 8, Michigan

FROM: Motown Record Corporation
          2648 West Grand Boulevard
          Detroit, Michigan 48208 .

For additional information contact
Al Abrams (TR 1-3340)

FOR IMMEDIATE RELEASE

HARVARD-TYPE FOLK SINGER

OPENS AT DETROIT'S CHESSMATE

Booker Bradshaw, probably the only major folk singer to hold a Harvard Degree opens a 13 day engagement at Detroit's Chessmate Club beginning Tuesday, March 2nd. In addition to his Harvard education, Bradshaw studied at London's Royal Academy of Dramatic Art.

The young folk-singer and actor recently cut his first album for Detroit's Motown Records. Label president, Berry Gordy, Jr. is greatly enthused over the range of Bradshaw's ethnic folk material. Bradshaw's album marks Motown's entry into the area of folk music.

The Chessmate is located at McNichols and Livernois.

Show times at the unique folk club are: 9:30 PM, 11:00 PM; and midnight.

opposite: Booker Bradshaw, the Harvard educated folk singer who later wound up on the Tarzan TV series and starred as Dr M'Benga in Star Trek. He was a personal favorite of Esther Edwards, so I curried favor by getting him coverage -- hence the totally unjustified press release about him.

Chapter 3

THE BEST THINGS IN LIFE ARE FREE

opposite: Brian Epstein cops for some free albums! Neither Berry nor I were thinking in terms of future posterity that day. Did you know that to make money, we (Motown) sold Beatles memorabilia at a booth at the Michigan State Fair? Ah, the things I wish I'd kept.

THE LAST LAUGH!

The only physical confrontation I ever had with anyone at Motown happened, of course, over a woman. But I got the last laugh.

I was on the road with Barrett Strong promoting "Money" and we were in Gary, Indiana. Gary was a very important market for us because then, as now, it has a majority African-American population and some hot R'n'B radio stations.

While Barrett was on stage, I hooked up with a young and very attractive woman in the audience, which was my standard operating procedure. When Barrett came off stage, he saw us together and walked over. I introduced them and Barrett started hitting on her. When I told him she was leaving with me, he said "Hell no. I'm the star, not you, and she is going with me," as he put his arm around her and pulled her toward him.

I told Barrett that was bullshit and to find his own woman. I snatched her back and started to walk off with her. That's when Barrett grabbed me, spun me around, and hit me in the mouth. "I said I'm taking her. I'm the star, not you. You work for me," he said, then took her arm and left. He also took the car.

I was pretty stunned, not from the blow, but by Barrett's actions. We had never had a problem before. I called Berry collect, he was furious. He ordered me to leave Barrett and the car in Gary and take a Greyhound Bus back to Detroit immediately.

When Barrett drove back to Detroit, Berry really tore into him. Barrett apologized to me and I accepted and never mentioned the incident to him again. I wasn't exactly turning the other cheek. Berry had told me that when he confronted Barrett about the incident Barrett had told him "That fuckin' bitch gave me a dose of clap."

"It's What's In The Words That Count"

TAMLA

2648 W. GRAND BLVD.

Jobete Music
BMI
Time 2:24

Detroit 8, Mich.
TR 1-3340

54027
(G1)

MONEY
(THAT'S WHAT I WANT)
(J. Bradford & B. Gordy)

BARRETT STRONG

BARRETT STRONG

Personal Management
BERRY GORDY, JR.

BARRETT STRONG

Personal Management
BERRY GORDY, JR.

BI...

Barrett St...

attended and ...

City. He con...

the age of e...

with his four...

played the piano for the church...

With the upsurge of the rock and roll craze,

Barrett, like many other teenagers, formed a rock

and roll group. He was only thirteen at that time.

Barrett later auditioned for hitmaker, Berry

Gordy, Jr., manager of Marv Johnson and writ...

of Jackie Wilson's greatest hits. Gordy, Jr. t...

an interest in Barrett's style and signed him t...

recording contract.

Barrett's first record, a mild success,...

followed with the smash recording "MONE...

(that's what I want).

Barrett weighs 140 lbs, stands 5'9" ta...

is a talented, versatile young artist who...

accompanies himself at the piano.

THE BILLBOARD

ARTISTS' BIOGRAPHIES
JOCKEY PROGRAMMIN...

Strong Makes 'Mone... On Disk Debut

Barrett Strong, new recor... artist on the Anna label, is a ... tive of Detroit. He attended ... completed high school in ... Motor City.

Strong comes from a music... family, and at the age of eight w... the lead singer in a group wit... his four sisters singing spirituals... He also played the piano for the... church choir.

With the upsurge of rock and ... roll, Strong, like many other teen... ers, formed a singing group. He ... was only 13 at the time. He later ... auditioned for Berry Gordy Jr.,... Marv Johnson's manager and writer ... f Jackie Wilson's big hits. Gordy ... ook an interest in Strong's career ... d signed him to a recording con... ct.

Strong's disk debut on Anna, ... oney," is moving 'strong' on the ... t 100.

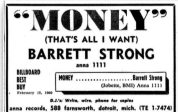

There were two early trips to New York City in 1959 that I will never forget.

THE FIRST INVOLVED accompanying Berry and Raynoma (Berry's wife and partner) to New York City so that Berry could take a meeting with United Artists about additional distribution of our records. Berry already had made a deal for Marv Johnson but was looking to expand it. I jumped at the chance to go with them. Why? Because it meant I would be taking my first flight and making my first visit to New York.

While Berry would be meeting at United Artists, I would be visiting the music trades, *Billboard*, *Cashbox* and *Music Vendor*. But there was one hitch. Berry thought it was important that we present a successful image which could be underscored by our staying in a first class hotel. If we left a message for anyone to phone us back at our hotel, it couldn't be one up in Harlem. So Berry chose the Park Sheraton. The problem was that we only had enough money to pay for one room. After we had made our rounds that day, we met back at the hotel. There was only one bed in the room and Berry was determined to let me sleep in it.

"You take it and Ray and I will sleep on the floor," insisted Berry.

I told Berry absolutely not. There was no way I was going to let my boss and his wife sleep on the floor while I slept in the bed. Especially with my being a white boy. Berry kept insisting. I kept countering his arguments. Raynoma just sighed and kept looking at her watch. It was getting later and we were getting nowhere. Frustrated, I told Berry we'd just flip a coin. He agreed and I pulled a quarter out of my pocket.

"Heads" said Berry and I nodded in agreement. I flipped the coin and put it on my wrist.

"You win," I told Berry while looking at the coin. "Let's do two out of three," he said.

"No, c'mon, Ray's tired," I replied, quickly putting the quarter back in my pocket without letting Berry see it. I actually had won the coin toss. Early the next morning, I heard a noise and saw a sliver of light. I didn't immediately know from where it was emanating. From my vantage point on the floor, I could see that Berry and Ray were still asleep in the bed.

Then I looked at the door. There stood one of the black hotel maids with the door ajar. Her mouth was wide open as she took in the strange sight - a black man and woman asleep in the bed and a young white boy lying on the floor. Before I could say anything to her, she had shut the door. I fell back asleep. But not for long. Maybe a half-hour later, I again heard sounds and saw a wider sliver of light. Looking immediately at the door, I saw a gaggle of hotel maids with the maid who had arrived earlier standing to the side. I'm sure the first maid had gathered everyone working on the floor that early morning. They had all come to see the strange sight. After what seemed like minutes in which I decided to feign sleep, they closed the door and left. Not a word had been spoken.

Berry didn't know he had lost the coin toss until five years later when we were being interviewed for a news story and I told the reporter. Berry laughed when he heard it.

My second memorable trip involved Barrett Strong's recording of the iconic "Money, That's What I Want."

WHEN BERRY PLAYED the record to me for the first time, I joined him in exclaiming "Smash! It's a Smash!" Because I was in charge of national record promotion, Berry asked me what disc jockey I would choose to "break" the record. Almost instantly, I replied, "Alan Freed." Yes, the legendary DJ who coined the term "Rock'n'Roll." Freed was then broadcasting over WABC in New York.

Berry asked me to check on access to Freed. We knew Freed would ask for money but just how much cash would he expect? A call to one of my promotion buddies in New York gave me the answer.

"You slip him a $100 bill when you give him the disk. That's not for playing it on the radio," I was cautioned, "It is only for Freed to give you his expert opinion about the merits of the record."

So with an oversize acetate dub and a $100 bill in hand, I flew to New York. Taking a cab from the airport to the WABC studios, I was excited about meeting Freed. When I got to the station, I was ushered into a long waiting room. Packed like pepperonis on a pizza and sitting on the benches were promotion men, all with a record in hand. As the line slowly dwindled, I listened to Freed's show on the speakers.

Then it was my turn. While a record was on the air, Freed put the acetate on a turntable and listened to the opening lines of the song. "The best things in life are free. But you can give them to the birds and bees," sang Barrett. Freed had heard enough. He folded the $100 bill and put it in his pocket. "I'm going to wail on this right away," he said. "I am the first in the country, right?" I assured him that he was and my audience with him was over. As I walked into the waiting room I heard Freed's voice on air saying, "Just give me money, that's what I want."

Months later, when I realized that this had all taken place while Freed was under federal investigation for taking payola, I wondered if those had been just the words FCC investigators had been waiting to hear.

Outside, I flagged down a cab. Because money was tight, Berry had suggested I stay at the Hotel Theresa in Harlem. That's the place Fidel Castro and his flock of chickens stayed when he addressed the United Nations. The white cab driver looked at me like I was crazy.

"I'm not taking you to Harlem. Are you nuts?" he asked. "Well, how far will you take me?" The cab driver thought for a minute. "I'll take you up to Columbia University. You're on your own after that." I agreed and got into the cab. I walked the rest of the way from Columbia University to 125th Street. I was the only white person on the street. But no one stared or stopped. I got to the hotel and checked in. With the cab money I had saved, I had enough left over to go to Tommy Small's Jazz Club that night.

The next day I learned that "Bad Girl" by the Miracles had broken onto the Billboard magazine Top 100 charts and sent Berry a Western Union telegram. Later that day, I called Berry figuring he'd be happy and send me some money. Two days later I got a letter from Berry on his blue Berry Gordy Jr. Enterprises letterhead. He sent me his thanks – and five bucks.

BERRY GORDY, JR. ENTERPRISES
2648 WEST GRAND BOULEVARD
DETROIT 8, MICHIGAN
TRINITY 1-3340

Al Abrams

BERRY GORDY, JR. ENTERPRISES
2648 WEST GRAND BOULEVARD
DETROIT 8, MICHIGAN
3340

CLASS OF SERVICE		SYMBOLS
This is a fast message unless its deferred character is indicated by the proper symbol.	**WESTERN UNION** TELEGRAM	DL = Day Letter
		NL = Night Letter
	W. P. MARSHALL, PRESIDENT SF-1201	LT = International Letter Telegram

The filing time shown in the date line on domestic telegrams is STANDARD TIME at point of origin. Time of receipt is STANDARD TIME at point of destination

```
(1107 PME OCT2 59) DEC725
SSD665 DE GMA587 (SY KRA224) 6 COLLECT LN 1 ATTPT
KR NEW YORK NY 2 305PME
BERRY GORDY JR
2648 WEST GRAND BLVD DET (RTE DY)
"BAD GIRL" BROKE NUMBER 78
   AL.
```

209

307

Berry Gordy, Jr./gb

Detroit Courier
THEATRICALS

Four Tops 'Reach Out' For Nation's Number

"BABY I NEED YOUR LOVIN'"
"WITHOUT THE ONE YOU LOVE"

"ASK THE LONELY"
"I CAN'T HELP MYSELF"

THE TV JOURNAL   June 26 - July 2

Detroit Does It Again

Four Tops at the Top

One Detroit sound gave way to another last week when The Four Tops' recording of "I Can't Help Myself" became the No. 1 record in the U.S.

Only one week previous, The Supremes' disc, "Back In My Arms Again," reached the number one spot, and became the fifth consecutive number one

record for the Detro...

The members of the Tops, who have been together since 1954, a Fakir, Levi Stubbs, Benson, and Lawrence

They have been the record the theme song TV spectacular "It's Happening Baby." The "You're What's Baby," was written Gordy, Jr., president of Recording Corporation, Tops' U.S. label.

The show is being d operation with the Unit office of Economic Oppo and will be aimed at teens and young adults with job and school pro

Also appearing on the ute special are The Sup Martha and The Vandella Temptations, and The Mi all Detroit artists.

FOR IMMEDIAT

FOUR TOPS ARE BACK AT THE TOP AGAIN

"I CAN'T HELP MYSELF," a Moto Detroit's Four Tops has returned to position in the nation this week, a board Magazines's ratings of the nat records. "I CAN'T HELP MYSELF" was nation two weeks ago, but dropped fr tion last week.

This is the second time this year th cording by a Detroit group has returned to one slot after yielding the lead. The Supre recording of "COME SEE ABOUT ME" accomplishe feat in January.

Ironically, The Four Tops recording ori reached the top of the charts by moving the Su fifth consecutive number one record "BACK IN MY AGAIN" from it's chart topping position.

Ergo! The Supremes are supreme, but the e tops!

AN INDUSTRY PHENOMEN

Motown Crashes N For Single Recor

BY HARVEY TAYLOR
Free Press Staff Writer

Detroit's Motown Record Corporation has emerged as an amazing Number One in total single record sales for the year 1965, according to compilations which Billboard, the international music-industry newsweekly, will publish next week.

The largest independent record manufacturer in the United States, Motown came from fourth place in "singles" sales in 1963 to second in 1964 led only by Capitol, holder of all U.S. rights to the Beatles.

The new supremacy in singles sales represents what is perhaps the most impressive achievement to date of the Detroit Sound.

The 1965 sales charts showed three Motown Records in the Top Ten, led by The Supremes' "Back in My Arms Again," the Four Tops' "I Can't Help Myself," and The Supremes' "Come See About Me."

MOTOWN'S NEW BIG STARS OF Tops as they appear on the cover of their

vin Gaye recorded "I'll be Doggone" and "How Sweet It Is," also high in the national rhythm and blues charts. Mo...

orized that why Moto in the sale that the year in re

June 9, 1965

FROM: Motown Record Corporation
2648 West Grand Boulevard
Detroit, Michigan 48208
For additional information contact
Al Abrams (TR 1-3340)

<u>FOR IMMEDIATE RELEASE</u>

One "Detroit Sound" Gives Way To Another

For the second week in a row, a Detroit singing group has the nation's number one best selling record. The Four Tops Motown recording of "I CAN'T HELP MYSELF" becomes the top record in the country effective Monday, June 14th (according to Billboard Magazine).

Last week, The Supremes Motown recording of "BACK IN MY ARMS AGAIN" reached the number one spot, and became the fifth consecutive number one record for the Detroit trio.

The members of the Four Tops, who have been singing together since 1954, are Abdul Fakir, Levi Stubbs, Renaldo Benson and Lawrence Payton. They have been chosen to record the theme song of the CBS-TV spectacular "It's What's Happening Baby". The show will be televised on June 28th over WJBK-TV, Channel Two in Detroit. The theme, which is titled "You're What's Happening Baby" was written by Berry Gordy, Jr., Motown President.

The show is being done in co-operation with the United States office of Economic Opportunity, and will be aimed at giving teens and young adults help with job and school problems.

Also appearing on the 90 minute special will be The Supremes, Martha and The Vandellas, The Temptations, and The Miracles, all Detroit artists.

"I CAN'T HELP MYSELF" is the fifth Motown recording to reach the number one position in the national charts this year. Of the five, three were by The Supremes, the other by the Temptations. In addition, two other Motown recordings reached the number two position this year (one by Martha and The Vandellas, the other by Junior Walker).

On the subject of number one records, Detroit's Marvelettes, who were one of the first female vocal groups in the nation to have a million-selling record ("PLEASE MR. POSTMAN" in 1960), and recently had the number one record in Singapore, Malaysia; will embark on their first

opposite: I wonder what happened to Brian Epstein's autograph book? Here he is getting the signatures of the Four Tops on his visit to Hitsville.

Al Abrams

RAISING THE STEAKS

During my stint as national promotion director at Motown, I could always count on a group of African-American DJs in major cities to break a new record for me so that I could use the tag line "Already a hit in ... CHICAGO" (for example) in a trade magazine ad.

One of those DJs was Dave Dixon of my favorite-named (by call letters) radio station: KATZ in St. Louis. But everytime Dave agreed to "wail" on a record for me, I had to promise him a steak dinner. Well, one time I didn't get back to St. Louis for quite a while and I wound up owing Dave eight steak dinners. Then I heard he was coming into Detroit for a gathering of African-American DJs from across the country that Berry had organized.

Whew, I figured this was going to cost me a pretty penny at Carl's Chop House - then one of Detroit's most-expensive eateries and one of my favorite hangouts - when Dave arrived for the convention. And I knew Berry wouldn't front me the money.

So I had a brainstorm. I went to my neighborhood supermarket and bought a package of eight frozen "minute steaks" the kind you would stick in an oven and serve up at dinner. Then I wrapped the package so it looked like an expensive gift.

When Dave arrived at the convention, I waited until he was in front of a large group of people including Berry. Then I walked up to him and said, "Hey Dave, are you ready to eat all those steak dinners I owe you?" Dave replied "That's one of the reasons I came to Detroit." Then I handed him the package. Dave looked at it curiously and unwrapped it. Inside, I had placed a card reading "Here's your eight steak dinners Dave...enjoy!" When Dave saw the card and the thawing frozen steaks he broke out laughing. Actually, so did everyone else.

Berry was not amused.

"It's What's In The Words That Count"

The Men Who Made Motown

THE CARE AND FEEDING of radio DJs was all-important to me from the first day Berry hired me as promotion man for his Jobete Music catalogue.

Along the way, I met some great people and made some very good friends. I also met my fair share of racist pricks as well. I'll tell you about both groups back in the day before I became disillusioned with the changing image of record promotion and yearned for the relative respectability of being a press agent.

Much later, my major responsibility was to get the white DJs to play our product. But I started working with the tremendous talent bank of Detroit Rhythm and Blues DJs on WCHB and WJLB.

Frantic Ernie Durham, Joltin' Joe Howard, Senator Bristol Bryant, 'Long Tall Lean Lanky' Larry Dean and Bill Williams are all still legends who belong in an R&B Radio Hall of Fame. But they deserve even greater immortality because they are the Men who Made Motown. How? By loyally playing Berry's records at a time when few, if any, white DJs would put our black vinyl on a white turntable.

I had the good fortune of meeting those greats on a different level - not just as a fan. When I was 15, I approached the editors of the *Detroit Tribune*, a black weekly newspaper, and asked if I could contribute a regular column highlighting news of my racially mixed high school. And thus the aptly-named *Central Chatterbox* was born. I wanted to keep the column alive after I graduated that year, so I converted it into a weekly *Top Ten Records* column for which I regularly alternated between the WCHB and WJLB DJs.

And so by the time I was hired by Berry, it was an easy transition to talk to and deal with these DJs. Make no mistake about it, I was a fan of these DJs and the music they played.

Lying about my age and always stalling on requests that I produce my birth certificate, I

above-right: Larry Dean Falkner; above-far left: 'Frantic' Ernie Durham was hired first by the Handleman Company, the distributor that provided Tesco among others with records - which I could buy every week at a substantial discount. I later worked in the mailroom of the giant McCann-Erickson Advertising Agency where I held the glorified title of "trainee." I still have a proposal I typed for one of the agency honchos (a character right out of TV's *Mad Men*) advocating advertising in the *Detroit Tribune* to sell Buicks to "Michigan Negros" (sic.)

That was the job I gave up to go to work for Berry Gordy for $15 a week and all the chili I could eat. The hardest part was giving up the shiny1959 Buick I was allowed to take home every weekend as long as it was back at the office with a full tank of gas (cost: $3.00) by 6 AM Monday. Somehow I never remembered to change the radio dials from WCHB to white-bread WJR. It probably jolted many an executive driving the vehicle on weekdays.

Indeed, it had been a white DJ, Mickey Shorr of WXYZ, who first told me about "the young black guy who owned a small record company and needed someone to drive his artists around to record hops on weekends." Record hops, emceed by DJs, featured lip-syncing appearances by recording artists, in return for which the DJs would "wail" on the artist's new record. Subtle payola, it was indeed.

Shorr, whose station operated on a tight Top 40 list, could not play Berry Gordy's records if he wanted to - and he loved R&B. Because he was unable to play those disks which he received from promotion men, he would take a stack with him to a Detroit deli where he regularly held court. Young fans of the music such as me knew we could approach him there and walk away with a pile of some of the hottest sounds imaginable.

One can only imagine what those soul promotion disks would be worth today.

Unfortunately, Shorr was to fall victim to the payola scandals and unable to find a job he moved to California and recorded novely songs with Dickie Goodman under the name of Spencer and Spencer. Returning to Detroit, he opened a chain of mobile electronics stores. Although Shorr died in 1988, the stores (and Shorr's legacy) live on as the car audio and stereo unit of the ABC Warehouse discount stores.

I was delighted to get the records that I would hear being played nightly by John R. and "Hoss" Allen on Nashville's powerhouse 50,000 watt clear channel WLAC radio station. That signal would come in loud and clear on my transistor radio every night.

Before I learned I could get the records free from Shorr, I would take a streetcar to downtown Detroit and walk to the record shop of Joe Von Battle on Hastings Street where for a buck I could buy a 78 rpm gem and safely carry it back home. When I first met John Richbourg and Allen at a DJ convention, I was virtually speechless seeing these two icons in the flesh – and realizing they were both white men.

One of my closest friends among the Detroit R&B DJs was Larry Dean Falkner, who one night shared with me his family archives showing that he was truly a relative of the Mississippi-born white Nobel Prize winning author William Faulkner. Note the difference in the spelling of the surname between the white and black sides of the family.

When Larry and many of the other DJs lost their jobs in the terrible times of 1959-1960, I set up a primitive job bank by seeking jobs for them through columns in the music trades.

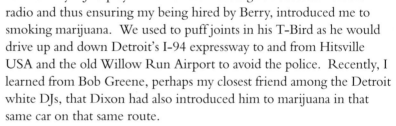

Larry Dixon, the first and only DJ to play Mike Powers "Teenage Sweetheart" on the radio and thus ensuring my being hired by Berry, introduced me to smoking marijuana. We used to puff joints in his T-Bird as he would drive up and down Detroit's I-94 expressway to and from Hitsville USA and the old Willow Run Airport to avoid the police. Recently, I learned from Bob Greene, perhaps my closest friend among the Detroit white DJs, that Dixon had also introduced him to marijuana in that same car on that same route.

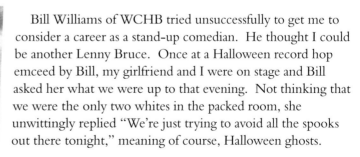

Bill Williams of WCHB tried unsuccessfully to get me to consider a career as a stand-up comedian. He thought I could be another Lenny Bruce. Once at a Halloween record hop emceed by Bill, my girlfriend and I were on stage and Bill asked her what we were up to that evening. Not thinking that we were the only two whites in the packed room, she unwittingly replied "We're just trying to avoid all the spooks out there tonight," meaning of course, Halloween ghosts.

above-right: Larry Dean Falkner and his wife Greer Simms; above-left: two of America's biggest DJs Robin Seymour (WKMH) and Ed McKenzie (WXYZ); lower-left: 13-year old Freda Payne wins one of McKenzie's talent contests

Powers Cuts Disc

★ ★ ★   ★ ★ ★

City Singer Launched on Tour

Eighteen months after he arrived in Canada with his pockets full of music—and not much else—Mike Powers has his first recording on the market, an organization of more than 3,000 fans, and high hopes for the future.

This week, the 28-year-old baritone (who lives at 539 Church St.) began a promotional tour which will take him to 26 cities in Canada and the U.S.

His record, "Teen-age Sweetheart" has already shown signs of clicking. Both it and the song on the reverse side, "I Left My Love in Paris," were written by Mike and are recorded on the Zelma-Quality label.

Mike was born in Yugoslavia, where his father worked in foreign embassies for seven years, following the war. He learned English and American-style singing from listening to records at the embassies.

In 1958, Mike headed for Canada, and Windsor was his first stop. He had no American visa, and the towers of Detroit were tantalizingly close and inaccessible.

He joined a male quartet in Toronto, and began singing on the night club circuit. He made a few television appearances (singing one of his own compositions, "Christmas Away From Home," which drew favorable comment), washed dishes when things were slack, and scraped together every cent he could for the professional arrangement of his music.

Then he came back to Windsor, and found a Detroit company willing to risk a recording.

Now that he's been "discovered," Mike's not washing dishes but he's working hard at his career. So far, his promotional tour has involved appearances in night clubs, teen centres and on television programs in Detroit and Windsor.

Mike sings with a pleasant, unforced light baritone voice and is slowly learning the rudiments of stage appearance. Intense, quiet, sincere, he has avoided picking up the off-stage mannerisms of professional entertainers.

"I've tried to develop my own style," he explains. "I don't want to be a copy of Como or Boone or Sinatra.

"For me, the money isn't the important thing. I feel I have something to give the world, and that's all I care about."

His local fan club numbers more than 3,000 members (mostly teen-and-twenty-year-olds) who are particularly active in helping promote Mike's records.

One record—even a successful first record—don't mean a career in the rocky entertainment field, but Mike's fans are sure he'll end up on top sooner or later. So does Mike.

There was dead silence. At the time, "spooks" was also a derisive slang term for Negroes. Bill saw the embarrassment and panic on her face and quickly came back with a quip that brought everyone in the room to laughter. However, we still made a hasty exit. In another essay, I'll write about other good friends like Chuck Daugherty, Harvey the K, Joel Sebastian, Tom Clay, the other Bob Green, Ollie McLaughlin and more radio legends.

But not everyone loved me or the black music I was trying to get them to play. Once, when I approached Lee Alan of WJBK, he told me - in front of a group of my promotion men peers - to "Get the hell away from me with that G-d damn N----r shit music."

I didn't tell Berry. In fact, I've never told him.

But because it was the midst of the payola scandals, I wrote a Western Union telegram to George Storer, the powerful Washington-based owner of WJBK, and suggested he investigate Lee Alan for payola. Then I signed it with a made-up League of Concerned Detroit Citizens tag, walked over to a phone booth in the Cunningham's Drug Store near Hitsville where we all ate lunch, and phoned in the telegram.

The next day, the headlines read that Alan was fired. Over the years, he repented and began passing himself off as a longtime early champion of Motown. But don't you believe a word of it. The League knows better.

above: WXYZ playlists plus a night at the Flame Show Bar featuring the cream of Detroit DJs and a very young Berry Gordy (far right)
opposite: extract from The Windsor Star, Windsor, Ontario, Canada

UNSCRUPULOUS

MR. GEORGE STORER
1605 Biscayne Blvd.
Miami, Florida

CAPS

WJBK

IN THE INTEREST OF PROTECTING THE PUBLI[...]
THOROUGH INVESTAGATION BE HELD INTO THE[...]
LIKE PROCEDURES OF ONE LEE ALAN, DISC J[...]

INDIVIDUAL

AS MR. ALAN HAS ALREADY ADMITTED TO HA[...]
T.V. SHOW AND ACCEPTING MONEY UNDER TH[...]
HE ALREADY HAS PROVEN HE IS A PERSON W[...]BLE
POSITION WITH A STATION OF ALREADY PRO[...]
STANDARDS HAVE BEEN LOWERED ONCE... AND [...]
THAT OCCASION...IN FACT, HE USED THAT OCCASION FOR PURPOSES TO HIS
ADVANTAGE IN FURTHERING HIS OWN PUBLIC IMAGE, AND HAS SHOWN THE
PUBLIC WHAT HIS ETHICS ARE MADE OF AND INFLUENCED BY— WHAT IS THERE
TO PREVENT HIS AGAIN BEING TEMPTED BY THE PROMISE OF FAST, EASY,
UNHONESTLY EARNED......MONEY.

AS GUARDIANS OF THE PUBLIC MORALS WE DEMAND SOMETHING BE DONE IN THE
WAKE OF THESE REVELATIONS. IF YOU DO NOT DO YOUR OWN "HOUSECLEANING"
WE WILL HAVE TO DO OUR CIVIC DUTY AS CITIZENS ,AN[...]
AND THE HOUSE COMMITTEE, AND POSSIBLY BOYCOTT ALL [...]
ON WJBK.

DETROIT CITIZENS

"BOBBIN
WITH ROBIN"
on
WKMH
radio
Every Day
MON. thru SAT.
3:00 to 6:30
1310 on your dial

ROBIN SEYMOUR

MUSIC FEATURES

X JOX

—UNE BUNDY

...eelance record promoter, a
...y were to discontinue a...
...ny hits would be found ar...
...at this could happen anyhow. With the current r...
singles sales slump is affecting many disk jocke...
...rs lose their excitement and enthusiasm—and it's...
...em—their lethargy is somehow transmitted to...

...d Abrams, of Tamla Recording Company, Detro...
...—in "an open letter to broadcasters"—: "As the indirec...
...f 'the payola furor' that has made promotion men...
...non grata' by most radio stations, I realize what I...
...refusal to give certain individuals their unquestion-...
...t to another chance and by continuing to hold...
...em their past mistakes, many of the top stations...
...oasts are in actuality depriving not only themselves...
...audiences as well of the services of some of...
...ly outstanding disk jockeys."

...THAT: S...

WXYZ Radio-Dial 1270
TV-Channel-7

"ED McKENZIE'S
SATURDAY PARTY"
Sat. 12-2 WXYZ-TV

"RECORD MATINEE"
Daily 3-6:15 P.M.
WXYZ-Radio

"Mickey Shorr's
RECORD ROOM"
Daily 4:30-5 P.M.
WXYZ-TV

"Mickey Shorr's
NIGHT TRAIN"
Nightly 7:20-10 P.M.
WXYZ-R...

"Johnny Slagle's
DANCE MATINEE
Sun., 2:30-3:30 WXYZ

"AROUND THE TOW...
Daily 1-3 WXYZ Rad...

TEEN LIFE

Monday, May 6, 1957

'Just Lookin' Fabulous'...

WCAR
Conrad Patrick

CKLW
Bud Davies

WWJ
Bob Maxwell

WEXL
Ben Johnson

'Casey' Kasem

...atic...
Yo...
...ute...
Ne...
...lds.
...t 5:...

..., Ol...
a...
...goe...
an...
...t ta...
...dcast...

Sand...
...y 2...
...from...
disk p...
...wate...

in Person!
The King of Rock 'n' Roll!
ALAN FREED
ON STAGE WITH HIS
SUMMER
FESTIVAL
OF ROCK 'N' ROLL

CHUCK BERRY
Clyde McPHATTER
The MOONGLOWS
JOE TURNER
EVERLY Brothers
Screamin' Jay Hawkins
TEDDY RANDAZZO
ALAN FREED and his GREAT ROCK 'N' ROLL ORCH.
Sam THE MAN TAYLOR · BIG AL SEARS · PANAMA FRANCIS

La Vern BAKER
FRANKIE LYMO...
& TEENAGERS
JODIE SANDS
LEWIS LYMON
& TEEN CHORDS
JOHNNIE and JOE
PAUL ANKA

BRENDA HOLLOWAY
Tamla Recording Artist

Direction:
International Talent Management, Inc. (ITMI)
2652 W. Grand Boulevard
Detroit, Michigan 48208

August 16, 1965

FROM: Motown Record Corporation
      2648 West Grand Boulevard
      Detroit, Michigan 48208

For additional information contact
      Al Abrams (TR1-3340)

<u>FOR IMMEDIATE RELEASE</u>

MOTOWN ARTIST BRENDA HOLLOWAY
ON BEATLES U.S. TOUR

Brenda Holloway, the 18 year old popular vocalist whose recording of "Every Little Bit Hurts" was a hit record in 1964, is one of the featured recording artists performing with the Beatles on their second American tour. Brenda, a native of Los Angeles, and a Motown recording artist, is the envy of many teenagers, as she will be flying across the country with the Beatles during their two week visit.

The Motown or "Detroit Sound" recording artists have long been favorites of the Beatles. During their last visit to America, the moptop quartet singled out the Supremes, Smokey Robinson and the Miracles, and Marvin Gaye as their personal favorites. The Beatles have also recorded several songs which originally achieved popularity in the form of recordings by Motown artists.

The opening concert by the Beatles held at New York's Shea Stadium Sunday, August 15th was taped by a crew from the Ed Sullivan CBS-TV show. Highlights of the concert will be shown by Sullivan in a special show entirely devoted to the Beatles, which will be televised on Sunday, September 12th. Brenda Holloway may thus very well make her debut on the Ed Sullivan Show in the very good company of the Beatles. (The Ed Sullivan Show is carried locally by WJBK-TV, channel two, at 8:00 P.M. E.S.T.)

Incidentally, Detroit's singing Supremes are featured in the repeat telecast of ABC-TV's "Hollywood Palace" this Saturday, August 21st. This show is carried locally by WXYZ-TV, channel seven, at 9:30 P.M. E.S.T. That same night, the Supremes will be appearing live, in concert, at the Meadow Brook Pavilion of Oakland University at Rochester, Michigan in a program designed to raise money for scholarships for the University.

On Tour with the Beatles: Our Brenda Files Her Report

BY GLENNA McWHIRTER
Free Press Staff Writer

"The Beatles never calm down, never relax. The whole trip was like a crazy, wild vacation.

"Ringo planned all the menus and we ate green beans every night for two weeks!

"In Portland the kids caught up with us. They were pushing and screaming. You feel like you're going to be killed.

"On the plane we sang, and talked, and had pillow fights.

"George never combs his hair; I don't know if he'll ever get married because of that hair."

The words tumbled out, bubbled over each other in a disorganized litany, a declaration of faith, a prayer of thanksgiving. Brenda Holloway was remembering the two weeks she spent on tour with the Beatles in August.

Like half the world's teenagers, 19-year-old Brenda is wiggy (as they say) about the Beatles. Unlike most of those teens, though, Brenda is a recording star in her own right. "Every Little Bit Hurts," "When I'm Gone," and "Operator" are among her hits on the Tamla label for Detroit's burgeoning Motown Records.

Brenda started violin lessons at the age of seven, kept at them for 10 years and still is a talented violinist. She also plays the flute, cello, and piano. But her key to fame is the way she can sing the hot "rock" with a bluesy sound that mellows the biting edge.

When the Beatles' tour of the States was about to start this summer, there was a widely circulated story that the Beatles had insisted on Brenda's joining them after hearing one of her records sent them by a disc jockey in Texas. The story, according to Brenda, was false.

What actually happened was that Motown president Berry Gordy suggested to the Beatles' manager, Brian Epstein, that Brenda go along, and sent him some tapes of Brenda's work — possibly "Put Your Head on My Shoulder," which has been a big hit in England. "I don't think the Beatles knew anything about me until it was all settled," said Brenda modestly.

At any rate, Brenda was the only girl singer in the troupe, which also included five dancers, the eight-member King Curtis band, Cannibal and the Headhunters (four of them—eeek!), and a British instrumental group called Sounds, Inc.

The tour began at Shea Stadium in New York City and continued—inexorably—through Toronto, Atlanta, Houston, Chicago, Minneapolis, Portland, San Diego and Los Angeles. It ended two weeks later in San Francisco's Cow Palace. There were two shows a night, one- and two-night stands to sell-out crowds of 15,000 to 50,000 ecstatic disciples of THE sound. A real blair!

Through it all Brenda's devotion to the Beatles shone bright and constant. For a while afterward she suffered from a slight sore throat picked up on the tour, but she sighed, "I'll never be able to tell you how wonderful it was, how really nice the Beatles are.

"Ringo is my favorite. He's so friendly. On the plane he talked and joked all the time, even with the dancers. He didn't have to; he just likes people.

"Music is his whole life and he's always talking about it. He wants to be a really good drummer.

BRENDA HOLLOWAY: "Ringo is my favorite."

August 23, 1965

Mr. Alex Freeman
Number Two, Horizon
Fort Lee, New Jersey

Dear Alex:

Here's an interesting report from Our Girl with the Beatles,
Brenda Holloway, that I wanted to pass on to you.

"RINGO BORROWED MY HAIR DRYER TODAY".

Early Sunday morning, a very excited Brenda called me from
Minneapolis to tell me about a highlight of her two week cross country
tour with the Beatles.

Saturday afternoon, just prior to the tours appearance at
Metropolitan Stadium in Minneapolis, Brenda heard a knock at her hotel
room door. Opening it, she found Beatle Ringo Starr, with his ample
hair pinned up in rollers and curlers. Ringo explained to a startled
Brenda that he would like to borrow Brenda's portable hair dryer.
Brenda agreed to loan Ringo her dryer, provided Ringo would autograph
it upon return. Brenda was Ringo's only chance to borrow a dryer, as
the 18 year old singer is the only female performer with the tour.
Besides, how many other girls can say that Ringo Used their hair dryer,
and autographed it too!

Since pincurls and rollers are a way of life to the Bealtes, you'd
think they would have their own hair dryers. Perhaps one of the other
Beatles was under their dryer when Ringo had to borrow Brenda's.
George perhaps?

Many thanks for the item on Brenda in last Friday's column.

                              Best regards,
                              MOTOWN RECORD CORPORATION

                         By _____
                              Al Abrams
                              Press Relations

AA:met

September 3, 1965

Mr. Mort Persky
Sundat Feature Editor
Detroit Free Press
321 West Lafayette Ave.
Detooit, Michigan 48231

Dear Mort:

This letter is to confirm our telephone conversation regarding Brenda Holloway.

I hope that you will be able to personally talk
with Brenda. I know that you'll enjoy meeting her. I'll
be more than happy to bring Brenda down to the Free Press,
on either the afternoon of Monday the 13th or early Tuesday the 14th, whichever date should be most convenient for
you. Please be assured that Brenda's story will be an exclusive for the Free Press.

I sincerely appreciate your interest in Brenda.
I know that she will make a very good and interesting story
for "Detroit" magazine.

I hope that the photographs of Barbara McNair
which I sent to you Thursday were satisfactory. I'll check
out the dates that she will be in town to record and, if
you have the time, I'll be glad to bring her over to the
Free Press so that you can meet had talk with her. I had
the pleasure of meeting her a short time ago, and I was
quite impressed by her personality. If anything of interest,
that might be worth a story, should result from her interview, this too would be an exclusive to the Free Press.

Thanks again for your interest...and for your help.

Best regards,

MOTOWN RECORD CORPORATION

Al Abrams - Press Relations

106

AA:kh

November 15, 1965

Dear Mr. Abrams,

When I received the copies that you sent of the Detroit which featured Teens In Detroit. And I looked and saw my picture. I just could believe it. I was so happy I cried.

They have in Los Angeles a similar magazine, and never have I seen any teenagers with the exception of the Beatles on the cover. So of course you know this floored me.

you are definitely in my corner Al, and if _____

proud to know t___
_ your corner. And _
forever grateful to y_
the things to are b_
succeed.

May God c___
_ss you and keep
_m

P.s.
_ recorded a
_ album
_ the "Boss Club"
_ Hollywood on the
stripe.

Gratefully Yours
Brenda Holloway

9543 Bandera St
Los Angeles 2 California

SPECIAL ISSUE:
Teens In Detroit

DETROIT
The Magazine of Michigan's Metropolis   November 7, 1965   The Detroit Free Press

BRENDA and Those Beatles   NADINE and Those Clothes

LOS ANGELES, CALIF. 88
PM
16 NOV
1965

8¢
U.S. AIR MAIL

Mr. Al Abrams   Boulevard
2648 West Grand Avenue
Detroit 8, Michigan

November 16, 1965

Mr. Van G. Sauter
Hotel Caravelle
Saigon, South Vietnam

Dear Van:

The germ of a good human interest story just crossed
my mind.

Are you aware that Mary Wilson of The Supremes has a
brother now serving in Vietnam. His name is Roosevelt Wilson,
and he's in the Army.

This might make for a good local story and would be of
interest nationally as well on the strength of The Supremes

We could work something out with Mary by sending him a
gift, album, etc., Via yourself.

Please let me know your comments on this idea.

I am preparing a copy of my new book "How To Cheat Tic-
Tac-Toe" for you, but how can I claim 10% of the winnings?

                    Best Regards,

                    Al Abrams
                    Press Relations

AA:rmp

Sidney Poitier, rising singer Liz Lands, comic Dick Gregory were part of million-dollar talent at the Freedom Festival.

Liz Lands Gospel Lyric Soprano, Waxes JFK Tribute
A special song tribute to the late President Kennedy called *May What He Lived For, Live*, was recorded by gospel lyric soprano Liz Lands, for the Motown Record Co. in Detroit.

Remember When J.F.K. Said:
"*If an American, because his skin is dark ... cannot enjoy the full and free life which all of us want, then who among us would be content to have the color of his skin changed and stand in his place?*"

NOW YOU CAN HEAR THE HISTORIC WORDS THAT ENDEARED HIM TO AMERICA'S NEGROES

Available in a 12-inch Long Play High Fidelity Recording   *7 Civil Rights Speeches*

John F. Kennedy

JOHN F. KENNEDY AND THE NEGRO captures much of the late President's personal views on civil rights. This long-playing recording can be purchased through the EBONY BOOKSHOP, 1820 S. Michigan Ave., Chicago, Ill., 60616 by mail order. Send $2.00 for each record.

FILL OUT COUPON

WE SHALL OVERCOME
(Arr. By: Fowler, Paul)

Promotional
Not For Sale

G-7023
Jobete-BMI
DM B-052104

GORDY

Produced By
FOWLER
& PAUL
Time: 3:15
Vocal Accomp.
Voices of
Salvation
45 RPM

LIZ LANDS
Excerpt from Gordy Album
908—"The Great March
to Washington"

20c JET   DEC. 12, 1963

THE LEGACY
JFK LEAVES
TO NEGROES

20c JET   JAN. 9, 1964

WILL [...] FOR NEGRO[...] IN 1964?

Dinah's
Best Kept—
Secret

LIZ LANDS—Records by this young Detroit singer is vocal tribute to President John F. Kennedy, "May What He Lived For Live," were distributed to over 2,000 delegates on the floor of the Democratic Convention in Atlantic City last week. Through the efforts of Joseph Lieberman, Administrative Assistant to Democratic Chairman John M. Bailey, the records were made available to the delegates during the memorial program honoring the late President. The record was enthusiastically received by the delegates, and was heard by millions when it received play on a national network.

HITCH HIKE
MARVIN GAYE
Tamla 54075
December 19, 1962

Al Abrams
PICKS

Hi, I'm Marvin Gaye. You know, the Free
good with Teen Beat. That's a special pa
record beat, the what's-happening beat,
beat, the clothes beat ... the who
Beat every Friday in the Detr
all the action is.

Come on, Teen Beat
Comin' on
Come on, Teen Beat
Comin' on
Free Press, Teen Beat

What's way in
What's way out
Who's talking to you
What's the talk about?

Come on, Teen Beat
Comin' on
Come on, Teen Beat
Comin' on
Free Press, Teen Beat

TAMLA RECORDS, DETROIT, MICHIGAN
AUDITION COPY
NOT FOR SALE

45 RPM
Jobete
BMI

Time 2:31
NO8W-4160

HITCH HIKE
(Stevenson, Paul, Gaye)
MARVIN GAYE
Produced by William Stevenson

#77

Not for
commercial
purposes—Not
to be Sold

THE TEE
MA

AIN'T THAT PECULIAR

Words and Music by
WILLIAM ROBINSON, WARREN MOORE, MARV TARPLIN and ROBERT ROGERS

Recorded by MARVIN GAYE on TAMLA Records

JOBETE MUSIC CO., INC.

75¢

Recorded by MARVIN GAYE & KIM WESTON on Tamla Records

WHAT GOOD AM I WITHOUT YOU

by WILLIAM STEVENSON and ALPHONSO HIGDON

custom

JOBETE MUSIC CO., INC.

75¢

d Corporati
nd Bouleva
igan, 4820
ion
1-3340)

MARVIN GAYE REVUE
RETURNS TO 20 GRAND

Marvin Gaye, popular Detroit recording artist, opens a ten
engagement at Detroit's Club 20 Grand on Friday, February 19th.
tured on the bill with Marvin are: songstress Kim Weston,
Spinners, and the Earl Van Dyke Band. Last year a similiar
broke all existing house records for the 20 Grand according
owner, Bill Kabbush.

gotiations are currently underway for Marvin Gaye to
ny of the nightclub engagements left open by the death
These include New York's Copacabana, and major
Miami Beach clubs. Tentative plans are also
n to sing the Academy Award best song
wn" on the national telecast of
"My Kind Of Town" is from
Seven Hoods" which starred
ed by Marvin in his best

t Free Press
CTION PAPER

SIDE 1
Copyright 1966—
Detroit Free Press

77

tio
"Rob
tune
"Hell

BEAT SONG
N GAYE

of Motown
Corp.)

hat's 'Teen Beat'!

When you're trying to sell
teen-agers, you gotta talk their
language.

And there's little doubt that
the Free Press is talking their
language in a new radio commercial that promotes our Friday "Teen Beat" page.

The voice on the commer-
cial belongs to teen record idol
Marvin Gaye. The music is by
Johnny Allen, a regular
writer for Gaye and his co-
performers at Motown Rec-
ords. And the 11 musicians all
are well-schooled in the
"Detroit sound" that Motown
has made world-famous.

To a large extent, Sunday
Editor Mort Persky is responsible for it all. Spurred by a
request from the Promotion Department, Persky worked out
the deal with Motown's public
relations man, Al Abrams.

The Free Press advertising
agency also did its bit, pro-
viding the words for the
commercial.

It was recorded at the Artie
Fields studio—and what you
hear in the one-minute and
30-second versions of the spot is
the result of a hard afternoon's
labor by Marvin Gaye and his
musician friends.

DREW PEARSON AND STEVIE WONDER
Drew Pearson's Big Brother BAR-B-Q)

Direction:
International Talent Management
2652 West Grand Boulevard
Detroit 8, Michigan

Chapter 4

I CALL IT PRETTY MUSIC
BUT THE OLD PEOPLE CALL IT THE BLUES

opposite: The only way I could get a photo of Little Stevie Wonder into white newspapers would be to pose him with Drew Pearson, the famous muckraking political columnist. Accused frequently of printing bullshit about politicians in his Washington Merry-Go-Round column, Pearson began packaging cow manure and selling it from his farm.

FINGERTIPS!

Tammi Terrell was not the only Motown artist who liked hanging out in my office. In her case, it was to meet the male artists who regularly stopped by with news for me.

But Stevie Wonder had another reason for making a stop-over in my office. The story gives a new twist to Stevie's recording of "Fingertips."

I was always thrilled when Stevie would navigate his way to my office to stop in, if only just to say hello. However, I soon learned that the then still 'Little' Stevie Wonder had an ulterior motive.

My very efficient secretary at that time was named Rosie. Unfortunately, most people who remember her will do so because of her enormous breasts.

That message somehow got to Stevie. When he would walk in my office, he would stretch out his arms and start groping the walls and feeling his way around. Somehow, his groping always brought him straight to Rosie and her breasts. He'd stand there copping a feel with his hands on her breasts and with a grin on his face and say, "Now I know I'm in the right office."

For her part, Rosie was a great sport everytime it happened. However, once Stevie's visits were observed by some of the male artists and producers, it launched a series of suddenly-blinded visitors to my office all trying to find their way to me in the same manner.

"It's What's In The Words That Count"

I've always wished I had a primitive movie recorder on the day when Stevie Wonder performed a free concert at my home.

I HAD HITCHED A RIDE back home with Stevie and his driver after we had done a *Detroit Free Press* interview. I had called my then-wife Sharri to tell her I was on the way home with Stevie. She mentioned it to several of the kids in the neighborhood. By the time we arrived, there were at least 20 kids milling around in front of my home.

Stevie heard all the commotion and asked me what was going on outside the car. I told Stevie about all the kids waiting just to see him and he asked if I had a porch. I told him I did and escorted him there. I had no idea what he was planning.

Stevie acknowledged the cheers of the kids in the audience - we lived in an integrated neighborhood - and Stevie proceeded to sing four of his hit songs for the kids. When it was over, he thanked everyone.

I had met my wife, Sharri, when I used to visit WJBK to drop off records and talk to DJs during their on-air commercial breaks. Sharri worked at the radio station in the Traffic Department and would walk back and forth across the lobby's waiting room in a miniskirt showing off her great legs. I obviously paid close attention but we didn't connect until after she "accidentally" bumped into me on Detroit's Woodward Avenue one Friday evening on the strip where Detroit's record distributors had their headquarters. I always thought of Sharri as the best benefit of my years as a promotion man.

Wednesday, August 26, 1964

STEVIE WONDER, fourteen - year - old Detroit-born blind singer, will perform in a one-man show for the patients at the Rehabilitation Institute on Wednesday, August 26, at 8 p.m. Stevie, a Talma Recording artist, has been featured in several motion pictures as, well as having appeared on the Ed Sullivan Show. The Rehabilitation Institute is located at 261 Mack Boulevard (formerly Brady) near Harper Hospital.

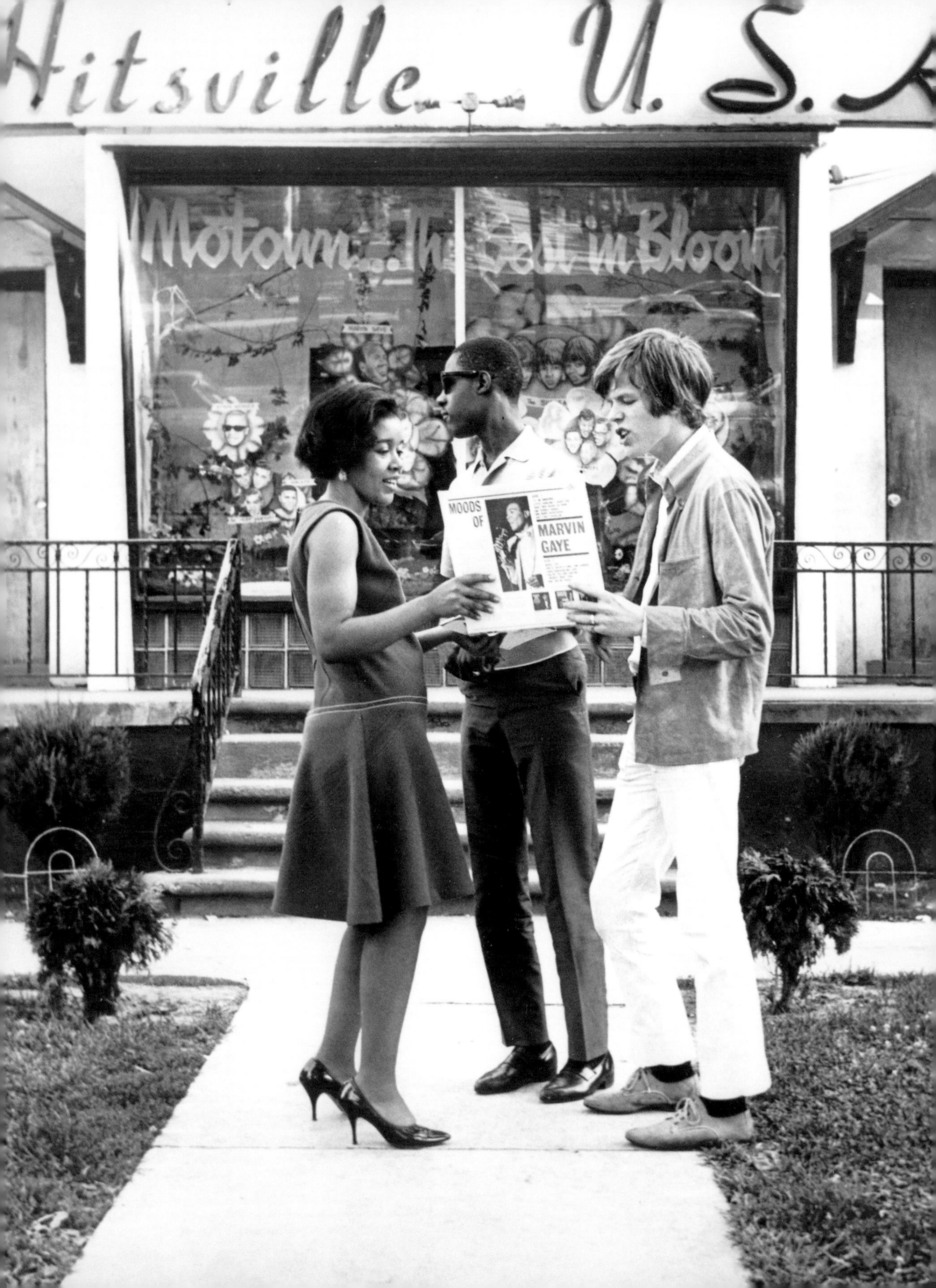
Hitsville U. S.
Motown
MOODS OF
MARVIN GAYE

Outrageous Stunts

DURING MY RADIO DAYS, my original stint as a record promotion man for Motown, I realized early on that if I applied some of the same concepts to record promotion that were then in vogue for getting movies publicized (remember, this is all in the prehistoric pre-Internet Era), I would not only get the records played on the air, but could also get some publicity in print media.

So, I opted for outrageous stunts. One such involved a two-part instrumental on Tamla titled "Snake Walk" by the Swinging Tigers - in reality Beans Bowles and many of the Funk Brothers studio musicians. In keeping with the title, I showed up for work wearing a turban, a phony beard and one of my mother's white sheets. Of course I had to wear my wristwatch and shades.

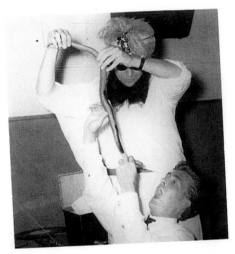

I carried a snake charmer's basket and a very phallic-looking rubber snake, as well as a flute. It never dawned upon me that a white guy showing up for work at a black-owned company dressed in a white sheet like a Ku Klux Klan member was bound to raise eyebrows.

With my young photographer pal Doug Ashley (later destined to become a White House photographer) in tow to record my encounters with Detroit's DJs; we set off to make history. The record did not become the smash I had predicted, but the photos of DJs like Tom Clay deep-throating the rubber snake were priceless and many made the national music trade publications. The DJs who received national promotion were also thrilled. And I made my reputation.

I owed a huge favor to Chuck Daugherty who spun records on WXYZ's All Night Satellite show. Earlier in the evening, before his regular nightly stint, Chuck had a short program sponsored by Coca-Cola. And he was able to talk about and play any record he

opposite: By now, Herman Noone of Herman's Hermits knew the only way he'd ever get his picture in any black publications would be if he were posed with Stevie Wonder. So I decided we'd make him happy. The lady on the left is Margaret Phelps of the Hitsville USA fanclub and the voice that introduces the Tamla Motown Appreciation Society record reproduced with this book.

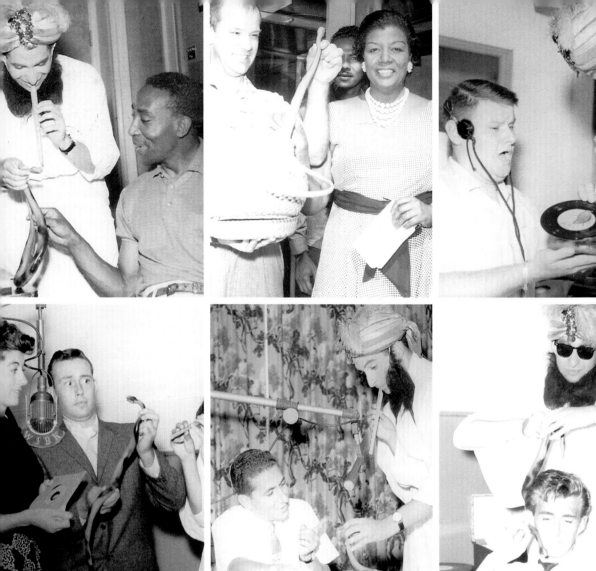
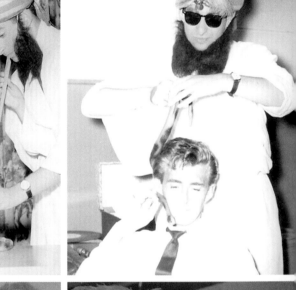

wanted - even if it wasn't on the station's Top 40 list. Chuck could do live on-the-air interviews with recording artists. Thus, he became the first white DJ to interview a Motown family artist on a mainstream radio station that appealed to white listeners. In fact, he interviewed two of our Jobete artists, Barrett Strong and Marv Johnson.

Chuck also had a propensity for pulling off attention-getting stunts like dying his hair green for St. Patrick's Day. When a brief illness necessitated his stay in a local hospital, my DJ pal Bob Greene and I visited Chuck and grabbing white hospital gowns and pretending to be doctors, put him onto a gurney which we proceeded to wheel madly up and down the corridors of the hospital with Chuck laughing like a mad man.

Chuck was also a good photographer and he shot many of our early artist publicity photos. He really proved his worth to me whenever any attractive young woman whom I had approached with an offer to be on a Motown album cover started pressing me for a photo session with our "art director." I would just take them to Chuck's "studio" and the pressure would be lifted. One red-headed stewardess photographed by Chuck actually wound up in *Playboy*.

Late one Friday afternoon, Chuck called me and said, "Hey, you know a lot of black guys. Do you know anyone who might be willing to help me move?" I only had to repeat the query to Berry once. Seeing Brian and Eddie Holland and Lamont Dozier standing in the studio, Berry pointed to them and said "There's your crew."

Chuck never knew for years that his moving crew was actually the same trio who would soon be hailed as America's Most Successful Songwriters. Chuck was an important DJ and a friend to us, and spending a Saturday helping him move was just another small way of keeping him happy.

opposite: Al amuses Detroit DJs in his fake snake-charmer garb as part of his infamous "Snake Walk" promotion;
above: legendary DJ Chuck Daugherty

But the high-priced talent of Holland-Dozier-Holland didn't impress the owner of a suburban Detroit bar when we all stopped in to grab beer and burgers. "I'll serve you two," said the owner gesturing to Chuck and me, "but not these black guys." The five of us ate in Chuck's car in the bar's parking lot. That bar was in a strip of Grand River Avenue in Farmington Hills, today some of Detroit's priciest suburban commercial real estate. As valuable as it is, I'm sure Holland-Dozier-Holland have enough change in their pockets to buy the entire block.

Bob Greene, now living in Thailand, broadcast over WAAM in Flint and WPON in Pontiac, two cities north of Detroit that were part of the 1960s GM auto factory boom. (Today, both are literal ghost towns.)

One night when we were all sitting in a Detroit bar, Bob decided to perform a wedding ceremony for me and Judy Robinson Berger, the woman I was dating - the same one from the Bill Williams "spooks" story. Alas, it had no validity.

There was another Bob Green on Detroit radio - originally Bob Greenstone; he worked at WKMH (later known as the powerhouse WKNR) in Dearborn. He also lived in Dearborn, one of America's most racist cities. His landlord never quite figured out Bob was Jewish, and I never visited Bob when his landlord was around. I'm certain Bob was the Town Jew. Bob Green, like Bob Greene (with three e's if you please) both became my close friends. Bob is still active in the industry and currently resides in Dallas, Texas.

Another young Jewish DJ who became a good friend was the successor to Tom Clay as "Jack the Bellboy" on WJBK. Calling himself "Harvey K, the Invisible Rabbit with the Musical Habit" - a riff on the popular "Harvey" film about James Stewart and an imaginary rabbit - Harvey K. regularly played our songs on his popular 7 PM to Midnight show.

Harvey gave up an incredibly promising career in broadcasting to move back to New York to join his family's garment industry business. On one of my trips to New York, Harvey invited me to have lunch at his family's palatial mansion in Forest Hills where we were waited upon by the family's black servants. I bit my tongue and didn't say a word about it to Berry when I got back to Detroit. For those of us who were working so hard to make a difference, it was another perspective on black-white relations in the pre-civil rights era.

above: Dearborn DJ Bob Green

On the opposite end of the spectrum was Ollie McLaughlin, a black DJ at the otherwise all-white WHRV in Ann Arbor, Michigan - home to the University of Michigan, He is better remembered today as a talented record producer, having discovered Del Shannon, who had a megahit with "Runaway." The success with Del launched Ollie's career as a record producer. It's nice to know that his record labels, Karen, Carla and Moira, named after his three daughters, are to this day revered by Soul fans.

Joel Sebastian of WXYZ was one of the most talented DJs I ever met - and one of the nicest people to boot. I encouraged Berry to record Joel on our Miracle label not because it was a payback for playing our records, but because I thought Joel was a tremendous talent. The radio world thought so as well, and Joel became a big hit on Chicago radio. He died young, a great loss to the industry and to the world. Rest in Peace My Friend.

Dave Shafer, who also became "Jack the Bellboy," before moving on to Canada's CKLW, was one of the gutsiest DJs I ever met. He was hosting a record hop at the tony Detroit Yacht Club one weekend, and I said I'd bring Mary Wells out to perform. Judy, my aforementioned girlfriend, was with us (every one of the Detroit DJs loved her company) when we arrived at the swanky private club. I'm sure we made quite an impression, two Jews and a black woman walking in the doors of the private club that barred minorities as members.

Dave introduced Mary to the crowd of cheering teenagers, scions of some of Detroit's top auto industry executives, and Mary prepared to take the stage to lip-synch her big hit, "Bye Bye Baby."

Suddenly the club manager approached Dave and began whispering into his ear. I asked Dave what was the matter, and he said the manager told him Mary couldn't perform because she was wearing a pants suit.

My girlfriend spoke up. She was the exact same size as Mary and was wearing a skirt. She offered to change clothes with Mary and the two of them headed toward the ladies' room.

above-right: Dave Shafer; above-left: Mary Wells

"PLEASE MR. POSTMAN"
THE MARVELETTES

A Personal Letter From The Marvelettes To You:

The last time Mr. Postman walked by our house he delivered to us the happiest letter we've ever recieved. In it was the news that you have made "Please Mr. Postman" our first hit record and given us the reason for presenting this album to you.

After listening to our album we would really appreciate your helping us to decide what your favorite song in this album is and maybe your favorite will be our next single release. Just write us a letter and let us know which song you liked best. So why not give Mr. Postman your letter today and be sure to tell him:

"Deliver De Letter; De Sooner De Better"

SIDE A

1. **ANGEL**
   Bateman-Saunders-Leverett

2. **I WANT A GUY**
   Holland-Gorman-Gordy

3. **PLEASE MR. POSTMAN**
   Brian Bert-Garrett-Dobbins

4. **SO LONG BABY**
   Brian Bert-Young

5. **I KNOW HOW IT FEELS**
   Brian Bert-Bradford-Wylie

SIDE B

1. **WAY OVER THERE**
   Gordy-Robinson

2. **HAPPY DAYS**
   Gordy-Knight

3. **YOU DON'T WANT ME NO MORE**
   Berry Gordy, Jr.

4. **ALL THE LOVE I GOT**
   Holland-Gordy-Bradford

5. **I KNOW HOW IT FEELS**
   Brian Bert-Bradford

6. **I APOLOGIZE**
   Gordy-Robinson

* WHICH IS YOUR FAVORITE?

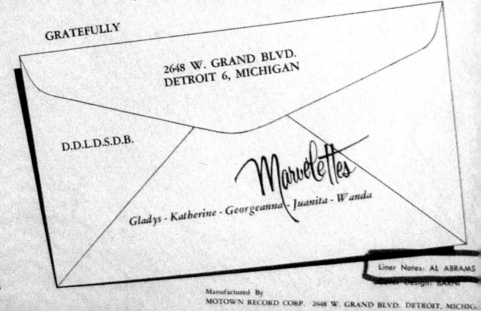

GRATEFULLY

2648 W. GRAND BLVD.
DETROIT 6, MICHIGAN

D.D.L.D.S.D.B.

Marvelettes

Gladys - Katherine - Georgeanna - Juanita - Wanda

Liner Notes: AL ABRAMS

Manufactured By
MOTOWN RECORD CORP. 2648 W. GRAND BLVD. DETROIT, MICHIG

That's when the club manager yelled out at them to stop and blurted out the truth. Mary could not sing at the club because she was black.

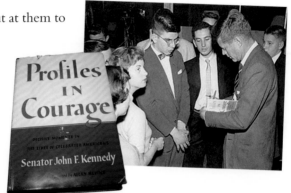

Without missing a beat, Dave looked at the manager and said, "If she can't sing here, then I can't DJ," and he began packing up his equipment. We all helped him and left together. The kids were silent.

Dave's courageous action at that time in American history - the civil rights struggle was still in its infancy - was the kind of thing that had brought people recognition in President John F. Kennedy's *Profiles In Courage* book.

I know that the club manager must have called the WJBK station manager Monday morning and ranted and raved. But Dave never said a word about it until we talked almost 50 years later, shortly before his death. Dave Shafer truly believed in racial equality at a time when it was still a dream for many of us. More than that, he was what we call a mensch.

In addition to making friends with some of the DJs, I also became close with a couple of promotion brethren! Record promotion was then a total male enclave.

BECAUSE MISERY LOVED COMPANY, usually any trip to promote records in Toledo, Ohio meant my talking as many other promo men as possible into sharing the boring drive.

Two of the most professional of the promo men were Dave Fox and Al Valente. On one of our trips south to Ohio, the other guys decided we'd make a detour to nearby Woodville, Ohio. There, above a restaurant frequented by truckers, was an old-fashioned red-light whorehouse. The denizens, all of whom were lounging about in various states of undress, knew and welcomed the promo men. That's when I learned about the barter system - the promo men would bring the women, 33 1/3 long playing albums and trade them for sex.

The women were eager to see what records the guys brought up. I had a handful of the

opposite: original printers proof sheet for "Please Mr Postman" album back cover featuring liner notes by Al Abrams.
above-right: John F Kennedy signs a copy of his "Profiles In Courage" book.

123

Heh, heh, back in the good old payola days this is what we did to visiting DJs

Seated below at the 20 Grand Club: DJ Lee Lyons of Grand Rapids (guest of honour), Al Abrams, Al Valente, Sir Mack Rice, Joe Stubbs, Jackie Wilson, Berry Gordy

early Motown releases including the Marvelettes "Please Mr. Postman," for which I had penned the liner notes attributed to the group. I proudly pointed this out to the most attractive of the women but they had no interest in my wares or in a 19-year-old promo man.

Instead, the guy who got the most action was the one who had a batch of Mitch Miller's *Sing Along* albums. So I sat in the cathouse waiting area and listened to the stereophonic sounds emanating from the nearby rooms - and they weren't old standard song lyrics.

Afterward, the guys took orders from the women for albums to bring up on their next trip. Everyone got a wish list but me. Even my small stick-on labels I created for DJs and pasted onto the disks reading "Thanks for the Spin" were worthless as currency. Somehow I don't think the Woodville barter system was quite what the record companies intended when they stamped "Promotion Copy - Not for Sale" on the album covers. It's also why Woodville, Ohio may today be the worst spot in America to look for Northern Soul classics.

Whenever a visiting DJ from upstate Michigan like Lee Lyons of WMAX in Grand Rapids would come to Detroit, Berry and I would show him a good time. Al Valente would be the only promo man I'd invite to join us at our table at Bill Kabbush's famous 20 Grand night club. Our table guests frequently included Jackie Wilson, Levi Stubbs and Sir Mack Rice of the Falcons. Of course, I was breaking laws left and right by hanging out nightly in bars like the 20 Grand, Baker's Jazz Lounge, the Club Alamo and the Minor Key - Detroit's greatest jazz venue - with my being three years under the "Michigan Must Be 21" liquor law. But it was always fun, especially seeing our acts perform live with a full band at the 20 Grand. I even enjoyed the Chittlin' Circuit comedy act of Washboard Willie and his Supersuds of Rhythm.

Amazingly enough, within the first six months of my working as a record promotion man, two other young white boys who were interested in promoting black music, wound up as my protégées. One of the duo, Bill Hennes, is today the publisher of America's leading Country and Western online newsletter. Bill still remembers an afternoon in 1959 at the Michigan State Fair when I had dropped my little black book and Bill found it. For a couple of hours, he thought he was in heaven. He had also learned a new meaning for the word "payola.' Subsequently, it was just that aspect of the business that turned me off on record promotion. The other was Bob Patton, who before his untimely death in 2009 had become one of the best of the white R&B DJs and a trusted friend and advisor to James Brown. I am proud that I helped give both of them a jump start in the industry.

But certainly not every DJ was looking to promotion men as a source of nubile female companionship. Quite the opposite was Eddie O'Jay of Cleveland - yes, the legendary DJ who lent his name to the popular singing group he discovered. On one of my driving trips back from the East Coast, I got a message that Eddie wanted me to stop in Cleveland and see him at the radio station. I set up an appointment and when I arrived, Eddie played matchmaker and introduced me to a stunning young woman who lived in upscale Shaker Heights. She was personable and attractive, but she was also Jewish - and I already had one of those at home in the person of my girlfriend.

Of all the many DJs I met traveling on the road, the R&B jocks in Washington, D.C. were my favorites. I would make the rounds of the radio stations when our acts like Smokey and the Miracles would play the legendary Howard Theatre - Washington's version of the Apollo. I would stay in the same rooming house as our acts.

BUD DAVIES

DAVE PRINCE

One person whose kindness toward Motown and our artists that I will always remember is Calvin Jefferson of radio station WOOK. I'd be remiss not mentioning other DJ friends like Dave Prince (née Pringle) of WKNR, Ray Otis, also of WKNR, whom I helped move to Detroit from Cleveland, Bud Davies of Windsor, Ontario's 50,000 watt powerhouse CKLW broadcasting across the Detroit River in Canada, Ed McKenzie, the great "Jack the Bellboy" on WJBK who invited me to his home where we spent hours immersed in the fascinating world of amateur ham radio, and even radio station salesmen like Carl Porter of WAAM in Flint.

Carl and I later became partners in Noisy Minority, Inc., a company created to merchandise golf balls with an image of soon-to-be-disgraced United States vice president Spiro Agnew on every ball. Agnew had beaned professional golfer Doug Sanders with a golf ball, and we were playing on the novelty value of the event. We tagged the golf balls as "Guaranteed to Go Right," a wordplay on the conservative Agnew who was Richard Nixon's VP. Noisy Minority was a catchphrase used to deride Nixon opponents, and our black and white partnership fit right into that mold.

Al Abrams
PUBLIC RELATIONS

A TAILOR'S TALE

Berry had ordered a suit from a tailor on one of our visits to New York in 1960. He was waiting and waiting for the suit to arrive in the mail and getting quite frustrated. One morning he said to me, "Look, you and that tailor are both Jewish. Maybe you can get him to listen to you and find out what's going on with my suit."

I told Berry I'd take care of it and asked him for the tailor's phone number. Then I sent the tailor a one-word Western Union telegram with instructions to "Deliver, do not phone."

Three days later, Berry's suit arrived. It was a perfect fit. Berry was overjoyed. "What did you tell the tailor to get him to move so quickly?" he asked. I showed him my confirmation copy of the telegram. It read simply "Nu?"

"Nu? Nu? What is that, some kind of magic Jewish word," asked Berry. Playing along, I told him "Well, maybe. But it worked, didn't it?" What I didn't tell him was that "Nu?" is simply Yiddish for "So?"

The next week Berry decided to show off his new suit at the ARMADA convention in Atlantic City. Most, if not all, of the record company executives attending were Jewish. During the opening cocktail party, I saw Berry going from group to group. He would approach the executives and with a knowing look on his face say a loud "Nu?"

Noting the amused looks on the faces of the executives, I ran over to Berry, took him by the arm and whispered in his ear, "Nu? isn't a Jewish magical word. It just means So?" Berry seemed pleased with his new-found knowledge and went back to the groups of executives, still asking them "Nu?" I have to admit it did break the ice as a conversation-starter.

I later taught Berry a few basic words of Yiddish so he could converse with my mother if he called my home looking for me. The instant my mother heard his garbled Yiddish, she would always say "Hello, Mr. Berry" and ask him "Nu?"

"It's What's In The Words That Count"

Motown Records, Man,
Which Is Big, Really Big

BY VAN G. SAUTER
Free Press Staff Writer

Eight doors open off the first floor hallway at 2652 West Grand Boulevard and when they are closed, the tiny passageway grows eerie. You are alone there, but with a distant sound of music—a music that is part blues, part gospel and a lot of rhythm.

It takes a keen perception to open the right door to the music.

That's the story of Berry Gordy, Jr. and the empire of sound he built from West Grand Boulevard to the lucrative listings of Billboard's "Hot 100" chart—Motown Records. Berry Gordy knows the door to the right sound.

Who is Berry Gordy? What is the sound? Where is the empire?

Like the correct door, they are elusive.

Berry Gordy

The short, wiry Negro with the handsome, almost cherubic face moved from behind the expensive desk with the grace of the boxer he once was.

"You," he said, thrusting out a well manicured finger.

"You probably haven't any voice but there are probably three notes you can sing. I can take those three notes and give them an arrangement and some lyrics. That makes a song. And your song will sell."

He paused, then quickly relaxed, becoming almost self-conscious.

"I don't want to sound conceited," said Berry Gordy as he moved back to the desk. He seemed embarrassed. "Really. I'm not a conceited guy."

Berry Gordy is not conceited but he is confident —and always has been. Some men spend precious years fighting in tank clubs or riding on team buses between minor league towns wondering if they have it.

Berry Gordy can never recall being without it. He is now a champ and thinks like a winner.

The Sound

Sound—the articulation of the it—comes from a small circular piece of black plastic called a 45 or a single. Most of these discs are bought by teenagers— teenagers in love, often unrequited love. These teenagers—in a gaudy Southfield development or an exhausted Blaine Street tenement—have something in common. Energy. They like to dance and move to music.

So, the song must have a great rhythm, and the arrangement is conceived first. Then come the lyrics, which must say something to a teenager in love.

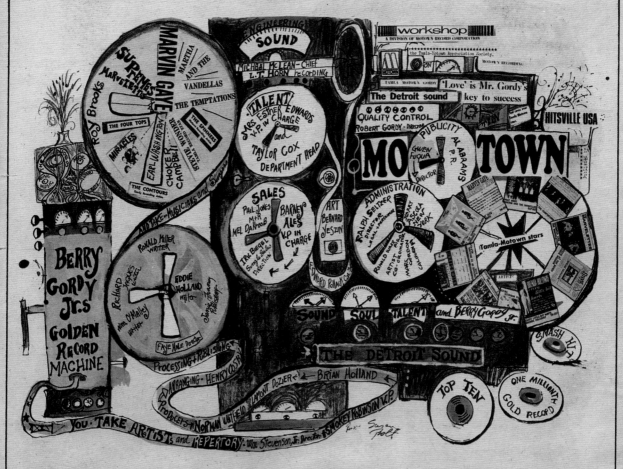

Illustrations by Susan Bolt

CASTLES IN THE SAND
LITTLE STEVIE
WONDER
Tamla 54090
January 16, 1964

"He can invent a tune one day, brush his teeth for ten more days without humming it again, and then non-chalantly remember and commit the notes to tape."

TAMLA RECORDS, DETROIT, MICHIGAN

DJ
COPY

Not For
Sale

TAMLA 54090
Jobete – BMI
DM B-064225

Produced by
Davis & Gordon
Time: 2:10
45 RPM
Vocal

Al Abrams
PICKS

CASTLES IN THE SAND
(Wilson-Davis-Gordon-O'Brien)
LITTLE STEVIE
WONDER

Stevie's Talented—and Lovable

13-Year-Old Singer Swings Through Dubbing Session

Put a harmonica in Stevie Wonder's hand and you've got a jam session in the making.

Stevie could be in a newspaper office, talking about [...] playing his [...]

[...] evie, blow something," [...] a man in the second [...] booth.

[...] ie blew.

[...] hey Love Him

[...]'s a great little guy," [...] one young lady who [...] at Hitsville. "We all [...] him."

[...] d it isn't hard to under[...] d the Hitsville people's [...] ngs for this boy who's [...] blind since birth and [...] hit the top in the popu[...] music field.

[...] evie has a warmth and [...] rm seldom found in [...] lt performers. He has a [...] le for anyone—and a [...] le for all he talks with.

recently, adding vocal and instrumental tracks to two tunes already partly recorded.

It didn't seem like work for Stevie. He was having fun, and so were the people [...] king with him.

Stevie's love for Detroit and feeling for all the people he meets is outshone by only one thing—his music.

When Stevie plays his harmonica he seems to lose track of where he is and what's around him. All there is for him is music.

And when he sits at the drums the concentration is even more intense.

At the end of the dubbing session Stevie played for 15 minutes more without pausing for a deep breath. The result was amazing—more listenable and likeable than some of the tunes he's released.

He Improvised

Stevie's been playing the harmonica for eight years now, and the drums for six.

Music was just a part of everyday life for Stevie — along with school and playing with his two older brothers (he also has two younger brothers and a baby sister)—until one day he visited a playmate. The boy's brother Ronnie White sang with the Miracles.

Ronnie took Stevie to Hitsville president Berry Gordy Jr. for an audition. Gordy was impressed, signed Stevie and changed his name from Stephen D. Judkins to Little Stevie Wonder.

Since then Stevie's had at least one million-seller, "Fingertips." He's made four long-playing albums and toured the United States and Europe.

(Despite the trips Stevie still studies. When he's on tour he "goes to school" with a tutor. Back in Detroit he commutes to the Michigan State School for the Blind in Lansing.)

Stevie's not little any more. Now he goes by just plain Stevie Wonder. But he's really an unusual young man—with talent and heart.

Record Corner

YOU'LL HEAR THIS ON RECORDS
Stevie and Harmonica 'Dub'

[OR IMMEDIA[...]

Stevie Wonder, fourteen [...] [...] [...] [...]it born blind singer, will perform in a one-man show for the patients at the Rehabilitation Institute on Wednesday, August 26, at 8 P.M.

Stevie, a Tamla Recording artist, has been featured several motion pictures, as well as having appeared on Ed Sullivan show.

The Rehabilitation Institute is located at 261 Mack [...]rmerly Brady) near Harper Hospital.

above-left: STEVIE WONDER RECEIVES BMI AWARD
L to R Joanne Woodward, Stevie Wonder, Paul Newman, Ruby Dee and Tony Bennett.

STEVIE WONDER
Tamla Recording Artist

Direction:
International Talent Mgt., Inc. (ITM
2652 W. Grand Boulevard
Detroit, Michigan 48208

VAN G. SAUTER
1366 NICOLET
DETROIT, MICHIGAN 48207

March 25, 1965

Dear

One of the most unusual show business success stories of
recent years is Motown Record Corporation's, which was formed
in 1957 by a young Detroiter who quit an auto assembly line to
begin writing songs.

Berry Gordy, Jr. has built Motown into the nation's second
largest record company in terms of single sales, and has developed
such talents as the Supremes, Marvin Gaye, the Temptations and
Martha and the Vandellas.

As a writer for the Detroit Free Press, I have watched the
emergence of Motown's so-called "Detroit Sound". This sound
resulted in 1964 record sales in excess of 12,000,000.

Motown and the Supremes (who have had four hits in a
row and will headline a July show at the Copa) were written up
last week in Newsweek, and soon will be featured in such diverse
publications as Time, Business Week, Look, Vogue and Esquire.

I would like to provide for you, on a free lance basis at
your rates, articles about Motown and the Supremes. This
material will provide good reading for your subscribers, and
also give your amusement section a jump on the Motown articles
in the national press.

I am also covering a European tour by some of the Motown
artists, and will send for your consideration articles about
the trip and the impact of American music abroad. (The Marvelettes
for instance, have the No. 1 record in Singapore, Malaysia this
week).

Attached is the Motown story, and the others will arrive
during the next few weeks. If you have any particular story
or photo requests, please let me know.

Sincerely,

Van G. Sauter

Van G. Sauter

133

THE STEVIE WONDER STORY
by Van G. Sauter
Detroit Free Press

People walking past a tenement building in Detroit used
to stop and smile at the blind boy who sat on the front porch
playing a harmonica and a battered set of drums.

Now they have to pay to see him play.

For Stevie Wonder---blind from birth--has emerged as
a professional entertainer with several hit records to his credit
and an unusual capacity to communicate with audiences he can't see.

A tall, lanky youth of 14, he now enjoys a life that
used to be exclusive with the scions of wealthy families. He is
well traveled. He is educated by private teachers. His future
seems solidly assured.

But he has no chance of gaining sight, and thus can't
enjoy the sweet life of the performer who lives in the best hotels
and is warmed by the applause of thousands.

Stevie, the son of a baker, began his career at the age
of 4 when a friend gave him a small keychain harmonica. He played
it so well he was given a better harmonica and then a set of
drums for Christmas.

"I used to sit on the porch playing," he recalls, "and
then I'd walk down the street singing. 'Give me a nickel and
I'll sing for you,' I used to say. I'd get that nickel and make
it to the store.

"But that certainly wasn't professional singing."

Stevie went professional three years ago when a member
of the Miracles, a popular vocal group, heard the blind boy playing and introduced him to Berry Gordy Jr., founder of Motown
Records.

"This kid is fantastic," Gordy declared.

He was right. One of the first Stevie Wonder records, "Fingertips," soared to the No. 1 spot in the best seller charts. Subsequent songs have also made the best seller lists, and Stevie now appears with the country's top performers.

During a recent tour of England, Stevie startled music critics by his capacity to completely engage an audience and keep it firmly within his grasp.

"I don't know for sure how I do it," he said, "but I'm always happy and I try to make the other people happy too. We have a good time together. We get in the groove."

While on tour, Stevie is accompanied by Clarence Paul, his music director, and Ted Hull, his private teacher. But the smiling youth is always "adopted" by members of the other groups appearing on the same bill.

In spite of his life of darkness. Stevie is unusually per-ceptive and sees a great deal. On the road he takes time out to visit museums and shrines. At the Tower of London, for instance, guards removed a glass case so he could feel the suit of armor worn by Henry VIII.

"I always listen to people," he said, in describing how he evaluates the many individuals he meets on tour. "I pay close attention to what they say and I can tell if they care about other people's feelings."

Stevie is not touchy about his blindness, which is in
fact, a source of humor between him and his friends.

During one talk session on a bus between appearances, Stevie
responded to a piece of new information with a conventional slang
phrase.

"Boy," he said, "am I seeing things."

"You better not be," joked Mr. Hull.

"You're right," Stevie responded, "because if I am you're
out of a job."

Many people are amazed that Stevie maintains his good sense
of humor.

"Blindness isn't worth being bitter about," he said. If
you can't see you can't see. Sure, I'd like to see my mother and
I'd like to see the girl I'll someday marry. But it's not worth
making my life miseable.

"I'll have a good time all my life as long as I'm thankful
for what I have,"

STEVIE WONDER, moustached now, recording at Motown's Detroit studios:"I think one day he'll be the biggest star who ever walked through these doors," says Motown's administrator.

Free Press Photos by Bud Johnson

BY JEAN SHARLEY
Free Press Staff Writer

There was a time when the blind child of Detroit's inner city had only to be seen to be loved.

The look of him, scrawny-shouldered and eleven years old, walking toward a spotlight that offered no solace, turning to an audience whose presence he could only feel, singing of beaches and fingertips and trees he had never seen; these were enough.

The talent in Stevie Wonder's fingertips was gravy. They loved him before he played, before he sang. They closed their eyes and spun his records—and saw him.

"Little Stevie" isn't anymore.

There's a trace of a moustache and the lithe figure of a basketball player. There are trust-fund coffers that run over, blotting out the blue-jean aura and the appeal of a city boy singing for his supper. There's a new maturity.

How is it now—at 15—for Stevie?

On a Saturday night, in Jacksonville, Fla., it was another $1,000 or so in the pot. A silken evening suit of white. A lace shirt. The smell of a new town; standing in front of Municipal Auditorium breathing it in. Waiting in the wings,

wondering "How will these cats swing?"

Sunday: Atlanta, Ga. The Sunday before: Lansing, Mich. The next Sunday: Washington, D.C. a town that digs Stevie.

To the people at Motown Record Corp., who discovered him when he was 9 and who protect him, Stevie is now a more provocative personality. Things are not so sure with him. His future is less predictable between now and age 20 than it was between 10 and 15. His potential is greater.

Of all the rocking, rollicking, tongue-in-cheek,

zesty young people storming the entertainment gates. Stevie is among the most interesting in depth.

This is partly because he is talented; able to play the piano, organ, harmonica and drums and to sing without reading music and without lessons. Because he can invent a tune one day, brush his teeth for ten more days without humming it again, and then nonchalantly remember and commit the notes to tape.

There's more.

WHETHER THE OCTAVE DROP in his voice in the past year will hinder or help. Whether he'll succeed as an adult entertainer. Whether, in the more important transition, he'll move from blind childhood into blind adulthood with assurance and spirit.

When Stevie leaves on a Motown tour, a lot more than his drums and harmonica go with him. He takes enough educational gear to outfit a one-room schoolhouse, carrying a good deal of it himself.

"He's a kid," said Ted Hull, the articulate young Lansing teacher who has been Stevie's tutor and business manager for two years. "He sits in the back seat and he helps carry bags. Once, Stevie walked into a plush hotel carrying all the luggage. His fan club couldn't find him. They thought he

> "He can invent a tune one day, brush his teeth for ten more days without humming it again, and then nonchalantly remember and commit the notes to tape."

Continued on Page 16

Stevie Wonder's Growing Pains:
Backstage, the 3Rs in Braille

STEVIE, with his mother, Mrs. Paul Hardaway, and brothers Timothy, 6, and Larry, 11, and sister Renee, 3.

"They lived in a public housing project and the piano was next door. He just sat down and played... Music lessons were not a concern. Eating was the concern."

Continued

was the bellhop."

With Hull and Stevie are four print textbooks, five braille volumes, a cue board for arithmetic, a typewriter, tape recorder, braillewriter, slate and stylus for braillewriting, paper, a talking book machine, talking books from the Wayne County Library (C. S. Forester's 'Age of the Fighting Sail') and a small organ which can be hooked into a car's cigaret lighter for practicing and composing.

In recent weeks, Stevie has finished "The Will Rogers Story," "Exodus," and "A Man Called Peter." The study of space fascinates him, as it does many 15-year-olds, and he is continually frustrated by the lack of reading material available.

"Stevie reminds me of myself at his age," said Hull. "His interests are much higher than his reading ability."

It is doubtful if any show-biz prodigy has ever had a more elaborate schooling setup. Or if any youngster has ever been more receptive. While he lags in some areas, notably spelling and math, Stevie is running well ahead of other blind students enrolled in ungraded programs.

"It isn't that we go so fast," said Hull. "It's that they go slower. Three weeks ago, for instance, the youngsters at the Michigan State School for the Blind in Lansing had only two-and-a-half days of classes because of a National Education Association convention. Stevie and I worked five full school days."

Half of the year, when he is not on tour and not in Detroit cutting records at Motown, Stevie goes to school in Lansing with 265 other blind boys and girls, living on the campus.

In Detroit, he studies in an apartment that Hull set up on the seventh floor of the Chatham Apartment Hotel. In the living room are a piano and tape recorder for song composing; and in the bedroom, a typewriter where Stevie sits hour after hour typing five lines each of "authority, necessity, northwest, publish, beneath, appreciation, explained, bringing, inquire, cruel, improve, hotel, doubt and attending," with straight margins.

In Lansing, he is learning braille musical symbols with the intention of someday doing his own arranging and, of course, reading translated musical scores.

He does his homework at 18074 Greenlawn where he lives with his mother, Mrs. Paul Hardaway, his stepfather, and three brothers and sister. Sometimes he studies in the basement; sometimes

at the kitchen table while dipping into [a] box.

Which seems fairly normal except th[at] ago Christmas Stevie did his fractions [...] at the Olympia Theater in Paris, and las[t] he landed the first English settlers while [...] to go on at the Apollo Theater in New Yor[k].

AT 15, HE IS EMERGING as a young charm and gentleness. When a crowd of [...] and producers recently arrived at the Motown's main recording room and [...] locked, it was Stevie who went back for [...] When he goes upstairs at home, he bo[...] stairs at a time. In strange places, he [...] around trying to find chairs and doors [...] aid. He laughs a lot.

The Billboard award of August 10 [...] naming him the "Number One Artist in [...] tion" is written in English for other peop[le] in braille for Stevie. It represents, prim[...] record called "Fingertips," which sold 1 [...] copies and brought international stature to [...] at 13.

Stevie's earlier and subsequent records [...] gone as well, but they've gone, with tota[l] here and in Europe close to two million. H[is] sonal appearances are big.

When he sang "Fingertips" in Chicago's [...] iskey Park last year, and then slid into "High [...] Sneakers," the police were needed to qu[...] enthusiasm. After stopping the show cold, [...] went back to the dressing room for a prob[...] the British caste system.

Stevie started out early, banging a pan [...] mother's kitchen in Saginaw. His name was St[...] Judkins and his parents were separated. La[...] a Detroit public housing development, h[...] just one more poor, hungry, skinny kid—[...] that he also was blind.

He has a big brother, Calvin, now 16 a[nd] student at Mumford High School and yo[...] sister and brothers, Larry, 11, Timothy, 6, [...] Renee, 4. His stepfather works in a bagel ba[kery].

"I always had a feeling about him," his m[...] said. Pretty, with a good alto voice herself, sh[e] called the first day he played the piano. [...] lived in a public housing project and the p[iano] was next door. He just sat down and playe[d...] was a gift the family accepted. Music lesson[s were] not a concern.

Eating was the concern.

HE WAS DISCOVERED by a singer who ta[...] about him to Motown's founder and owner, B[erry] Gordy Jr. Among Motown's 100 singles, dou[...] triples and quartets, he is special: The first [...] town artist to go overseas. The first in a me[...] The first on network television.

"He did two pictures in Hollywood and it [was] fun—but he was disappointed," Hull said. [...] wanted to be an actor. Singing and playing w[...] fine, but he wanted a line."

As he grew richer, Stevie found himself in [...] odd circumstance of having plenty of money i[...] federally supervised trust fund — but nothing [...] take home. His family, until 18 months ago, liv[ed] in a house with no refrigerator. Later, he was a[ble] to buy them a house. But most of his money [re]mains intact.

"I think one day he'll be the biggest star w[ho] ever walked through these doors," said Mrs. [...] dena Johnston, Motown's administ[...]

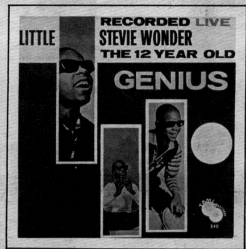

"Our problem is trying to help him live as normal a life as possible. It's not easy when he's in an adult environment. We're not allowing him to be too dependent—and we want him to keep pace with the average 15-year-old. He's remarkable in his adjustment, possibly because he's blind. I believe he sees ten times better than we."

Two years ago, with Stevie's musician-inspired conversation growing in flavor ("We took the music into Boston but those cats couldn't read") but his spelling floundering, Gordy asked Dr. Robert Thompson, superintendent of the Michigan State School for the Blind, about a tutor.

Thompson recommended Hull, a Michigan State University graduate who holds a special degree for teaching the blind. In two years, he and Stevie have covered three years of work. He thinks Stevie can finish high school in two years. He thinks association with young people is vital.

"His career is a fact and we take it from there," Hull said. "We work our lessons in with the tours and the recording sessions.

"He sleeps eight to nine hours a night. If he is in bed after a show by midnight, we're up at nine and studying to 12. If things get too rough, I may tell the office 'We have to slack up now, we're getting behind in our work.'"

"In show business, you're not really doing anything a lot of the time. You're waiting for a guy to tell you to do something," said Stevie. "That's

when I try to read books.

"I want to be ready in case I do want to go to college. Music is something I know a lot about. I used to think I'd major in electronics but that's not practical. If I don't make it, I can always teach music."

"In Europe last year, he interviewed the newsmen and performers he met," Hull said. "He used a tape recorder and asked questions on the racial situation and, in England, about the different classes of people. It's part of a social studies assignment."

Preferring that he concentrate on braille writing and braille music reading, Hull has not taught Stevie to do more than write his name.

"He normally autographs in braille. When someone insists on a signature, I take his hand and help him. It's difficult when he's being jostled by a crowd."

"We saw him on television," brother Larry said. "My mother said his head looked funny. It looked okay to me. We go into the basement sometimes and turn on the tape recorder and change our voices. Stevie changes his good. Then we start wrestling."

"I always like to be at home," Stevie said. "And I like standing on the stage, too, feeling the audience. The first time was in New York. I thought, 'Oh man, I'm moving.'

"I don't like all of it. I'll never drink. I don't believe in it. I've seen enough of it.

"The tours are good but everybody likes coming back. The last one, they said to me, 'Man, you won't need your white cane tomorrow. The suction's going to pull you into the plane.'"

On Nov. 14, at the end of a three-week tour in Kansas City's Municipal Hall, the slender boy with the proud, slim figure and the musical gift put his harmonica in his pocket and walked off stage.

Then he came home. A little richer. A little wiser. A little behind in math. And with his weekly $2.50 allowance.

"We've talked about college, but he's in such an unusual position," Hull said. "In order to stay on top, people have to see you.

"What you want to do you can't always do," Stevie said. "Whatever's poppin', you've got to pop with it."

No. 1, in Braille.

Chapter 5 ➤

NOW THAT WE'RE ON OUR WAY

opposite: The Supremes in my office. Shots for a Sunday magazine supplement.

AL ARONOWITZ

Al Aronowitz showed up at Hitsville for his interview with the Supremes for the Saturday Evening Post. I brought them into the room and introduced them to Al. We were all seated around my desk, and Al's first question to the girls was "So, which one of you is fucking Berry Gordy?"

I don't know who jumped up first, but Diana ran out crying and came back with Berry. By then, I had torn into Al who was trying to justify himself. Berry ran in and said "Get him out of here right now. Fuck the damn story. I don't ever want to see this cocksucker in here again."

I told Al to leave. And he did. I called his editor the next morning. He offered to assign it to another writer. But we turned it down.

However, six months later, we had a change of heart and decided that we needed to reach the large number of readers of the Saturday Evening Post. That's when I wrote their editor and suggested a more "friendly" writer, Marshall Jay Kandell, who had done a bang-up job on his Motown story for the Los Angeles Herald-Examiner. Even later, I tried to get Berry to hire Kandell to work in what I saw as an expanded Motown PR department, but it never happened. You'll find my letter to the Post on Page 159.

"It's What's In The Words That Count"

They were still the Primettes when I met them and there were still four in the group.

THE NAME CHANGE TO THE SUPREMES had not yet occurred, but soon after it had, I began driving them around to DJ record hops on the weekends.

At least the Supremes were spared the indignity of being delivered soaking wet to a record hop. Unfortunately, Eddie Holland wasn't as lucky.

One night as a sudden rainstorm hit, the top of my convertible stuck and would not go up. We were totally drenched, but like the trouper he has always been, Eddie took to the stage when we got to the venue and lip-synced his songs.

However, I vividly remember an early Motown Christmas Party in the Hitsville studio. The company had given the Supremes some sort of award in a presentation. When they took the stage and sang live with Earl Van Dyke's Orchestra, it was pure magic and everyone in the room knew it. That was the first time I had ever heard them perform live as all artists lip-synced at record hops and on *American Bandstand*-like local TV shows.

Once there were four. In 1960, these teenagers "just sang," says Diana (top), "and I had a high soprano voice." The others, from left, Barbara Martin (now married), Mary Wilson and Florence Ballard.

After Berry finally put me in charge of Motown artist and company publicity in May 1964, my main assignment was Mary Wells. I had told Berry the company was missing the PR boat by not properly promoting her in print media.

Shortly afterward, it became evident that Mary Wells was leaving Motown. I didn't have to look far to find my next assignment.

It was August of 1964, the Supremes had just returned from the Dick Clark Tour with "Where Did Our Love Go?" as the nation's Number One record. I couldn't even get them a story in their hometown daily newspapers. Why? Both dailies, the *Detroit Free Press* and the *Detroit News,* were on strike.

There were several temporary strike newspapers that jumped in to fill the void. This was still back in the day when most people depended upon their local newspaper as their primary news source. One of the best of these papers was the *Detroit Daily Press* which provided a home and a paycheck to many of the journalists displaced by the strike.

I took Florence, Mary and Diana to the offices of the *Daily Press* and the next day the paper ran the first local coverage of the Supremes and their first Number One hit record.

By the end of the year, the Supremes already had three Number One hits in a row and couldn't be ignored. Their mothers implored me to use my connections to get the strike settled so their friends and family and former classmates could read all about it in the "real" newspapers. Of course the news was reported all over the world, but that didn't count for much in

Mrs. Ross, Mrs. Ballard, Mrs. Wilson — *mothers whose achievements were Supreme.*
Free Press Sunday Magazine: January 24, 1965

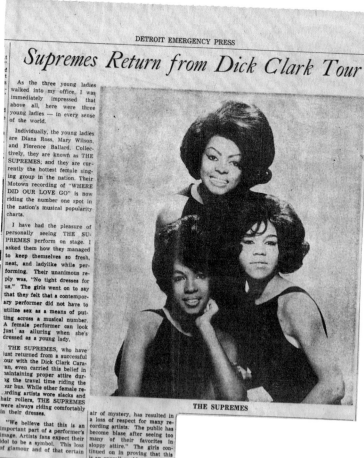

DETROIT EMERGENCY PRESS

Supremes Return from Dick Clark Tour

As the three young ladies walked into my office, I was immediately impressed that above all, here were three young ladies — in every sense of the world.

Individually, the young ladies are Diana Ross, Mary Wilson, and Florence Ballard. Collectively, they are known as THE SUPREMES; and they are currently the hottest female singing group in the nation. Their Motown recording of "WHERE DID OUR LOVE GO" is now riding the number one spot in the nation's musical popularity charts.

I have had the pleasure of personally seeing THE SUPREMES perform on stage. I asked them how they managed to keep themselves so fresh, neat, and ladylike while performing. Their unanimous reply was, "No tight dresses for us." The girls went on to say that they felt that a contemporary performer did not have to utilize sex as a means of putting across a musical number. A female performer can look just as alluring when she's dressed as a young lady.

THE SUPREMES, who have just returned from a successful tour with the Dick Clark Caravan, even carried this belief in maintaining proper attire during the travel time riding the bus. While other female recording artists wore slacks and hair rollers, THE SUPREMES were always riding comfortably in their dresses.

"We believe that this is an important part of a performer's image. Artists fans expect their idol to be a symbol. This loss of glamour and of that certain air of mystery, has resulted in a loss of respect for many recording artists. The public has become blase after seeing too many of their favorites in sloppy attire." The girls continued on in proving that this is an overall problem that show business must face—be it Hollywood, television, or recording artists.

THE SUPREMES, who hail from Detroit, Michigan, are just that. They're supreme in talent, in personality; and now, with the number one song

THE SUPREMES

THE SUPREMES, who are now in California taping a Steve Allen Show soon to be released, have a new record, "Baby Love," which seems to be heading for No. 1. Shown receiving their Shooting Star Trophy from Jean Pierre Aumont, they are (l. to r.) Florence Ball, Mary Wilson and Diana Ross.

Our Supremes Take 'Shooting Star' Prize

The Supremes, Motown Recording Artists, were presented with the coveted "Shooting Star" trophy by the distinguished French motion picture star Jean Pierre Aumont, who made the award on behalf of the London (England) Press Exchange Ltd.

The "Shooting Star," trophy was awarded to the Supremes for their record of "Where Did Our Love Go", which has made the greatest progress in England and Europe of any commercial recording. The record was the Number One song in the United States for a number of weeks.

The Supremes, all of them hail from Detroit, are currently embarking on a European tour —prior to which they will receive a gold recording to commemorate the sale of one million copies of "Where Did Our Love Go", as well as a Billboard Magazine Award which will be presented to The Supremes on the Steve Allen Television Show.

the Supremes' hometown of Detroit.

When the strike finally was settled in time for the dailies to benefit from all the Christmas advertising they might have lost, it started a spirited battle between both dailies to be first with a Sunday magazine feature story on the Supremes. However in those days, Sunday rotogravure printing process magazines required several weeks of lead production time, which moved the publication date for either story into January 1965 – six months after it made news.

Thus a battle of the titans was launched as the competing stories were written by two giants of Detroit journalism. Mort Persky of the *Free Press* was the newspaper's Sunday editor and was ready to launch his innovative *Detroit* magazine – but not until the following weekend.

Arnold S. Hirsch was one of the stellar writers at the *News*. His claim to fame was that he had taught the legendary Barbra Streisand how to drive while she was booked into a Detroit club early in her career.

Both newspapers pulled out all the stops in their layout and photo coverage. You'll find extracts from both stories overleaf – and you can judge for yourself who actually won the competition.

Persky became Motown's cheering section at the Freep. He and his staff of talented reporters quickly recognized that Motown was a Detroit phenomenon. Within months, the paper was reporting on "Our Supremes."

However, Hirsch also was to play a key role in making possible the incredible breakthrough not just of the Supremes and Motown into major daily newspapers, but of opening the gates to equal coverage of African-American entertainers.

Thanks to both of these men, the white stranglehold on reporting of pop music was broken forever.

The Supremes—Diana, Mary and Florence

Inside the Mansion That John Dodge Built

Virna Lisi: From Italy, with Cash and Class

The Supremes—3 Detroiters Who Have Captured the World

The Supremes aglow: from left, leader Diana Ross, Florence Ballard and Mary Wilson

By Mort Persky
FREE PRESS SUNDAY EDITOR

It begins, not strangely, with a clapping of hands, after which a sinuous but sturdy feminine voice begins curling around the lyric, lapping at it—

*"Baby, baby, please don't leave me,
Ooooohhh, please don't leave me, all by myself;
I've got this burnin', burnin' yearnin' feelin' inside me,
Ooooohhh, deep inside me, and it hurts so bad;
You came into my heart . . ."**

At this point two other feminine voices join in, a circumstance which makes it very nearly impossible to make out what the first voice is saying. And, further, making it somehow very difficult to care. The two new voices are singing:

*"Baby, baby,
Where did our love go?
Baby, baby
Baby, baby . . ."* *

And so forth. As if it matters What makes it so difficult to care about the words you miss is that the two new voices have filled out a musical printed circuit, and the juices are flowing. The words, make them out or not, have become part of a river of sound which has been knowingly, painstakingly shaped on Detroit's Grand Blvd. (by three relatively anonymous song wizards, none of them girls, who are known in the record credits as Holland/Dozier/Holland). It is a river of sound which has engulfed one continent, made a good start on

another, washed heavily across an influential little island, and is still on the move.

Most relevantly, it is the sound of the Supremes, who do the singing and make the whole equation balance as cleverly as you please. The song is on a record, it is called "Where Did Our Love Go," and so far it has sold a million copies in the U.S. and half a million copies in England.

The figures do not include the sales of their long-playing album of the same name, which is doing ever brisker over-the-counter traffic and contains two more tunes that the Supremes have more recently piloted into top-ten status: "Baby Love" and "Come See About Me." (This combination gave them two added distinctions: They became the first Americans with three No. 1 singles since Elvis Presley, and the first female group of any nationality ever to pull off that trick.)

The Supremes are three Detroit girls who are probably better known in England than they are in Detroit. They grew up in housing projects—where the families of two of them still live—but last year each of them grossed about $100,000, mainly from record sales, with some added gravy from a movie and some potent personal-appearance tours. One of these tours took them to England, where they apparently—if unbelievably to Americans drenched in Beatle lore—turned out to be more popular than the Beatles.

"Where Did Our Love Go" had the magic spark that made the motor catch. Diana Ross, a sensuous-faced 22-year-old who owns the

sinuous, sturdy voice that makes her leader of the group, was talking about it the other day at Hitsville's Detroit studios, where she and her two partners found their fortune. "Nobody really had that much confidence in the song, really," she said. "And then it hit. This, right now, is the most fabulous part of our careers." Mary Wilson and Florence Ballard smiled, a little mischievously, and nodded in agreement with their colleague.

The girls don't remember the day they recorded "Where Did Our Love Go" as anything special. But they remember this: They sang the song, with Diana doing the lead. There followed a huddle involving the girls and members of the songwriting-producing team of Holland/Dozier/Holland (producer Bryan Holland, melody-maker Lamont Dozier and lyricist Eddie Holland). Eddie Holland was dissatisfied with Diana's singing, felt the tune should be done with Mary's softer voice. Dozier said, "No, wait a minute, listen to this girl again. I think she's right. Let's give it to her. They listened again. And what may have been the crucial decision went to Diana.

About three weeks after the record was released, the group was on a tour of Pennsylvania towns. One night they sang "Where Did Our Love Go," and the response was so good they asked the audience to join in. To the girls' surprise, the audience knew the words. After that, asking the audience to join in became a ritual. And everybody everywhere knew the words. Four weeks after its release, the song was No. 1.

*©1964 JOBETE/BMI *Continued on Page 12*

Supreme's the Word for the Supremes

By ARNOLD S. HIRSCH

The Detroit News
Sunday
Pictorial

THEY DON'T scream, holler or wail incoherently. An adult can actually understand nine out of every 10 words they sing. And, most astounding, melody can be clearly detected in every song.

The real phenomenon, however, is that with all these strikes against them, three Detroit girls known as the Supremes are the hottest thing in teen-age recordom.

● Item: They are the first female vocal group ever to have three consecutive No. 1 records — each a million seller. And all since last June.

● Item: They have two L.P. albums in the top 15, a feat exceeded only by the Beatles, with four.

● Item: Their appeal is international, if not yet universal. They've made the top 10 in Norway, Eire, Holland and Singapore. They are great favorites in Japan, were overwhelmingly received on a personal appearance tour last fall in England, where their record sales also rated them No. 1, a first for a female vocal group.

Ironically, until a pair of television appearances early this month, the girls have been virtually unknown by anyone under 21 in their own home town. "Now," says lead singer Diana Ross, "when I walk down the street people recognize me and say they've been fans of ours for a long time."

Not that Diana or colleagues Florence Ballard or Mary Wilson are doing much strolling in their home town these days.

Ever since their first big record — "Where Did Our Love Go?" — clicked last June, the girls have been in as much a spin as any of their discs. "In the last six months," sighs Mary, "we've spent 14 days in Detroit."

Besides the trip to England and the Continent, they've been on a theater tour through the south, made a movie ("Bikini Party") and appeared on the Ed Sullivan and Les Crane television shows.

And even when the girls are home, there is little time for rest.

Days are spent at the studio of their arranger and musical director, Maurice King, who is preparing them for major nightclub appearances and the pilot of a new Dick Clark TV show with Connie Francis and Johnny Mathis.

Nights are occupied cutting new records at the Motown Records studios on West Grand Blvd. The sessions start at 6 p.m., often last well past midnight.

Chief differences between the Supremes and the hundreds, if not thousands, of other vocal groups is what is coming to be called the "Detroit Sound"— meaning, according to the girls, that the music is "less wild but still has a beat." **(Continued)**

⊙ Perry Como-type stools at Motown studios, Diana Ross rests on back of chair, Mary and Florence Ballard perch on piano. They sing to pre-recorded music.

February 16, 1965

Motown Record Corporation
2648 West Grand Boulevard
Detroit, Michigan, 48208

tional information
Al Abrams (TR 1-3340)

DIATE RELEASE

SUPREMES PAY RETURN
VISIT TO ABC-TV'S "SHINDIG"

Supremes; Diana Ross, Mary Wilson, and Florence
ill perform their new Motown recording "Stop! In
f Love" on ABC-TV's "SHINDIG" Television Show on
February 24th at 8:30p.m. E.S.T.

! In The Name Of Love" has sold over 500,000 records
week of release. From all indication-
h consecutive -

March 18, 1965

wn Record Corporation
West Grand Boulevard
oit, Michigan 48208

nal information
Abrams (TR 1-3340)

FOR IMMEDIATE RELEASE

SUPREMES BREAK THE RECORD

Detroit's Supremes, the nation's hottest new
sensations, have shattered a long standing record
ing both the first American vocal group, and the
male recording artists ever to have four consecutive
ne recordings.

The record that did the trick for the Supremes,
N THE NAME OF LOVE" goes to number one in the nation
onday, March 22nd according to Billboard Magazine.

The only other recording artists to achieve this
ction have been England's Beatles. Even in their heyda
Presley and Fats Domino never quite made it four straig

The Supremes; Diana Ross, Mary Wilson, and Florenc
will celebrate their unprecedented honor while in
ngland, where they are currently appearing with othe
t recording artists as part of THE TAMLA-MOTOWN
kage.

November 23, 1964

Motown Record Corporation
2648 West Grand Blvd.
Detroit, Michigan 48208

tional Information contact:
Al Abrams (TR. 1-3340)

FOR IMMEDIATE RELEASE

Lightning Strikes Thrice

ree young Detroit girls, the Supremes, have accom-
the remarkable feat of hitting the Number One spot
national record charts twice within a few weeks. Their
ng of "Baby Love", places them in line to receive their
Billboard magazine award, the first being for their
ng of "Where Did Our Love Go", for which they received
record denoting sales of over a million records. In
on a third recording, "Come See About Me" is rapidly
ng the charts, and is listed as Number 13 in the current
ard magazine.

he Supremes record of "Baby Love" is simultaneously
One in both the United States and England. They are
he first American group to have two tunes in the British
enty at one time, and they have made British disc his-
y becoming the first female vocal group ever to reach
mber One position in the New Musical Express charts,
it's inception in 1952.

he Supremes, Diana Ross, Mary Wilson and Florence Ballard,
ly returned from a three week tour of England and Europe
their appearances on British television shows caused
scenes reminiscent of the Beatles reception in America.

June 1, 1965

OM: Motown Record Corporation
2648 West Grand Boulevard
Detroit, Michigan 48208
additional information contact
Al Abrams (TR 1-3340)

FOR IMMEDIATE RELEASE

Detroit's Golden Girls Make It Five Straight

Well, they did it again!

etroit's Supremes, who have now become the top-
female vocal group in the history of the record
ustry, have added another notch to their already
ive track record of chart making record perfor-

of Monday (May 31st), the Supremes Motown record
IN MY ARMS AGAIN" becomes the nations number one
ing record. (This is according to Cashbox Magaz
d is expected to become number one in both Cashb
ard magazines in their next listings, effective

is the fifth consecutive number one record, and
fth million seller for Diana Ross, Mary Wilson,
e Ballard, and it's all happened in less then
ime. Only England's Beatles have had more con-
ber one records (10), but no other American
tist has ever had more then four consecutive
the top position.

remes have also joined the ranks of the
r on poverty fighters. A televisio
Detroit on June 11th
the Supremes, Marv
the Marve

But first there was still a major hurdle for me to overcome.

By the summer of 1965, the Supremes were regularly appearing on network television shows like the *Ed Sullivan Show*, *Shindig* and *Hullaballoo*.

However, when it came to the actual television program guide listings for the shows, virtually every other act – make that white act – would be listed in the pages.

The *Free Press* was already solidly promoting us, but at the News, Motown was frequently seen by some editors as the news value equivalent of a high school band.

The *News* produced their own weekly television digest as well as the digests for other major newspapers in New York City, Washington, D.C. and Houston, Texas. Shortly afterward, they added a Boston newspaper.

One day on a visit to the editors at the *News*, I asked why the Supremes, now with four consecutive Number One hits, couldn't be featured on the cover of the TV magazine during a week when they would be appearing on a network TV show.

The editor shook his head and said, "We can't do that. We can't put colored people (that, along with Negroes, were the terms then in use) on the cover of a TV magazine."

"Why not? I asked innocently.

"People keep this TV magazine handy in their living rooms all week long. You can't expect them to look down at it and have black faces looking up at them," he replied.

"Well, then they could turn the magazine over and just keep the ad on the back cover visible," I suggested. The editor shook his head. It was just not going to happen.

I thanked him and started to walk away. That's when he stopped me and said, "You know, there's something I've always wanted to ask you. Can you come into my private office for a minute?"

I followed him and he shut the door. Then he turned to me and said, "I've been curious about this for a long time. What is a nice Jewish boy like you doing working for a bunch of n-----s anyway? Shouldn't it be the other way around?"

I had been waiting for this moment for a long time and had rehearsed the scenario in my head.

Turning to look him straight in the eyes, I began to tell him my story.

"You know how those n-----s like to shoot crap?" I asked him, playing right into his racial stereotypes.

He shook his head acknowledging that claim and I continued.

"Well, I actually founded Motown Records," I told him and paused to give it time to sink in.

"You did?" he asked.

"Yes, I did." I said and continued, "And one night I got into a crap game with Berry Gordy. Well, I lost everything to him that night, including the company."

Then I paused again.

I knew this would be my big test. If he believed what I had just told him, I'd be home free. But would he buy it?

The editor sat there wide eyed. Again, he repeated, "You did?"

I shook my head affirmatively. "Yes, I did. But they still let me hang around the company and do things like I am doing here today just to stay close to and still be a part of what I had started."

Would he buy it?

After what seemed like hours he said, "That's the saddest thing I've ever heard. Sit here for a minute."

He got up and went into the hall where he called out the names of the entertainment editor, the TV editor and the feature editor.

"Come in here for a minute," he told them.

When they entered his office he repeated his comment telling the editors, "I've just heard the saddest story I've ever heard. From now on, I want you to do everything you can for this guy."

When I got back to Hitsville I told Berry and we fell on the floor laughing.

Needless to say, the Supremes made the TV cover with a great inside story by Arnold S. Hirsch. Not only was it a breakthrough for the Supremes, it was a major breakthrough for all African-American singers, actors and entertainers. It opened a door that had been shut for a hundred years. And in its own way, it ultimately helped make possible the election of Barack Obama as President of the United States.

Having the Supremes become the first black artists ever to be on the cover of a TV guide-like magazine was a civil rights victory of the first magnitude. And I've always been glad that the Supremes made history that week with my help.

THE SUPREMES' SUCCESS SECRET: A UNIQUE SOUND OF MUSIC

By ARNOLD S. HIRSCH

THEY ARE neither gimmicky nor unprepared. And that—along with their unique sound—is why the Supremes are rising as rapidly in television as they did on their way to the top rung of the record industry.

The three Detroit girls have achieved international prominence as singers with an unprecedented string of four consecutive records that won No. 1 ratings in national record charts.

And what record buyers have heard —and bought by the millions—is what ever-larger TV audiences are learning to appreciate. It is simply the Supremes' sound—a hard-to-resist blend of Negro gospel, strong beat and harmonies that are pleasing if not always pitch-perfect.

Most importantly, it isn't hokey. Unlike vast numbers of fast-blooming groups who have used hit records as stepping-stones to TV, then fallen flat without their echo chambers and multiple-recording tricks, the Supremes, who've been singing together since high school days, sound the same on TV as they do on discs. They have their own name for it.

"We call it 'sweet music,'" says the trio's lead singer, Diana Ross, whose flashing eyes are her trademark—and something of a problem.

"Before we got on TV, nobody ever said anything about my eyes," she says. "Now my friends tell me to stop flashing them so much. But I'm not doing anything with them now that I didn't do before."

Although the girls — Diana, Florence Ballard and Mary Wilson, all 21 —have appeared on such teen-slanted shows as ABC's "Shindig" and NBC's "Hullabaloo," they have proved equally successful on so-called "adult" shows. These include Ed Sullivan, Steve Allen and Les Crane shows.

More are coming up soon. On July 21, before their three-week engagement at the Copacabana, the girls will be in New York to tape an appearance with Al Hirt, who's Jackie Gleason's summer replacement on CBS. In August, they'll fly to Hollywood for a Dean Martin special on NBC.

In addition, U.S. audiences may get a look at the one-hour special they did in England this spring. Called "The Sound of Motown," after the name of the company they record for, the show was taped during a personal appearance tour in England, France and Germany. They are negotiating with ABC now.

Though their TV fees are rising, money isn't everything to the girls. They have their own gauge: time.

"We used to go on, do our number and be gone in less than three minutes," says Florence. "Now they're letting us stay on five or six minutes."

HE SUPREMES: Mary Wilson (L), iana Ross and Florence Ballard

3

May 17, 1965

FROM: Motown Record Corporation
        2648 West Grand Boulevard
        Detroit, Michigan 48208
For additional information contact
        Al Abrams (TR 1-3340)

FOR IMMEDIATE RELEASE

The Supremes, who are now well on their way to their fifth consecutive number one best selling single record will headline the bandshell show at the 1965 Michigan State Fair. The Supremes will be performing from September 2nd through 7th, alternating with popular vocalist Jack Jones.

Preceding this engagement the Supremes will tape a segment for the new NBC-TV Dean Martin Show on August 29th in Hollywood. The show will be aired in early fall.

The Supremes will appear on the CBS-TV Al Hirt Show on Saturday, July 24th. This show, the summer replacement for the Jackie Gleason Show, will be televised locally over WJBK-TV, channel two, at 7:30 p.m. E.S.T. The Supremes will open at New York's Copacabana on July 29th, performing there until August 18th.

The Detroit trio taped a series of radio spot commercials for the Coca-Cola Company this week. Their picture is now appearing on all Hudson napkin boxes (along with pictures of other musical stalwarts such as Benny Goodman and Roger Williams.) Inside each package are four color photo cards of the Supremes, Marvin Gaye, and The Miracles.

Along with The Temptations and The Choker Campbell Orchestra, the Supremes recently taped a television pilot show for possible ABC-TV syndication. Hosted by WXYZ-Detroit disc jockey Lee Alan, the show is of the "Shindig" variety, and is tentatively titled, "That Swinging Kind". The Supremes will be performing at a debutantes coming-out party in Detroit's fashionable Grosse Pointe Woods on June 18th. (Whatever happened to Lester Lanin?) Three of their most successful albums are now being offered through the Columbia Record Club. All this and it's just a year, come June 17th, since the Supremes first million seller "WHERE DID OUR LOVE GO" was released.

On other Motown newsfronts; The Four Tops have become the first American vocal group to suffer retaliation at the hands of the British immigration authorities in represal for the attitude exhibited towards British groups by the American musicians union. The Detroit group "underwent great difficulty" in obtaining their work permits for their schedule of television and personal appearances in England, which runs through May 27th.

Motown Records will distribute all recordings by popular French vocalist Richard Anthony in the United States, under terms of an arrangement made by Motown President Berry Gordy, Jr. while in Paris last month with the Motown Revue. Billy Eckstine's first single recording for Motown "DOWN TO EARTH", written by Detroiter Ron Miller, will be released this week.

155

opposite: Even Michigan's then-governor George Romney came out to the Michigan State Fair to see the Supremes. Romney, who later served in President Nixon's cabinet, is the father of Mitt Romney, a former governor of Massachusetts and the leading Republican Party candidate to challenge Barack Obama in the 2012 U.S. presidential election.

AKRON BEACON JOURNAL
Preview
SUNDAY, MARCH 20, 1966

TV and Radio
Art Music
Books Theater

The Swinging Supremes—See Page 2

THE SUPREMES — DIANA ROSS (LEFT), MARY WILSON AND FLORENCE BALLARD — BEGAN SINGING AS TEAM EIGHT YEARS AGO

Now Everybody Loves Them

Super-Cute Pixie Named Diana Puts Supremes In Big Time

By JACK MAJOR

The first time I tried to figure out what life was all about —I was 5 and the year was 1943—my conclusion was amazingly simple and clear - cut: The Japs and Germans were the bad guys, we were the good guys, and God and Errol Flynn were on our side.

And things remained that way for awhile. Then, suddenly, everything got switched around. The Japanese (we didn't call 'em Japs anymore) were really great people, industrious and friendly. And the Germans? Oh, baby, you don't knock a bunch of brilliant scientists.

The mysterious Image Changer had struck again! That sneaky IC— it creeps in unnoticed and works unseen, and after it leaves, things are never the same.

LIKE WITH Rocky Graziano. Why I remember when people thought of Rocky as a dumb, no-good boxing bum who was always in trouble with the law. After the IC went to work, Rocky became America's lovable clown. Good ol' Rocky.

And I even remember when people booed Mickey Mantle because they figured he was such a disappointment — he didn't hit 60 home runs every year, his batting average occasionally fell below .300 and his fielding wasn't as flawless as Joe DiMaggio's. Then IC struck and people recognized Mickey as the great player he is. Good ol' Mickey.

And now it's the good ol' Supremes.

Before IC came into their lives, The Supremes were just another rock n' roll singing group. After IC, the three Detroit girls were the toast of the musical world—adult's as well as teen-ager's.

People who had been knocking popular music ever since Bill Haley's "Rock Around The Clock" were suddenly singing a few bars of "Stop In The Name of Love" and telling every-

one, gee, but The Supremes are the greatest female singing team since The Andrews Sisters.

When and why their image changed is still a bit hazy. The Supremes became very "in" shortly after their hit engagement at New York's Copacabana. A string of television appearances followed, and apparently grownups gave them a try — and liked them.

THE SUPREMES are definitely special. They've got something The Toys, The Shangri-Las, The Marvellettes, and the 112 other female singing groups will never have—and that something is a super-cute, big-eyed pixie named Diana Ross.

The big question, however, is just how much longer will The Supremes have her.

Diana is the lead singer and is

DIANA ROSS IN ACTION
...the eyes have it

considered good enough to be a top star in her own right. Her style is Eartha Kitt-ish, but Diana's voice is much more versatile and exciting than Eartha's.

Some fuss is being made of the fact The Supremes' itinerary hasn't changed in several weeks—their last engagement is still the Sept. 29-to-Oct. 19 date in Las Vegas.

Because of this there is a rumor Diana will quit the group in October and strike off on her own.

SHE DENIES IT. "We'll do whatever Mr. Gordy tells us to."

Berry Gordy is president of Motown Records and is Big Boss where The Supremes are concerned. He has been father, manager and guiding light ever since the girls began singing together eight years ago.

The relationship between the girls has always been, and remains, a close, friendly one, but Diana admits that in some ways she is growing apart from the other two, Mary Wilson and Florence Ballard.

Diana is the only one who has come completely out of the shell. Mary and Florence are still, basically, a couple of nice kids from Detroit. Diana is now thinking about moving to New York so she can be right there where IT is happening.

DIANA ALSO handles the bulk of the group's publicity, and lately has done almost all the interviews. Mary and Florence have a tendency to clam up when Diana is holding court.

Diana has also developed a completely professional stage presence. She constantly gesticulates and grimaces and uses those crazy big eyes.

She knows how to handle a crowd and appears at ease while doing it. Even if she weren't the lead singer, Diana would command attention.

Yet Diana Ross might never have become a performer if it hadn't been for the other two.

Singing was Florence's idea. Some of her friends had formed a male singing group called The Primes. They wanted a sister group, so Florence, Mary, Diana and another neighborhood pal, Barbara Martin, started a quartet called The Primettes.

They sang at school dances, amateur shows, super market openings— any place they could. And from the beginning, Diana had the lead, sometimes sharing it with Florence.

THE GIRLS auditioned for Gordy, whose record company had already helped many youngsters from the Negro tenement section of Detroit.

Gordy had one piece of advice: Finish high school. It was a way of testing the girls' sincerity about singing. It was also his way of looking out for the girls' welfare. He knew how important a high school diploma would be to the girls if they dropped out of show business.

Three years later the girls returned to Motown and signed a contract. A few months later they were a trio. Barbara Martin had left to get married and her replacement, Betty Travis, soon quit for the same reason.

The trio's first taste of fame came not from recordings, but from the 1961 Emancipation Day Talent Contest in Windsor, Canada. The girls won first place—and $5 apiece.

IN THEIR early recordings, the girls were used only to provide the do-wah background for other performers. When Gordy made the decision to spotlight the girls he decided at the same time to change

(Continued on Page 18)

Mr. John Appleton
Entertainment Editor
The Saturday Evening Post
666 5th Avenue
New York, New York 10019

Dear Mr. Appleton:

About six months ago, Mr. Alfred G. Aronowitz of your staff spent some time at the Motown Studioes compiling material for a story on Motown's President, Berry Gordy, Jr. At that time, a serious situation arose regarding Mr. Aronowitz's personal conduct while our guest, which made it necessary for us to terminate our co-operation with him.

Since that time, the Motown Record Corporation, through the success of the Supremes, has received a great deal of national coverage, and has made the "Detroit Sound" a household word.

I strongly feel that the Motown story which you authorized Mr. Aronowitz to create for you, is still sufficiently worthy of coverage in your magazine.

The enclosed article was written by Mr. Marshall Jay Kandell, for the Los Angeles Herald-Examiner, of which paper Mr. Kandell was recently the Sunday Editor. Mr. Kandell has since left the Herald-Examiner to concentrate on free-lance writing.

Mr. Kandell is already closer to the source insofar as regards the inner workings of Motown. He is an excellent writer and most important of all, we would be more than pleased to fully co-operate with him in the preperation of his story. Mr. Kandell can be reached c/o 3640 Los Feliz Boulevard, apartment 22, Los Angeless 27, California.

I have taken the liberty of bringing the above to your attention in the event that you still feel that the complete and definitive Motown story is worth telling, and worth telling well.

Regardless, I also appreciate having this opportunity to bring Mr. Kandell's talents to your attention.

Cordially,

MOTOWN RECORD CORPORATION

By_____

Al Abrams
Publicity Director

see pages 198-199 for a reproduction of the article written by Marshall Jay Kandell

THERE'S NO STOPPING
US NOW
THE SUPREMES
Motown 1103
Jan 11, 1966

SHOW
TIME

The Cleveland Press
FRIDAY, JULY 8, 1966

A Magazine
of the Lively Arts

MOVIES
NIGHT
CLUBS
DINING
BOOKS
RECORDS
TV-RADIO
COMMENT

TeenSeT

APRIL, 1966   35 CENTS

COLOR PHOTOS: THE ROLLING STONES!
THE SUPREMES! DAVID McCALLUM!
DAVE CLARK 5! WALKER BROTHERS!
GARY LEWIS!

please let us

"LOVE IS HERE AND NOW
YOU'RE GONE"
(Holland, Dozier, Holland)
THE SUPREMES
© 1966 A TRADEMARK OF MOTOWN RECORD CORP.

"THERE'S NO STOPPING
US NOW"
(Holland, Dozier, Holland)
THE SUPREMES

Al Abrams
PICKS

YOUR TV STAR ALBUM

The Supremes

FROM: Motown Record Corporat[ion]
2648 West Grand Bouleva[rd]
Detroit, Michigan 48208

For additional information
contact Al Abrams (TR 1-3340)

FOR IMMEDIATE [RELEASE]

SUPREMES RECORD NOMINATED
FOR "GRAMMY" AWARD

"BABY LOVE", the second m[illion-seller by]
Detroit's Supremes, has been nominated for a "GRAMMY" award,
the [recor]ding industry's highest tribute, as one of 1964's best
[record]s.

The "GRAMMY" award is presented yearly by The National
[Academy of] Recording Arts and Sciences to honor significant
[achievements] in various categories of recorded music. The finalists
[are selecte]d by a vote of the entire academy membership on April
[The] "GRAMMY" award is equivalent to the motion picture
[and t]elevisions "EMMY".

[Th]e presentation of the "GRAMMY" awa[rd]
[at] 8:30 P.M. E.S.T. Sunday Ma[rch]
[it] received high

[The] Supreme[s]
[rece]ived a "G[RAMMY"]
[nom]ination

after FOUR
TOPS IN ALL THAT'S TEEN

Do I have any regrets about my time at Motown?

TO THIS DAY, I still sometimes lament my decision not to accompany the artists on the Tamla-Motown Tour of 1965 when I had the opportunity of a lifetime.

However, from a pragmatic viewpoint, I must still defend my choice of sending Van G. Sauter, one of America's most respected journalists, as my surrogate to file reports to the media from the tour. Let me explain.

I was faced with a choice between personally doing something I really wanted to do and doing something for the greater good of the Motown artists. I chose the latter.

I could easily have gone on the trip and filed press releases on the road - although that task was a lot more difficult in 1965 than it is today in the era of instant communication using social media such as Twitter, YouTube and Facebook.

I decided that if Motown paid Sauter, then a *Detroit Free Press* reporter, to accompany the tour, my chances of getting major coverage in the Freep would be substantially increased. Although to be both realistic and callous, I saw it as earning me a valuable IOU with the ambitious Sauter.

DETROIT'S SUPREMES ON TOUR

Singing Their Way   Across Britain

BRITAIN in the spring. April in Paris, then possibly on to Italy, West Germany and the Scandinavian countries when the weather gets warmer. It sounds like a leisurely itinerary for the idle rich.

In reality it's the not-so-leisurely but nevertheless enjoyable — and enriching — itinerary for the Supremes, the three young Detroit ladies who are just about the biggest thing in records today.

The girls — Diana Ross, Florence Ballard and Mary Wilson — are abroad with a flock of other Detroiters who record for the Detroit-based Tamla, Motown and Gordy labels.

They're making extremely well-received stage appearances and doing "live" and taped TV shows throughout the British Isles. They've sung and done sightseeing from London to Glasgow, with other stops at Bristol, Cardiff, Manchester, Leeds and Liverpool, home of some of their biggest fans — the Beatles.

The Supremes will be back in the states early in May for NBC-TV's "Hullabaloo," will later headline Atlantic City's Steel Pier Memorial Day show.

The globe-trotting girls haven't forgotten where home is, however. They'll return to Detroit to cut some new discs, and in June they'll go up north for an appearance in Cadillac.

Mary posts a letter to home in a London mailbox as a "Bobby" strolls by.

opposite: The Supremes in London shot by Dezo Hoffman.
above: Harvey and Gwen Fuqua and the then happy Marvin and Anna Gaye departing for the UK.

TO YOU ALL FROM HITSVILLE
WE LOVE YOU TOO
TAMLA-MOTOWN APPRECIATION SOCIETY

So I decided to stay behind in Detroit and send out as many photographs as I received from Europe to get stories placed in publications across North America. Did that PR gamble pay off? You betcha' - the proof is in your hands as you look through the newspaper and magazine stories in this book.

Van Sauter filed many reports on the 1965 Tamla-Motown European tour, but unfortunately very few newspapers -- if indeed any -- picked up on his dispatches. One of the best of Van's stories is his take on Stevie Wonder. This article spins a great tale about Stevie visiting the Tower of London where the guards removed a glass case so Stevie could "feel" a suit of armor belonging to Henry VIII. Never heard that story before? That's because this example of Van's reportage was never printed. You're reading it in this book on Pages 134-136 for the first time anywhere in 46 years. And you'll also find in this book on page 129 an excerpt from the fantastic story Sauter later wrote for the Freep's *Detroit* magazine giving readers an inside look into the behind-the-scenes workings of the Motown Hit Making Machine.

Of course, that's just a coincidence, wink, wink, nudge, nudge.

Sauter continued to add laurels to his resume. He reported from the front lines of Vietnam for the Freep. When I staged the World's First Mod Wedding (see pages 238-239) featuring Andy Warhol and The Velvet Underground, it was Sauter's reportage that went around the world via the wire services. You probably saw it in the UK dailies.

Sauter's story even appeared translated into Hebrew letters in *The Jewish Daily Forward*, a Yiddish-language newspaper, along with a photo of the bride - who was Jewish - in her mini-wedding gown and thigh-high boots. What a PR coup that was!

After Sauter joined the staff of the *Chicago Daily News,* he came to Memphis to write a feature story that put the Memphis Sound of Stax/Volt on the map and called it the "New Motown". The story probably made Berry furious when he saw the copy I just somehow happened to send him.

Sauter then joined the CBS-TV station in Chicago as News Director and rose within the organization to become the president of CBS News. That made him Walter Cronkite's boss.

Along the way, Sauter married the sister of Jerry Brown, the governor of California who made a bid for the Democratic nomination for the presidency. Brown, also sometimes known as "Governor Moonbeam," is currently serving once again as the governor of California.

Was it worth giving up my trip? What do you think?

But I did miss the chance to interact once again with Dave Godin, the founder of the UK's Tamla-Motown Appreciation Society who did so much for us at Motown. I had met Dave on his visit to Motown and we stayed in close contact via Air Mail letters in those primitive pre-e-mail days.

DETROIT MEETS LIVERPOOL

Detroit's SUPREMES and four members of the DAVE CLARK FIVE pose during rehearsal for a TV program in London, England.

See the Supremes and your other favorites at the 1964 "Motor Town Revue" opening Christmas Day at the Fox Theatre - Detroit

Dave knew I was collecting early newspapers, and he never missed an opportunity to send

me some great British editions - especially from the Second World War. We stayed in touch even after I left Motown. I always considered Dave as a friend.

I also regretted not having an opportunity to personally meet Vicki Wickham of *Ready, Steady, Go* and to see the classic RSG tribute to Motown live in the studio. Vicki was always so helpful to me in getting Motown coverage in the UK music magazines.

But perhaps most importantly of all, I regret that I never had the chance to meet Dusty Springfield, or see her perform in person.

After the tour, when I heard that Dusty had named her beloved dog "Motown," I bought the most beautiful diamond-encrusted dog collar I could find and sent it to Dusty for Motown as a thank you from the artists for all she had done for us on the tour.

Dusty was thrilled and sent me a beautiful hand-written thank you note. Last year, when I tried to locate it for her biographer, journalist Sharon Davis, I found that someone had nicked it. I wish I had it to share with you in this book. I keep watching eBay and other online collector auction sites hoping it will show up one day.

DARTFORD 9 15 PM 4 NOV

139 Church Road, Bexleyheath, Kent, England.   November 4th.

Dear Al,

     How are you? Well, I hope. No doubt you heard of the sad suicide of Mick Page, who was such a help in running the Society, and it was a shattering personal blow, and even now nine weeks after the event I still feel a sadness from time to time. Why I am really writing though, is to tell you that I have mailed to you by surface post some old historic news-papers that I found in Mick's room when I went over there to help his Mum sort out all his things. I know he would have wanted you to have them as when I told him once of your hobby he told me that he had some such papers that I could send to you - I'm only sorry that it had to be under such sad circumstances that I had to collect them.

     I have been very very busy despite you all not having heard from me for a little while. Has Emily had her baby yet? Please let me know as soon as you know so that I can send her our greetings and best wishes.

     We are still faced with an uphill struggle to get Britain a bit hipper music-wise, but we keep on trying. There are two editions of the magazine this month so I must be breif and get on with them.

     Kindest regards to you all,
     Swinger & friend,
     Dave

↑To op

Sender's name and address:

Dave Godin
139 Church
Kent, Engl

HITSVILLE U.S.A.
GREETINGS TO TAMLA
MOTOWN APPRECIATION SOCIET

NOT FOR BROADCAST
ALL RIGHTS RESERVED

SIDE 1
DM 097311

th,

Produced
BRADSHAW, E
Time: 3:
45 RPM

↑To open slit along here

MARGARET PHELPS, BERRY GORDY, JR.
SMOKEY ROBINSON & THE MIRACLES,
STEVIE WONDER, MARVIN GAYE,
THE MARVELETTES, THE TEMPTATIONS

MOTOWN

Chapter 6 ➤

MARCH ON HITSVILLE

opposite: Tommy Good singing to the crowd from the Hitsville front porch with Berry Gordy, Jr., Ivy Joe Hunter and Norm Whitfield looking on. Also in that appreciative audience is the perpetrator of the PR stunt -- yes, that's me on the immediate right -- literally hiding behind the woman in the black dress in case anything went wrong.

Magazine

The Afro ⦿⦿ American

Section

WEEK OF APRIL 23, 1966

THE AFRO - AMERICAN
BALTIMORE
AFRO-AMERICAN
WASHINGTON
AFRO-AMERICAN
NEW JERSEY
AFRO-AMERICAN
RICHMOND
AFRO-AMERICAN

next week
4-YEAR-OLD
CHARMS
THE
WHITE HOUSE

HOW

this ventriloquist got the 'BUG'

By BRENDA L. THOMPSON

LESTER and WILLIE TYLER

Lester only has one name, he's made out of wood, and he has the stiffest leg in captivity.

But you would never know that the little fellow is not human once 20-year-old Willie Tyler sets the flashy little man on his knee and commences an act that has been applauded all over the United States, Canada, and Europe.

Began at 12

Willie, the ventriloquist, said he learned the technique through a home study course from the Fred Maher School of Ventriloquism at the age of 12.

"When my family got our first TV set, I saw the Paul Winchell - Jerry Mahoney Show, which was aired once a week. Right away I got the "bug."

His lips never move, but every word Lester utters is clear as a bell. Willie, one of 10 children, attributes this to the fact that he likes to keep his mouth shut anyway.

'I tried to confuse people'

"You learn more this way. Sometimes in the past I tried to confuse people by throwing my voice. This is very

Wears Size 2 Suit

Ventriloquist figures (dummies) are really like anything else; they can be purchased at all prices. They can wear children's clothing. For example, Lester wears sizes 2 and 3 suits.

difficult, and it has to be done very professionally — or you're sunk!

"Nowadays, I find if I'm around people, and there is a noise produced that can't be accounted for, someone usually shouts, 'that was Willie throwing his voice.'"

Willie's full-time job began as a hobby as mentioned when he was still in grade school. After a year in col-

About Willie

The ventriloquist has appeared on local Detroit television and also armed forces TV overseas. At the present, he has not appeared on any major national hook-up — but hopes to soon. Hobby-wise, Willie likes to write many of his own songs, photography, woodworking, paneling and watching people —when they don't know they are being observed. It really knocks him out!

lege, after completing high school, he enlisted in the United States Air Force.

'Pretty raw'

His early ventriloquistic efforts were "pretty raw," said Willie; but time soon changed that.

Then as a result of the wonderful reception from the many shows he did while in Europe, Willie Tyler decided to turn professional.

"My very first little wooden partner was self-made out of sister's discarded doll. His name, as I recall was 'J.J.'

Lester has grown up

"Now I have five other ventriloquist figures. These are the ones I have used through the years, including a small and medium Lester. He's grown up now. Little Lester I did not make; I had him specially ordered.

"The turban idea was my own. It came to me when I was in the service stationed in Tripoli, Libya."

Act within an act

As if to give a bonus to all of his fans, Willie taught himself to play guitar and coupled this with his melodic tenor voice to produce an act within an act.

"But," Willie reminds us, "Lester remains the most important quality."

Born in Red Level, Ala. the bachelor's (marital plans are

in the making for mid-summer) goal in life is to become the best ventriloquist in the world. And this may be easier than he thinks. For as Willie says:

'Vents' are few in number

"Off hand I can't estimate the number of ventriloquists today. I do know that professional 'vents' are very few and far between. And colored ventriloquists are even fewer in number.

"Right now, it's not a problem getting work in my field. It's not everyday one gets to see a ventriloquist of any kind."

'Knock on wood'

So far, nothing drastic has happened to upset Willie's act before a show. But one time Lester's eyes went haywire . . . this was during a rehearsal at home though. "So far — so good —," Willie comments, but added, "knock on wood."

Motown Act

Willie Tyler is a member of the Motown crew where they are not only rock n' rollers, but country and western singers, comedians, etc. — any kind of potential talent.

But all of the credit can't go to Willie. Reflect for a moment on little Lester, the dashing young wit who sparks up an entertaining act.

When Lester hits the stage, he instantly comes to life and it is difficult to remember that Willie is putting words into his mouth.

They laugh together, sing duets, and become thoroughly integrated — that is until Lester, raising his eyebrows, asks Willie: "How do you feel standing here talking to a dummy?"

When Lester was asked, how did he feel talking to his boss, he replied: "Are you talking about Willie Tyler — the dummy with two names?"

It was a stroke of good luck that in the long, hot summer of 1964 I shared my attic -- hidden away on the third floor of Hitsville USA -- with our talented art director Bernard Yeszin.

NOT ONLY WAS HE A GREAT COMPANION but he had just discovered and brought to Motown's attention a young white singer named Tommy Good. Yeszin had found him performing in a popular suburban bar with his group Tommy Good and the Tabs.

Motown had recorded Good but was sitting on actually releasing his records. Now it appeared that a single would be released and Yeszin, who co-managed Good with Motown songwriter/producer Clarence Paul, hoped that a successful promotional gimmick could be found to call attention to the record.

That was all I needed to hear. The situation - a white recording artist on a black label seeking support to have his record released during the height of civil right tensions - was made for PR. And I had a plan.

My concept was audacious. Because Good came from one of the all-white suburbs ringing Detroit's central city, I would organize his already existing fan base to mimic in reverse a staple of that summer's civil rights epoch being played out on the streets of American cities. I would create a *March on Hitsville* with placard-bearing white people picketing a black-owned company.

Teens March on Hitsville

In one of the most unusual demonstrations ever witnessed in Detroit, a group of two to three hundred shouting teenagers marched upon the Detroit "Hitsville U.S.A." offices of the Tamla-Motown Record Corporation.

The object of the march, which was organized by the Tommy Good Fan Club, was to force the Company to release a record by young Detroit singer (23) Tommy Good.

The march caught everyone at the Company completely off guard and succeeded in tying up rush hour traffic over a busy eight block area. There were two minor accidents as homeward bound motorists stopped to look at the unusual spectacle.

Many of the marchers bore signs reading "Release Tommy Good," "Bring On Tommy Good," "Give Tommy Good a Break," and "Tommy Good, Yea, Yea, Yea." One sign carried by a young girl read "Tommy Good For President."

Said Mr. Gordy of the demonstration, "Reaction like this by a singer's fans prior to his record released is unprecedented. We expect to have a record out on Tommy Good in the very near future."

JOBETE MUSIC COMPANY

"BABY I MISS YOU"

Gordy

IT'S WHAT'S IN THE GROOVES THAT COUNT

AUG

ON COPY

7024

310

29

cord

NOT FOR SALE

Produced By
Wm. Stevenson
Time 2:57
45 RPM

CT

CT

BABY I MISS YOU
(Wm. Stevenson)
TOMMY GOOD

TAMLA

BABY I MISS YOU
(Wm. Stevenson)
TOMMY GOOD

MADE IN CANADA BY PHONODISC

FOR IMMEDIATE RELEASE.........

TEENS MARCH ON HITSVILLE

In one of the most unusual demonstrations ever witnessed in Detroit, a group of two to three hundred shouting teenagers marched upon the Detroit "Hitsville U.S.A." offices of the Tamla-Motown Record Corporation.

The object of the march, which was organized by the Tommy Good Fan Club, was to force the Company to release a record by young Detroit singer (23) Tommy Good.

The march caught everyone at the Company completely off guard and succeeded in tying up rush hour traffic over a busy eight block area. There were two minor accidents as homeward bound motorists stopped to look at the unusual spectacle.

Many of the marchers bore signs reading "Release Tommy Good" "Bring on Tommy Good"; "Give Tommy Good A Break", and "Tommy Good, Yea, Yea, Yea". One sign carried by a young girl read "Tommy Good For President".

Mr. Berry Gordy, Jr., President of Tamla-Motown, had been recording a session with Tommy Good at the time of the demonstration. A spokesman he was attracted by the sound of the chanting marchers. A spokesman for the Fan Club presented a list of demands to Mr. Gordy which included an ultimatum demanding immediate release of a record by Tommy Good - or the marchers would continue picketing of the Company's offices.

After negotiation with a spokesman for the Company, the marchers said they would be pacified by an appearance by Tommy Good. Tommy was pleased to make this "Command Performance", and a speaker and sound system were rushed out to the front of the Company's offices. The marchers were then treated to a "Live" perview of Tommy's records, which the crowd greeted with wild, unrestrained enthusiasm.

At one point during Tommy's appearance, his fans mobbed him, causing him to retreat within the Company's offices. For the most part though, the marchers remained peaceful and orderly.

Tommy then appealed to the marchers to return home, and after Mr. Gordy promised them that a record by their idol would be released, the crowd dispersed.

Said Mr. Gordy of the demonstration, "Reaction like this by a singer's fans prior to his record release is unprecedented. We expect to have a record out on Tommy Good in the very near future".

176

As I write these words, I think my first reaction if I heard this today from anyone else would be to exclaim, "Oh My God!"

After all, this was just a year after Dr. Martin Luther King's historic *March on Washington*. And Dr. King was a personal hero to Berry, Esther and everyone within the Motown family.

What was I thinking?

The answer was simple – I would successfully pull off the greatest PR stunt in Motown history.

But how would I ever sell Berry on the idea?

That was actually easier than I thought. Berry, who was used to hearing many of my outlandish ideas for PR stunts (and killing most of them) smiled and laughed when I told him the idea.

But then he added, "If it backfires on the company, I'll have to fire you." And he meant it.

The reaction of Esther Edwards was another matter. She saw my idea as an affront to the civil rights movement, coming as it did from a black company. But Esther never had much of a sense of humor, especially where I was concerned. However, once Berry told her his edict that I would be fired if the stunt failed, she reluctantly gave it her blessing and probably secretly hoped for the worst.

I had never organized a civil rights protest and had no idea how to start. The closest I had come to being involved in a civil disturbance was when I ate the racist petition that would have kept black kids out of a suburban high school.

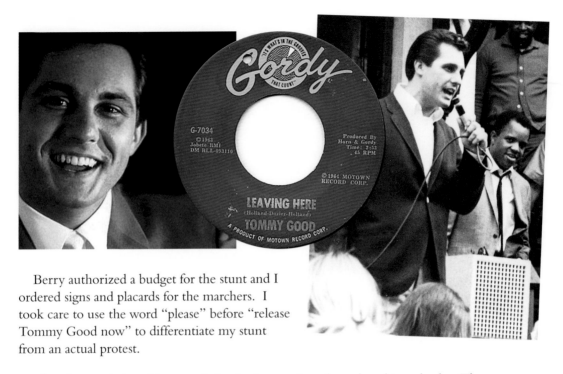

Berry authorized a budget for the stunt and I ordered signs and placards for the marchers. I took care to use the word "please" before "release Tommy Good now" to differentiate my stunt from an actual protest.

Then I commissioned buses to bring in the marchers from the white suburbs. They included Tommy's fan club and even his family members.

Everyone at Motown was in on the scheme. On the day the well-dressed and obviously well-heeled protestors (one placard-carrier was decked out in a suit and porkpie hat) descended upon Hitsville, I had Tommy hidden in my third floor office.

Everything went according to my plan. After the marchers walked the sidewalks and circled the building chanting, "Free Tommy Now," Tommy appeared on the Hitsville front porch. Miraculously, so did a PA system.

Berry and a number of staffers joined Tommy on the porch. Tommy sang a few songs to the crowd - including "Leaving Here" and "Ask the Lonely", his about-to-be-released single - and the crowd cheered.

Then Berry announced that Tommy's record would indeed be released by Motown and the crowd went wild.

The spectacle on busy West Grand Boulevard drew gawkers, snarled traffic and even

opposite: As you look at the signs carried by the well-dressed white people picketing Hitsville, USA, you'll note that I went to great lengths to prevent anyone from interpreting this as a parody on the contemporary civil rights marches. For instance, consider the unique "protest" signs to release Tommy Good's record that end with "please."

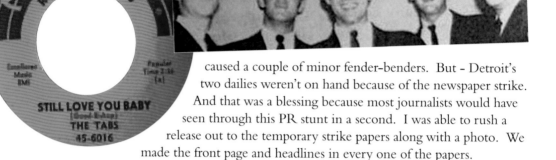

caused a couple of minor fender-benders. But - Detroit's two dailies weren't on hand because of the newspaper strike. And that was a blessing because most journalists would have seen through this PR stunt in a second. I was able to rush a release out to the temporary strike papers along with a photo. We made the front page and headlines in every one of the papers.

Tommy Good has called my stunt "ballsy." I was just glad it came off without any negative aspects and has gone down in music PR history as one of the greatest PR promotional stunts of the 20th Century.

There's another angle to the Tommy Good story that speaks volumes about the era in which we lived. We had to go through some great lengths to keep Southern record distributors from knowing that most of our artists were black. That's why we released records by Berry's brother Robert under the name of Bob Kayli and why you see a drawing of a mailbox and a spider and not a photo of the Marvelettes on the front cover of the *Please Mr. Postman* album. But were we really fooling them or humoring ourselves? This charade continued through the 1964 presidential campaign when Berry shot down my memo suggesting the company support Democratic president Lyndon B. Johnson in the presidential election (see page 61 for the memo.) In fact, Berry even made me take down a Johnson-Humphrey campaign poster just in case one of those Southern distributors happened to find himself in the unlikely situation of walking through my attic office.

The contrast between Tommy Good and his Gordy label mates the Temptations was even starker than just being white and black. While Tommy needed the *March on Hitsville* to help jumpstart his recording career, the Temptations just seemed to automatically flow onto the charts with every recording they released. Recognizing that they were almost immediately a crossover act with white audiences from the start, I wanted to create a strong bond with their loyal black audience base as well. Thus, I hit upon the idea of photographing each of the steps to the *Temptations Walk* on stage and putting them onto a photograph as a montage. One of the first entertainment reporters at a black weekly to enthuastically give the photo full coverage in his newspaper was Charles Henry of the Detroit edition of the venerable *Pittsburgh Courier* (reproduced on these page 185).

above: Rare photo of Tommy Good and the Tabs.

JOIN THE <u>MARCH</u> ON HITSVILLE!

why
won't
HITSVILLE
U.S.A.
release
**TOMMY
GOOD
RECORDS
NOW
?**

<u>M</u>arch: July 14th, 4:00 PM

Hitsville U.S.A. 2648 W. Grand Blvd. Detroit

for information call the
TOMMY GOOD fan club.
phone no. 382-7856

(Be there)

MY GIRL
THE TEMPTATIONS
Gordy 7038
December 21, 1964

Al Abrams PICKS

GORDY

GORDY 7038
©1964 Jobete BMI
DM WL L-109119
RK4M 6552

1964 Copyright
Motown
Record Corp.

Produced by
Robinson-White

Time: 2:55
45 RPM

MY GIRL
(Robinson-White)
THE TEMPTATIONS

Detroit Courier
THEATRICALS

tion Walk THE TEMPTATIONS

THE D...
by The...
Eddie...
and M...
Walk...

VOC...

THE WAY YOU DO
E THINGS YOU

by WILLIAM ROBINSON and BOBBY ROGERS
rded by TEMPTATIONS on Gord...

MY BABY
Words and Music by WARREN MOORE, WILLIAM ROBINSON, ROBERT RO...
RECORDED By THE TEMPTATIONS on GORDY Records

JOBETE M...

THE TEMPTATIONS

TOP TUNES—'My Baby' Is The Temptations' Latest
By RONNIE OBERMAN
Star Special Writer

If the Temptations ever tire
of singing, they can always
turn to playing basketball for

Paul Williams, 25. All live in
Detroit.
Height doesn't pose many
problems for the group,
recording to David. "When
we had our smaller

he's just concerned with
pleasing his fans. "When I go
out there to sing I'm out there
to perform for the people who
put us where we are," he

over to his house," David
explains. "He (Jackie) was in
the room but then just got up
and left. He left at noon and
came back at 3 p.m."

ONE MILLIONTH RECORD
THE MIRACLES

SHOP AROUND

FEBRUARY 12, 1961

Chapter 7

AIN'T NO PLACE LIKE MOTOWN

opposite: Why is this man smiling? Certainly Berry was happy that Tamla/Motown had its first million selling record. But this was also his "I told you so" moment. Now, with a million-seller, he could repay the $800 loan he received from the Ber-Berry Family Cooperative in January 1959 as seed money to launch his own label. Every Motown fan knows the story of how Berry was able to get the loan despite some skepticism by family members. This was the game changer.

WHAT A STEAL!

I've made a couple of references to the woman I was dating during my first few years at Motown. After I met her, I wanted to show her off to Berry as my catch of the day. Thus I brought her to Hitsville. Berry was impressed and then she saw Raynoma. They had a great reunion - Ray and Judy had been high school classmates. So pretty soon we were a foursome when it came to going to events and clubs.

I did hire Judy as my secretary which made her the first white female employee of Motown. She couldn't type or take shorthand but she was a whiz at answering phones. So her stay on Motown's fledgling payroll was prematurely cut short by Berry.

Christmas was coming and Berry and I wanted to get Ray and Judy a truly nice gift. Berry and I decided we'd get them both mink stoles to wear when we went out together. I had an uncle in the fur business - Fogelman Furs on Michigan Avenue for those old Detroiters reading this - and checked his prices. However, even with his best deal, the price was steep.

Berry said not to worry. He took me to a four-family flat where the upper floors were filled with clothing on racks. This was my first exposure to a "booster" - someone who stole clothes from stores for resale. We looked over the merchandise but didn't find anything we liked. So, we continued our Christmas shopping trip with a visit to another booster.

This time we lucked out and each bought a beautiful mink stole for a fantastic price. What a steal - so to speak.

I just hoped they hadn't been stolen from my uncle Harry.

When Christmas came, Ray and Judy were delighted. Of course, Berry and I told them we had shopped all over the city searching for just the right aptly-named stoles.

"It's What's In The Words That Count"

At that time, we were a long way from realizing how integral Motown music could be on a movie soundtrack.

AFTER MOTOWN HAD EXPANDED into three side-by-side houses on West Grand Boulevard, I would often find myself constantly running between Berry's office, my office, the studio and other departments. At one point, Irv Biegel of our sales department, whom I had worked with as a record promotion man, grabbed me by the arm in mid-run (after I almost knocked him over) and half-jokingly started pulling up my shirt sleeve.

"Let me see your needle track marks," Irv said, convinced that only someone high on drugs would be running around the office this way. I was not amused.

Still, I was not deterred in my daily rounds. One day, I decided that what I needed to get around the office quicker was a pair of roller skates. So I brought them to work and took off on my route. I can still remember the look of total amazement on the faces of some of the producers and writers as they first heard, then saw, me tunneling their way at mach speed. Several said "look out" (or much worse) as they jumped out of my path. Wow, did I really get up to 100 clicks between buildings?

Sure, Berry laughed the first couple of times he saw me trying to navigate the walkways between the buildings, but after a few days neither Berry nor Esther were amused. This was in the era before ramps for wheelchairs were required, and those certainly would have made my journey less treacherous, not to mention speedier.

However before I could retire my roller skates, fate brought a Hollywood movie executive to our office to meet with Berry and Norman Whitfield about creating some Motown music for the soundtrack of a proposed movie aimed at predominantly African-American audiences based around the wacky daily activities in a car wash.

I had just pulled off a PR coup in getting a full-page story in the Sunday edition of the *Los Angeles Herald-Examiner* (see page 198-199) on Berry and Motown that was titled Hitsville, USA. I was almost certain that was the motivation for the producer's visit to Motown as the story would have been widely-read in Hollywood.

above: Norman Whitfield

At that time, we were a long way from realizing how integral Motown music could be on a movie soundtrack. How far away were we from that concept? Simply visualize the *T.A.M.I. Show*.

As it happened, I came barreling into the room where Berry and the producer were meeting. Before Berry could yell at me, the producer started laughing. He asked if I always wore roller skates at work to get around the buildings. The producer started peppering me with questions about my age and being Jewish in a black owned company.

Then he delivered the coup de grace. "Maybe I ought to be making a movie about you two and this company, instead of one about a car wash. I couldn't make up a guy like you," he said, pointing at me. I took it as a compliment, especially when he said he wanted me to play myself in the movie. My name up in lights. Superstardom and bevies of Hollywood starlets awaiting me! By now Berry's expression had changed to beaming.

Like many other things back then, we talked and talked about it, but nothing ever came of either movie. So I retired my roller skates and muttered curses under my breath at Irv Biegel daily until he finally left Motown.

At that time in our history, the story of our exciting little company would have made one heck of a movie. Actually, it still would. And just think what I could have done back then had I known about roller blades!

above-left: poster for the T.A.M.I. Show, Marvin Gaye backed by The Blossoms performing on the show; above-right: two stills from the film 'Car Wash'

About ten years later, *Car Wash* became a big money-making movie, I'm almost certain it was produced by the same guy who came to Detroit a decade earlier. Why? Some of the jokes and shtick sounded just like what I had heard in Berry's office.

And guess who did the soundtrack for *Car Wash*? Norman Whitfield, who had left Motown and was working in Los Angeles with Funk Brother Jack Ashford. The soundtrack, which featured Ross Royce, the one-time back-up band for Edwin Starr, also became a big seller.

There weren't any Motown songs in the movie, but with Norm, you really didn't need them. It had THE sound.

Today your dream has come true, you're in charge of the entire company.

Berry Gordy was always ready to delegate authority - but not particularly in the way I wanted.

One winter, Detroit was hit with a record blizzard. So much snow piled up that even the city buses weren't running.

Unfortunately, it happened on a day when we were waiting anxiously for a phone call from United Artists Records in New York.

So, when Berry called me and told me he had no way of getting to the office that morning, I naively asked what about the expected phone call. This, of course, was in the era before telephone answering machines.

That's when Berry said, "Well, you're the second-in-command. Today your dream has come true; you're in charge of the entire company. Go in and answer the phones."

I protested, telling Berry there was no way I could drive my car, take a bus or even a cab to West Grand Boulevard.

"Then walk!" said Berry before hanging up on me.

I bundled up, put on a pair of snow boots and for almost two hours trudged through snowdrifts walking to the studio. I had a key to the building.

I got there, unlocked the door, turned the lights on and heard the phone ringing. I ran to answer it hoping the party on the other end wouldn't hang up.

It was Berry. "What took you so long?" he asked. Before I could answer, he said "New York's been hit with a blizzard too, and no one will be in the office at United Artists, so you may as well shut up the studio and go home. Now you know what it's like to be Number One." Then he laughed and hung up.

Berry had taught me my lesson about wanting to be the guy who ran things. The joke was on me and I laughed all the way home.

Usually, our phones were answered by Janie Bradford, the co-writer of "Money." One day I told her I was waiting for an important call from a reporter at *Cashbox* magazine. But I had to go the lavatory, so I asked Janie to take a message.

Sure enough, when I walked back to the reception desk Janie handed me a pink "While You Were Out" slip with a message from *Cashbox*.

I got back to my office and called him. The first thing he asked me was "Is everything all right?" I told him everything was fine and he started laughing.

He told me that when he asked for me, Janie had replied "Oh, Al's in the shithouse."

It took years for me to live that story down.

July 1, 1965

Mr. Frank Judge
Television Editor
THE DETROIT NEWS
615 West Lafayette Avenue
Detroit, Michigan

Dear Frank:

        I wanted to confirm the information which I
gave you today regarding the appearance of Berry Gordy, Jr.
and the Supremes on "To Tell The Truth" this coming
Monday, July 5th. (The show is carried locally over
WJBK-TV Channel two at 7:30 P.M)

        Three "Berry Gordy, Jr.s" will face the panel
as they attempt to determine which of the three
challengers is the Motown Record Company President.

        This show will also be the network "debut" for
Berry Gordy, Jr. and I understand that a great portion
of this show is being devoted to Detroit.

        Many thanks for your help.

                                Best wishes,

                                MOTOWN RECORD CORPORATION

                                By_____
                                   Al Abrams
                                   Public Relations

AA:met

1965 DISTINGUISHED SERVICE AWARD
NOMINATION FORM

RULES GOVERNING NOMINATION:

1. Nominee must have been 21 to 35 years of age during 1964. No one will be eligible who became 36 before January 1, 1964.

2. Nominee must work or live in the Metropolitan Detroit area (for these purposes in the counties of Wayne, Oakland and Macomb).

3. All information must be contained on the pages of this form.

4. Nominations should be mailed or brought to the Detroit Junior Board of Commerce, Detroit Leland Hotel, Detroit 26, Michigan.

5. All entries must be in the hands of the Detroit Junior Board of Commerce not later than December 28, 1964.

Nominee's Full Name _Berry Gordy Jr_ Birthdate _11-28-29_ Present Age _35_

Address _1342 Joliet Pl_ City _Detroit_ Home Phone _WO 2-4710_

Marital Status _Married_ No. of Children _4_

Occupation _Manufacturing_ Position or Title _President_

Place of Work _Motown Rec Corp_ Business Phone _TRI-3340_

Address _2648 W. Grand Blvd_ City _Detroit_

Schools Attended, Degrees, Academic Honors, etc. (Dates):

Published Work:

Nominator's Name _____ Signature _____

Address _____ City _____ Phone No. _____

Occupation, Business, or Junior Chamber Name _____

May 27, 1965

FROM: Motown Record Corporation
       2648 West Grand Boulevard
       Detroit, Michigan 48208
For additional information contact
     Al Abrams (TRI-3340)

FOR IMMEDIATE RELEASE

City Honors Berry Gordy, Jr.

Berry Gordy, Jr., the young music magnate who has made
the "Detroit Sound" a household word across the nation was
honored Wednesday (May 26th) as the City's "Small Businessman of the Year."

Detroit's mayor, Jerome P. Cavanagh presented the award
to Gordy, the 36 year old president of Motown Record Corporation. Motown is expected to gross $12 million dollars in
1965 through the sales of records by such popular Detroit
recording artists as the Supremes, Marvin Gaye, Martha and
the Vandellas, The Tmeptations and other teenage favorites.

Gordy founded his musical empire in 1958 in the living
room of his home, which at that time was on Gladstone Avenue.
He had his first big hit, "Way Over There" by Smokey Robinson
and the Miracles, in 1959.

Last year Motown sold 750,000 albums and 12 million single
records, outdistanced in single sales only by Capitol records
and it's quartet of mop-haired Beatles (who once called Motown's
rival Supremes their favorite singing group).

A Korean war veteran, Berry Gordy, Jr. attended Northeastern High School, and once boxed in golden glove matches
at Graystone Ballroom, which Motown now owns.

Motown Records and the "Detroit Sound" were profiled in
the May 22nd issues of Time and Life magazines. The June issue
of Fortune Magazine, and the June 15th Look magazine will also
carry feature stories on the talented young Detroiter and his
contributions to Detroit.

Gordy's award is one of a number sponsored by the Small
Business Administration to businessmen who have showed imagi=
nation and initiative.

overleaf 196-197: Berry the business man signs legendary singer Billy Eckstine

197

Winding Staircases, Narrow Halls and A Driving Sound, This Is...

The largest independent record company in the world, Motown scored 42 hits out of 60 tries last year and estimates set this year's take at about $15 million. Primarily a seller of rock and Gospel sound, Motown is diversifying to include jazz, blues and country and western.

TONY MARTIN

"Ours is
says Be
Motown'

...

ITSVILLE, U.S.A.

By MARSHALL JAY KANDELL

ncere sound,"
Gordy Jr.,
ng president.

DETROIT—WAITING in the reception room are a half dozen Negro musicians, a bearded guitar player and a violinist who speaks with a heavy Yiddish accent. Most of them are standing. The few seats do not encourage prolonged visits.

An attractive girl sits behind a glass partition. She tends the switchboard, handles appointments, greets visitors and pushes the buzzer which opens the door to the studios and offices of the most unusual recording company in the United States—the Motown Record Corporation . . . "Hitsville U.S.A.!"

The world's largest independent record company, Motown is second behind Capitol Records in U.S. single record sales. Capitol has the American distribution rights for the Beatles.

Once past the receptionist in the middle building of the three converted aged homes which make up "Hitsville" one embarks on a journey through tiny congested rooms, up winding, creaking staircases wide enough for only one person, under low slanting ceilings and beams and along a maze of passageways and past a dozen mysterious doors.

Behind each door and around every turn one finds desks and shelves—all piled high with magazines, albums, correspondence, etc. Every square inch of "Hitsville" is used. Public relations man Al Abrams shares an attic with the art department. In the basement of one building a team of young technicians makes all the equipment used in the studio.

Motown Sound

Motown is unusual in its location, its history, its organization and its success. In a time when the teenagers are dancing to the sounds of Liverpool, Motown is not only holding its own but pushing its own sound—a combination of rock and Gospel that

Before Motown, Berry was a plasterer and contractor with his father, and worked on Detroit's Lincoln-Mercury assembly lines for $85 a week. He once boxed in Golden Gloves matches in Detroit's Greystone Ballroom— which he now owns.

And he wrote songs and played the piano. "After writing the songs, though," says Gordy, "I didn't like the way other companies produced and recorded them." And so, using money saved by his family, he started producing his own records.

Why in Detroit? "The main reason for being here," jokes Gordy, "was because we were scared of the rest of the world. If we made a mistake we could run home to mama."

Gordy hasn't made any mistakes. Motown now consists of seven record labels, a talent man

December 1, 1964

FROM: Motown Record Corporation
         2648 West Grand Boulevard
         Detroit, Michigan 48208

For additional information contact:
         Al Abrams   (TR. 1-3340)

FOR IMMEDIATE RELEASE

Tony Martin Sings On Motown

Tony Martin, veteran singer and motion picture actor, has signed an exclusive recording contract with Detroit's Motown Recording Corporation.

His first recording for Motown, "Talkin' To Your Picture," is meeting with favorable response from the nation's disc jockeys.

Tony Martin and his wife Cyd Charisse will open December 8th in "First Edition '65', at Detroit's Fisher Theatre.

February 15, 1965

FROM: Motown Record Corporation
        2648 West Grand Boulevard
        Detroit, Michigan 48208

        For additional information contact
        Al Abrams (TR 1-3340)

FOR IMMEDIATE RELEASE

IT'S OFFICIAL!
BILLY ECKSTINE SIGNS WITH MOTOWN

Motown Record Corporation, the Detroit based firm that finished up 1964 as the second largest single record manufacturer in the United States, has signed veteran singer Billy Eckstine to an exclusive recording contract. Eckstine will arrive in Detroit this week to record several albums, which will be released in the near future.

The Four Tops, who are currently scoring nationally with their hit Motown recording "Ask The Lonely", have appeared with Billy Eckstine in many major Las Vegas and New York nightclub engagements.

CONFIRMATION COPY OF WESTERN UNION
MBELE 89 PD 2EX BFEB MAILED TO SENDER

DLY
CONFIRMATION
TO BE MAILED

SINGER BILLY ECKSTINE, WHO RECENTLY MADE NATIONAL HEADLINES WHEN HE DISAPPEARED DURING AN ENGAGEMENT AT NEW YORKS AMERICANA HOTEL, FLEW IN TO DETROIT THIS WEEK TO HUDDLE WITH MOTOWN RECORD COMPANY PRESIDENT BERRY GORDY JUNIOR OVER A PROPOSED RECORDING CONTRACT.

MOTOWN HAS ENTERED THE MOTION PICTURE SOUND TRACK FIELD WITH AN ALBUM OF THE SOUND TRACK OF "NOTHING BUT A MAN". THE HIGHLY ACCLAIMED INDIE-MADE FILM STARS IVAN DIXON AND SONGSTRESS ABBEY LINCOLN IN A DRAMATIC ROLE AND IS A STRONG CONTENDER FOR ACADEMY AWARD RECOGNITION.

AL ABRAMS PUBLIC RELATIONS MOTOWN RECORD CORP

(BOOK OF 9)

TRI 13340
BD FCJ MOTOWN RECORD CORP
CFN FURN

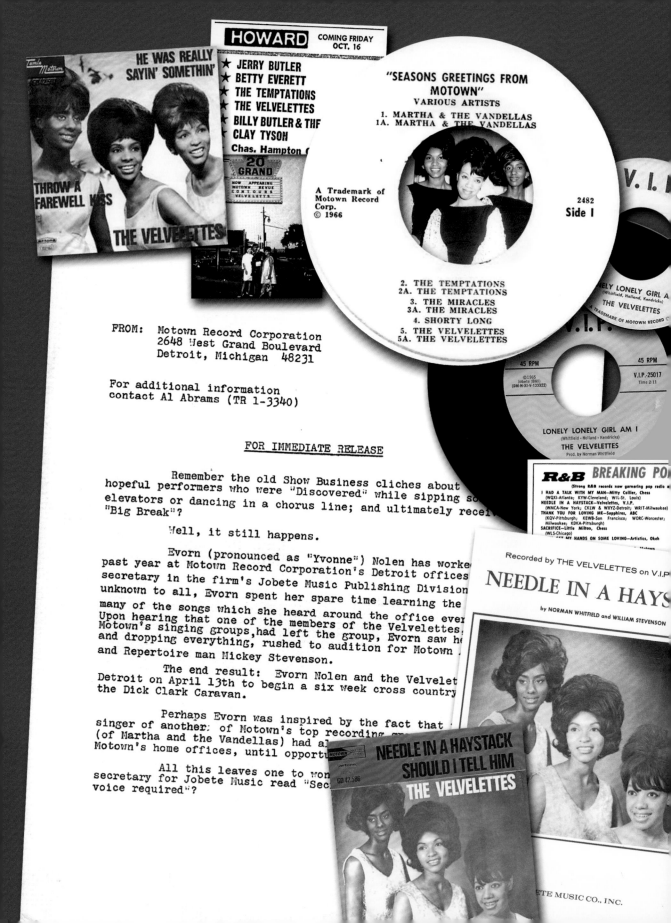

He Was Really Sayin' Somethin'

THROW A FAREWELL KISS

THE VELVELETTES

HOWARD   COMING FRIDAY
                       OCT. 16
★ JERRY BUTLER
★ BETTY EVERETT
★ THE TEMPTATIONS
★ THE VELVELETTES
★ BILLY BUTLER & THE
★ CLAY TYSON
Chas. Hampton

20 GRAND
NOW APPEARING
MOTOWN REVUE
CONTOURS
VELVELETTES

"SEASONS GREETINGS FROM
MOTOWN"
VARIOUS ARTISTS
1. MARTHA & THE VANDELLAS
1A. MARTHA & THE VANDELLAS

A Trademark of
Motown Record
Corp.
© 1966

2482
Side I

2. THE TEMPTATIONS
2A. THE TEMPTATIONS
3. THE MIRACLES
3A. THE MIRACLES
4. SHORTY LONG
5. THE VELVELETTES
5A. THE VELVELETTES

©1965
Jobete (BMI)
(DM-N-XI-V-133322)

45 RPM

V.I.P.

LONELY LONELY GIRL AM I
(Whitfield, Holland, Kendricks)
THE VELVELETTES
A TRADEMARK OF MOTOWN RECORD

V.I.P.

45 RPM
V.I.P.-25017
Time 2-11

LONELY LONELY GIRL AM I
(Whitfield - Holland - Kendricks)
THE VELVELETTES
Prod. by Norman Whitfield

FROM: Motown Record Corporation
        2648 West Grand Boulevard
        Detroit, Michigan 48231

For additional information
contact Al Abrams (TR 1-3340)

FOR IMMEDIATE RELEASE

        Remember the old Show Business cliches about
hopeful performers who were "Discovered" while sipping so
elevators or dancing in a chorus line; and ultimately receiv
"Big Break"?

        Well, it still happens.

        Evorn (pronounced as "Yvonne") Nolen has worke
past year at Motown Record Corporation's Detroit offices
secretary in the firm's Jobete Music Publishing Division
unknown to all, Evorn spent her spare time learning the
many of the songs which she heard around the office ever
Upon hearing that one of the members of the Velvelettes
Motown's singing groups, had left the group, Evorn saw he
and dropping everything, rushed to audition for Motown
and Repertoire man Mickey Stevenson.

        The end result: Evorn Nolen and the Velvelet
Detroit on April 13th to begin a six week cross country
the Dick Clark Caravan.

        Perhaps Evorn was inspired by the fact that
singer of another of Motown's top recording gro
(of Martha and the Vandellas) had al
Motown's home offices, until opportu

        All this leaves one to won
secretary for Jobete Music read "Sec
voice required"?

R&B BREAKING PO
(Strong R&B records now garnering pop radio a
I HAD A TALK WITH MY MAN—Mitty Collier, Chess
(WQXI-Atlanta; KYW-Cleveland; WIL-St. Louis)
NEEDLE IN A HAYSTACK—Velvelettes, V.I.P.
(WMCA-New York; CKLW & WXYZ-Detroit; WRIT-Milwaukee)
THANK YOU FOR LOVING ME—Sapphires, ABC
(KQV-Pittsburgh; KEWB-San Francisco; WORC-Worcester;
Milwaukee; KDKA-Pittsburgh)
SACRIFICE—Little Milton, Chess
(WLS-Chicago)
GET MY HANDS ON SOME LOVING—Artistics, Okeh

Recorded by THE VELVELETTES on V.I.P.

NEEDLE IN A HAYS
by NORMAN WHITFIELD and WILLIAM STEVENSON

NEEDLE IN A HAYSTACK
SHOULD I TELL HIM
THE VELVELETTES

ETE MUSIC CO., INC.

M E M O R A N D U M

TO: Mr. Ralph Seltzer

FROM: Al Abrams

DATE: November 22, 1965

RE: Suggested 1965 CHRISTMAS GIFT LIST

Special Gifts:

Mort Persky	Detroit Free Press
Miss Barbara Holliday	Detroit Free Press

Identical Gifts:

Ken Barnard	Detroit Free Press
Roy Stephens	Michigan Chronicle
Albert J. Dunmore	Michigan Chronicle
Arnold S. Hirsch	Detroit News
Van Sauter	Detroit Free Press
John Finlayson	Detroit News
Miss Jackie Korona	Detroit News
Frank Judge	Detroit News
Robert Lubeck	Detroit News
Miss Bettelou Peterson	Detroit Free Press
Peter Hoffmann	Associated Press
Jim Jones	Newsweek
Hugh McCann	Newsweek
Herm Schoenfeld	Variety (N.Y.)
Ray Oviatt	Toledo Blade
Chester Higgins	Jet (Chicago)
Charles Henry	Detroit Courier
Art Sears Jr.	Jet (N.Y.)
Virgil Medlin	Oklahoma Journal
Sandy Gardiner	Ottawa Journal
Alex Freeman	(Syndicated Columnist)
Stanley Brown	Fortune Magazine
Kevin Barry	Danbury (Conn.) News-Times
Mike Thompson	Miami News
Vernon Hoyt	Omaha World-Herald
Gary Johansen	Omaha World-Herald
John Frook	Life Magazine (Chicago)
Miss Jeanne Duran	Detroit Free Press
Robert M. Swift	Miami Herald

Earl B. Dowdy	Detroit News
Richard T. Cloonan	Detroit News
Bill Baker	Detroit Free Press
Warren Picower	Tuesday Magazine (N.Y.)
Miss Aida Chapman	Tuesday Magazine (N.Y.)
Miss Michaela Williams	Chicago Daily News
Richard Christiansen	Chicago Daily News
Ron Oberman	Washington D.C. Star
Gerry Baker	Toronto (Ontario) Star
George Micheal	K.B.T.R. Denver
Bill E. Burk	Memphis Press-Scimitar
Roger Elwood	Teen Trends Magazine
Miss Loraine Alterman	Detroit Free Press
Jack Burke	Phoenix Gazette

(total of 45)

I would like to go as high as $20.00 for some gifts (I am buying books this year, themes of which will appeal to the type of personality I am dealing with.)

Therefore, I would like to be allocated $950.00 for Christmas gifts. This is by far a liberal estimate, and of course, any monies left over will be returned.

The goodwill received from these gifts could not be purchased at that price.

Al Abrams

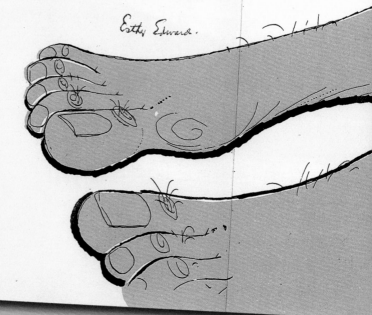

"YOU'VE GOT WHAT IT TAKES" TO FILL THE BOSS' SHOES

BIG FEET!

Esther Edwards

Esther Edwards always had a great sense of humor. But looking at this card, 51 years later, makes me wonder if maybe she wasn't also sending me a less-than-subtle message?

TO	FROM
Al Abrams	Ralph Seltzer
CC: Edw Pollack	

SUBJECT Your proposed Christmas Gift list

FOLD HERE

DATE

11/23/65   I have reviewed your proposal in the above regard, and it is my opinion that the amount involved exceeds what should be reasonably allocated for these purposes. In addition I am concerned that there may be some duplication with gift giving from other sources within the company, which should be avoided. Unless you feel strongly to the contrary(in which case let me know) I would think the sum of $500.00 should more than cover the situation. Please make appropriate arrangements with Mr. Pollack, regarding the financial arrangments. Attached please find returned your list.

SIGNED *[signature]*

FORM 1120. REGENT FORMS, PHILA., PA. 19130

SPEED - MEMO

207

This is a Sincere Wish

for a very

Merry Christmas

and a

Happy New Year

Many THANKS for making this,
my first year in the music business,
a year I'll never forget ...

Al Abrams
Promotions
JOBETE MUSIC CO., INC.

Memo

Date   *Dec. 25th*

Message ...

NO!

It's not another record
It's not another hype ...
BUT
Mr. D.J.

FROM: Hitsville, U.S.A.
2648 West Grand Blvd.
Detroit, Michigan 48208
871-3340 (Al Abrams)

November 15, 1965

FOR IMMEDIATE RELEASE

SUPREMES' CHRISTMAS RECORD
RELEASED THIS WEEK

Motown Record Corporation is releasing a new single recording by THE SUPREMES this week, titled "The Children's Christmas Song" b/w "Twinkle, Twinkle, Little Me". The songs are taken from THE SUPREMES' "Merry Christmas" album. Both songs are originals.

Diana Ross, lead singer of The Supremes, invites all children to sing along with her on "The Children's Christmas Song." On the record, she calls out to "Chico, Joy, Berry and Terry" to join with her, which the four children then do. "Chico" is Chico Ross, younger brother of Diana, and Joy, Berry, and Terry are the three children of Motown's President, Berry Gordy Jr.

Incidentally, Jobete Music Company, Motown's B.M.I. affiliate, which lead the nation's music publishing companies in 1964 with 42 tunes on The Billboard Hot 100 Chart, (making it the top music publishing company in North America), derives its name from the first two letters of the names of Berry Gordy Jr.'s children.

Top Tunes

By

RONNIE OBERMAN

Star Special Writer

Shortly after Marvin Gaye was graduated from Washington's Cardozo High School in the late 1950s, he packed up his bags and went on the road with a group called Harvey and the Moonglows.

Well, there's no more Harvey and the Moonglows today, but there sure is a Marvin Gaye.

In fact, the Tamla Records star, whose latest recording of "Ain't That Peculiar?" is one of his biggest, is being called by some, the heir apparent to the late Nat King Cole.

Marvin, who recently phoned from Hollywood, where he is appearing at a Sunset Strip nightclub, recalled that he was born in Freedman's Hospital 26 years ago and lived in the District for 18 years. He said his parents still live in Northwest Washington.

"Well, I had always wanted to sing," Marvin said, referring to his decision to turn professional. "I got the chance with Harvey and the Moonglows, who prompted me to go on the road. I thought it was a good opportunity, so I split."

Marvin Gaye and his wife, the former Anna Gordy, breakfast at home.

Father Is Minister

He added that his father, who is an Apostolic minister, was unhappy with his decision to leave Washington at first, "but things are rather peaceful now. If a man is a respectful and God-fearing man, then it doesn't matter what you do as long as you include God in it, and I do."

Marvin later left the Moonglows and went to Detroit in 1960 with Harvey Fuqua, leader of the group. It was there that the two met their future wives, both sisters of Berry Gordy Jr., president of Motown Records.

"At that time he didn't have a great record company going," Marvin explained.

"He was just sort of getting started."

Marvin's first big recording for Tamla, a subsidiary of Motown, was "Stubborn Kind of Fellow," and since then he has scored with such tunes as "Hitchhike," "Pride and Joy," "Can I Get a Witness," "You are a Wonderful One," "How Sweet It is to Be Loved by You," "I'll be Doggone," "Pretty Little Baby" and "Aint't That Peculiar?"

One of Greatest

Marvin said the last song was written by Bill (Smokey) Robinson, who is lead singer of the Miracles. "I consider him one of the greatest writers of our time," Marvin said. "He has a natural lyrical ability and a very melodic mind. He has a way of rhyming everyday words which make people feel they know the singer."

Marvin admitted that it doesn't matter whether Smokey or the great Motown writing team of Brian Holland - Lamont Dozier-Eddie Holland pens his songs "because I'm fairly adaptable to all types of songs. It doesn't matter who writes them as long as I can really get into it."

He said the favorite tune he has recorded is "How Sweet It Is," which was written by Holland - Dozier - Holland, as was "Pride and Joy."

Versatile Artist

As one who does not stick to singing rhythm and blues exclusively, Marvin said he likes to think of himself "as a versatile artist who can sing any type song. If I want to sing a ballad, I would like the public to listen and be attentive."

Marvin's latest album, a tribute to Nat King Cole, came about after Mort Persky, Sunday editor of the Detroit Free Press, likened the Tamla star to Cole and said the best tribute would be for Marvin to record an album of Cole songs.

Al Abrams, director of press relations for Motown, said Marvin was selected in a Cashbox Magazine poll this year as the top male rhythm and blues vocalist and also has been selected for inclusion in the 1965-66 edition of Who's Who in America.

Marvin, who has appeared on several network television shows, has been scheduled to open next June at New York's famous Copacabana.

In Loving Memory of

Marvin Earl Johnson

October 15, 1938 — May 16, 1993

SATURDAY, MAY 22, 1993
12:00 Noon

NEW BETHEL BAPTIST CHURCH
8430 C. L. Franklin Blvd. (Linwood)
Detroit, Michigan 48206

REVEREND ROBERT SMITH, JR., Pastor - Officiating

The Obituary

Marvin Earl Johnson was born on October 15, 1938 in Detroit, Michigan to the late Elizabeth and Johnny B. Johnson. He graduated from Cass Technical High School.

At an early age, Marvin showed an aptitude and love for music. He joined the Junior Serenaders and their debut was at the Michigan State Fair. Soon after, he joined a new group, The Downbeats. His first records were "My Baby O" and "Once Upon A Time" which were recorded with Kudo Records. There he met Berry Gordy and they produced his first composition featuring Marv on the piano, the first Motown Sound was born.

When one remembers "Marv", one remembers a gentleman with a sense of loyalty and compassion for his friends. He loved music, one of the many things he lived for. He composed music throughout his life. His career, once again, had begun to blossom. He was scheduled to tour Europe with the release of his new album, "The Best of Marv Johnson" recorded with United Artist.

Marv was a well-versed person who walked with great men and women of his day and travelled extensively around the world! He was exceptionally compassionate and loving when it came to his children, friends and his brothers and sisters of music.

Marvin E. Johnson made his transition on Sunday, May 16, 1993 at 8:30 a.m. in Richland Memorial Hospital in Columbia, South Carolina.

He leaves to continue his work and cherish wonderful memories: four children, Alice Little, Marvin Jr., Terrance and Terrell Russell; six grandchildren, Daniel, Deanna, Andrea, Antonio, Adrienne and Christopher; three brothers, Ronald Black, LaValle Norwood and Cornelius Black; one sister and brother-in-law, Bernadine and Rassie Cleary; one niece, two nephews, six aunts, one uncle, his extended family, Aretha Franklin, Irma Franklin, Doris Gordon and a multitude of life-long friendships with all who knew him.

A precious one from us has gone
A voice we love is stilled,
A Place is vacant in our home
Which never can be filled.

And after a lonely heartache
And many a silent tear,
But always a beautiful memory
Of one we love so dear.

"Don't cry when I'm gone for I have lived a good life. I have no regrets. Let there be celebration for my homecoming and I will rest with my wonderful memories of all of you, who've touched my life. Till down the road we'll meet agian"

— Doris

Order of Service

ORGANISTS .... Darryl Houston
Sweet James Epps
Teddy Harris

PROCESSIONAL

SOLO .... "Danny Boy" .... The Falcons
SOLO .... "Lord's Prayer" .... Norman Thrasher

SCRIPTURE
New Testament .... Rev. Edgar L. Vann, Jr., Pastor, Second Ebeneezer B.C.
Old Testament .... Rev. Robert Smith, Pastor, New Bethel B.C.

SOLO .... "One In A Million" .... Theron Hill

PRAYER .... Rev. Kenneth M. Moseley
Ass't. to the Pastor, Second Ebeneze B.C.

EXPRESSIONS (2 minutes) .... Esther Gordy Edwards
Terrance Russell
Robert Bateman

SOLO .... Kim Weston

ACKNOWLEDGEMENTS & CONDOLENCES

OBITUARY .... Ronald A. Black

SOLO .... "Fix Me" .... Sweet James Epps

RESOLUTION

SOLO .... Pat Lewis

EULOGY .... Rev. Robert Smith, Jr., Pastor , New Bethel Church

RECESSIONAL .... Ministers and Family

ORGAN POSTLUDE
(Final Rites at Cemetery Chapel)

"O sing unto the Lord a new song; for He hath done marvelous things" — Psalm 98:1

March 23, 1990

Dear Motowner, *Al Abrams.*

Join us, and help celebrate the
life and legacy of the late Marvin Gaye
on his birthday.

Event: MARVIN GAYE TRIBUTE
Date: Monday, April 2, 1990
Time: 12:00 Noon
Place: Fox Theatre Lobby
2211 Woodward (Downtown Detroit)

Marvin Gaye, III and Ms. Anna Gaye
will be in attendance along with
Mayor Coleman Young, other dignitaries,
artists, and friends.

Petitions will be available for
your signature to get Marvin Gaye
a star on Hollywood's Walk of Fame.

We hope you will be able to
attend this Tribute in the lobby of
the Fox Theatre.

Sincerely,

Kristina King
Coordinator

Esther Edwards
Director

214

P.S. Bring your family & friends!

THE
MOTOWN
MUSEUM

DETROIT

The Boston Globe
BOSTON, MASS. 02107

Dear Al,

Frankly, since your assignment has been changed at MOTOWN I think that their public relations-publicity machinery has broken down almost to the worthless stage. It used to be so hip.

Anyway, for old times sake, here's a clipping on the Supremes for your files.

If you see one of their new LPs kicking around, I'd love to have a copy.

You can send it to my home address listed below.

Dear Al:

Just between you and me I never received tha album(s). I'm at a loss to explain the Motown thinking...if they don't think an LP is worth all the publicity I've given them with our circulation daily and Sunday...well, to hell with them.

If it weren't for you, Motown could go over Niagara Falls in a Capitol bus for all I care.

But I just thought you'd like to know this...and maybe the company has offended xx many others in large cities where one day they might be looking for help.

Best,

Bill

Bill Buchanan

STAX

SOULSVILLE
U.S.A.

STAX
RECORD

Ph. 946-4282

SATE
Recor

Epilogue

SWEET SOUL MUSIC

opposite: I further endeared myself to Berry by sending out photos of the Soulsville USA sign designed to remind people (subtle, eh?) of the sign on the Motown studios.

Al Abrams
PUBLIC RELATIONS

DO YOU LOVE ME?

The Contours were always among my favorite people, both as individuals and as a group. Recently, Joe Billingslea, reminded me that back in the day when they would pass me going from Studio A to Berry's office, I would say, "Contours, Do You Love Me?" The Contours would reply, "No, cause' you can't dance."

"It's What's In The Words That Count"

Being Berry's "brother" didn't translate into getting big bucks for my breakthrough efforts to have Motown's music cross over racial lines.

OF COURSE I WAS PLEASED that Berry in his autobiography credited me for my PR work on the Supremes' first Copacabana appearance, as that indeed made and changed American musical history. The warm inscription Berry wrote in my copy of his book (see back cover) acknowledged my role in the early days. Alas, Berry missed the opportunity to tell many of these stories. That's why I am picking up the slack.

At first, paydays at Motown meant being handed whatever cash was available in Berry's pockets when you approached him. As Robert Bateman reminded me when we appeared together at a symposium at the University of Michigan, sometimes it was like getting bus fare from Berry. This is not to say that Berry was not generous if it didn't involve cash. I quickly learned that if I paid Berry a sincere compliment on something in his possession, he would immediately offer it to me as a gift. (And no, it didn't apply to his female companions.)

It began with my complimenting the sound emanating from his living room stereo at 1719 Gladstone. This was the same stereo on which I first heard Berry's music being played the night I showed up at his doorstep, hoping he would hire me instead of my friend. Not long after I was hired, I told Berry how much I liked the sound quality, and within minutes, I was packing the stereo into my car to take home. Then it was his brown corduroy sport jacket that I craved. At that time, Berry and I wore the same size (believe it or not) and could interchange our clothes if we were ever so inclined. From there, it progressed to Berry's ties – and I'm sure he literally and figuratively would have given me the shirt off his back, had I asked.

But the ultimate was when I complimented Berry about his Leicaflex camera and he ordered his assistant Donald Foster to give it to me. Yet, it didn't last forever. Berry finally got wise to my flattery and just took my compliments in stride.

> **QUICKI-NOTE** DATE July 16, 1965
> TO Mr. Berry Gordy, Jr.
>
> Received from Donald Foster, as per request of
> Berry Gordy, Jr., one Leica camera.
>
> SNAP-A-PART 47-332 NATIONAL MADE IN U.S.A.
> FROM Al Abrams

It was because of the often erratic methods of pay - much less the low salary I was receiving from Motown - that I frequently had to moonlight just to make some cash to maintain my expensive lifestyle. My successful PR stunt of dressing up like a snake charmer and getting photographed with DJs to promote "Snake Walk" by the Swinging Tigers (i.e. the Funk Brothers) had not gone unnoticed by other record companies. Even though the record was not a hit, you wouldn't know it from the photos that made the national music trades.

Sonny Bono (yes, THAT Sonny Bono), a young record promoter and producer, contacted me about doing a similar stunt to promote a record. I agreed. Decked out in a cowboy gunfighter's outfit (complete with six-shooter and phony moustache) - and with the six-foot-one red-head former stewardess I was then dating dressed as a dance hall queen, I set out to visit the DJs. Once again, my photographer friend Doug Ashley recorded it all for posterity. This did not sit well with Berry and Esther. And for a very short stint, I wound up working for Del-Fi Records through their distributor. All of Motown's sales and promotion department had worked at various times for Detroit-based record distributors - Barney Ales, Irv Biegel, Gordon Prince and me. I was thrilled to be inducted into the Michigan Legends Rock and Roll Hall of Fame class of 2011 along with Sonny Bono, Diana Ross, Suzy Quatro and The Romantics (see page 287 in the Addendum.)

However, I was becoming even more disillusioned as a promotion man. It may have been exciting for some of the other promotion men to go on double-dates (and I am using that term loosely) with big time touring recording stars like Tony Orlando, but I felt cheapened. Not that I was a picture of virtuous morality. When Berry and I attended our first national record business convention at the Hotel Traymore in

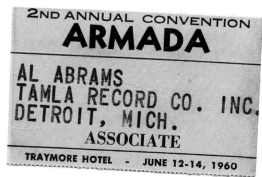

Jobete Music Company, Inc.

2648 WEST GRAND BOULEVARD
DETROIT 8. MICHIGAN
─
TRinity 1-3340

July 19, 1960

FOR IMMEDIATE RELEASE

Att: Ira Howard
Editorial: Music Dept.
Cashbox Magazine
1721 Broadway Ave.
New York, New York

"TAMLA NAMES ABRAMS PR HEAD"

DETROIT-Cleffer Berry Gordy Jr. upped Al Abrams, former national
promotion director for Gordy's Pubbery Jobete Music Co; To
Director of advertising and public relations for his twin diskerys
TAMLA and MOTOWN RECORDS. In addition to his new duties Abrams
will continue to supervise all promotion for both labels. Abrams
currently is seeking four experienced promo men to rep the diskery
on the road. He can be reach daily at TR 13340.

Label is currently hot with "WAY OVER THERE" by the MIRACLES, who
broke into the top 100 with "BAD GIRL" about this time last year;
and is currently preparing new singles for immediate release by
BARRETT (MONEY THAT'S WHAT I WANT) STRONG and thrush MABLE JOHN,
sister of hot R & B artist LITTLE WILLIE JOHN who was recently
inked by Gordy. Albums are also in preperation by the MIRACLES and
BARRETT STRONG.

In addition to managing the above Gordy manages MARV JOHNSON,
currently riding high with 2 sides in the HOT 100.

221

Atlantic City, Berry wanted us to be seen in the best possible light.

That was fine, until Berry heard that there was a prostitute plying her trade on the 7th floor of the hotel. Berry and I bade good night to the group of record company executives in the lobby. We said we were tired and needed to get some sleep and ostensibly took the elevator to our rooms. But Berry hit the button for the 9th floor. When we got off the elevator, we headed for the fire escape. Berry's logic was that if no one in the lobby saw us take the elevator to the 7th floor, they wouldn't suspect where we were heading. As Berry exited the fire escape - ass backwards - on the 7th floor, he was greeted with guffaws of laughter. Standing in the long line awaiting entry into the hooker's room were the very same record executives we had just left in the lobby.

When I ultimately told Berry I wanted to make the switch from record promotion to public relations fulltime, Esther blocked me. She said I did not have the formal education or the writing skills that were required. Incensed, I went out and got a job writing a local weekly television show, *House Detective*, on the former WWJ-TV (now WDIV-TV) - a show that is still on the air almost half-a-century later. The host of the show was an alcoholic who would turn up at the studio for the taping and disappear for the rest of the week. One week he went to the restroom before the taping and urinated all over his trousers. So he taped the show sitting at a desk with only his suit coat and shirt visible. A good thing too - he wasn't wearing his wet and stained trousers. I sat across from him giving him cues off my script while his nubile young wife (who had a thing for young boys) and was seated on the chair next to me, stroked my legs and thighs.

Eager to get away from this volatile situation, I began editing *P.S. Ink,* a house organ for a printing company. When my work won a national award, I took it to Berry and Esther. As you can see from this book, they were suitably impressed. Along the way, so were other major entertainment entities. At one point, Howard Pearl, the PR guru who handled United Artists movies, offered me a job to work on UA's James Bond films beginning with *Thunderball*. Needless to say, the pay was substantially more than I was making at Motown. I thought about the job and decided to approach Berry to see if he would meet the offer. Berry refused and wished me well. I gave it more thought and decided to stay at Motown.

Two weeks later, Berry gave me a raise. However, my salary was still far below what my peers in the industry were receiving, and ultimately that was my rationale for taking on Stax/Volt as a client after leaving Motown in 1966 and declining the offer of a Motown paycheck for life. Simply put, Stax/Volt paid more.

---

opposite: Al Bell and Jim Stewart before Stax/Volt crumbled.   **223**

SOMETIMES MY PR CAMPAIGNS benefited more than my clients. When I approached Al Bell a few months after leaving Motown about hiring me to do PR for Stax/Volt, I told him I would be asking US Senator Howard H. Baker, Jr. of Tennessee to write the liner notes for the Otis Redding/Carla Thomas now-classic *King And Queen* album. Al called me from an airport and probably thought, "Yeah, right, but I'll give this guy a try."

At that time, Baker was known primarily as the son-in-law of another US Senator, Everett M. Dirksen of Illinois, a great orator whose dulcet tones had led him to record "Gallant Men," which made it all the way to Number 29 on Billboard and earned him a Grammy. I knew this could give Baker a chance to go out on his own -- applying music business logic to politics.

This letter (opposite) from the senator's staffer who helped make it possible, shows how those liner notes boosted the recognition of Baker from being just one of 100 senators to a recognizable name and face. By 1974, everyone in the US knew his name and face, when, as Vice-Chairman of the Senate Watergate Committee investigating President Richard M. Nixon, he repeatedly asked "What did the president know and when did he know it?"

Getting a US senator to write Stax/Volt liner notes certainly helped propel the company into mainstream newspapers across the country. Mission accomplished!

For my next Stax album liner notes assignment (another classic, the *Stay in School* LP), I already had the Vice President of the United States, the great Hubert H. Humphrey, in my line of sight.

above-top: Carla Thomas, Otis Redding and Booker T Jones (at the piano), 1967
above: Otis Redding, Carla Thomas, Al Bell, Jim Stewart and a slew of Stax folks present a plaque to the Senator.
He was so inspired that he went on to ask "What did the president know and when did he know it?" at the Watergate Hearings and became a true American folk hero.
opposite: a letter from Senator Baker's staffer Edgar H Miller, Jr., 1967

United States Senate

COMMITTEE ON PUBLIC WORKS

September 26, 1967

Mr. Al Abrams
Al Abrams Associates
19490 Greenfield
Detroit, Michigan   48235

Dear Al:

If we could get a couple more pictures like the Otis-Carla-Baker all purpose presentation shot making the rounds, I believe we could get Baker elected President.

My count, too, makes this the third award that the picture has been used for. Probably there are more that we don't know about as editors scratch around for art to illustrate some new story about one or all of the trio.

Senator Baker is finally beginning to realize the impact having his picture on the record jacket is making. The other morning, about 4 a.m., he was waiting for his baggage at Dulles Airport. A porter came up to him and asked, "Aren't you a senator?" Baker admitted he was. "I thought so. I think I've seen you on television but aren't you the one who has his picture on the Otis Redding-Carla Thomas record?" Several senators still comment to him about the record from time to time.

Best regards,

Edgar H. Miller, Jr.
Press Assistant to
SENATOR HOWARD H. BAKER, JR.

EHMJr:dl

225

Inside the late and lamented Stax studio on East McLemore Street. Can you spot Isaac Hayes?

One Press Agent's Topsy-Turvy World: Nothing Fails Like Success

Al Abrams

. . . and client.

Al Abrams? Never heard of him, did you?

He's the man who gets on at the bottom, rides to the top, then starts all over again — at the bottom.

His press release, dated Aug. 21, 1967, read: "Stax-Volt recording artist Otis Redding has been selected as the World's No. 1 male vocalist by the readers of Melody Maker magazine, a leading British 'pop' music publication . . . Adding significance to the selection is the fact that Elvis Presley has for years dominated the poll, withstanding even the formidable onslaught of the individual members of the Beatles. It remained for a fellow American, and an exponent of a latter-day 'Memphis Sound' to topple Presley from this throne . . ."

Substitute 1965 for 1967 and change a few names, such as The Supremes instead of Otis Redding — the "Motown Sound" for the "Memphis Sound." This is the rhetoric of Al Abrams, who sang the praises of The Supremes until they were too big to need it — and was quietly eased out of his job as chief publicity man for Motown. This is the baroque but amazingly effective approach which brought Stax-Volt Recording to Al Abrams door until the late Otis Redding and the "Memphis Sound" became a part of the pop lexicon.

Abrams has the knack for making the unlikely possible. There was no way in the world to sell the disc jockeys around the country on something called the "Memphis Sound" — but he did it! It is the irony of his career that the more successful he is in promoting talent the faster he works himself out of a job. When the names get big, they want nationally known "praisers."

In 1959, Al Abrams became Berry Gordy's first employe in an enterprise called Rayber Music Co. (Ray for Gordy's first wife, the ber for Berry) located in Gordy's living room in a house on Gladstone off Twelfth St. The Rayber Music Co., for a consideration — like, say, $100 — would record your song and give you a few extra copies. It was strictly a small-time operation and Abrams left for other quarters. In 1964 he signed on at Motown — still a small, struggling firm — with singer Mary Wells as his assignment. When Miss Wells left the Motown stable, Abrams looked around, noticed a group called The Supremes and asked if he could assist with the promotion of their first album, "Where Did Our Love Go?"

"It was just luck," says Abrams now, "that that one turned into their first top seller." Luck or no, Abrams and the Supremes made all the record hops, and the girls even appeared free of charge on local TV shows "for the exposure."

By November, the record was a bestseller. Abrams flooded the media with free copies of the albums, publicity shots of the girls, and effusive thank-you notes for the barest public mention. By March, 1966, the girls had made the pages of that barometer of success, Time Magazine, with a Timesque caption: "Their Copa runneth over."

In December, 1966, Abrams had to leave Motown; he had lost most of his prerogatives to a newcomer. In February, 1967, he joined Stax-Volt, a company nobody knew about, and rode with Otis Redding to the top. Stax-Volt also went to the top, though, and instead of rewarding Al Abrams, dropped him in favor of bigger fish. That was in May, 1968.

Now Al has accepted an old friend as his top client and her name is Florence Ballard. Al Abrams, first and last, has proved to have an uncanny instinct for a winner. There's no reason to think he's lost it. But let's hope that next time he wins at least part of one of those big jackpots.

PUCCI

opposite: extract from the Detroit Free Press written by Barbara Holliday.

opposite: Flo Ballard poses for a Soul magazine layout during her solo career. The man with her is her husband and manager, Thomas Chapman. The building in the background is Detroit's St. Regis Hotel, once owned by a consortium

BUD BILLIKEN DAY, Chicago. Sponsored by the *Chicago Defender* (one of the few African-American daily newspapers.)
above-left: Flo Ballard with comedian Godfrey Cambridge
above-right: Flo and Greg Morris of TV's *Mission Impossible* at the Billiken Day Parade. This was one of the biggest PR events of Flo's solo career.

AL ABRAMS ASSOCIATES

publicity — public relations

19490 greenfield, detroit, michigan 48235

phone (313) 342-8447

Please direct all telephone
inquiries Monday and Tuesday
November 18 and 19 only to
(313) KE 7-0471.

Client: Patmon, Young and Kirk

November 15, 1968

FOR IMMEDIATE RELEASE

HOLLAND-DOZIER-HOLLAND ANSWERS MOTOWN
IN 22-MILLION-DOLLAR LAWSUIT

Holland-Dozier-Holland, the Detroit songwriting and

producing team recently tagged as the world's most successful

songwriters by a national music publication, filed a precedent

setting 22-million-dollar lawsuit in Wayne County Circuit Court

on Thursday, November 14th, against the Motown Record Corporation;

Jobete Music Company, Inc.; Motown President Berry Gordy, Jr.;

Motown attorneys Ralph Seltzer and Harold Noveck, and accountant

Sidney Noveck.

The suit, for the highest amount ever requested in a lawsuit

of this type, claims that Motown's acts of conspiracy, fraud,

deceit, overreaching, and breach of fiduciary relationships have

damaged the plaintiffs in the amount of 22 million dollars.

(more)

The lawsuit goes on to allege that Berry Gordy, Jr. built

his empire through exploitation of the famed songwriting and

producing team, whom the Detroit Free Press once singled out

as one of the major reasons for the success of the Supremes and

the Motown Record Corporation.

Edward Holland, his brother Brian, and Lamont Dozier,

together have written and produced the seven million selling

records for the Supremes, beginning with "Where Did Our Love Go,"

which launched the phenomenal career of the Detroit vocal trio.

Based on a tabulation of BMI awards, Holland-Dozier-Holland have

been responsible for 60% of the BMI awards received by Jobete.

Holland-Dozier-Holland has produced 25 of the 29 Motown acts,

and were the exclusive producers of the Supremes and the Four Tops.

The 31-page complaint was filed by lead counsel Frederick A.

Patmon, of the Detroit firm of Patmon, Young and Kirk Professional

Corporation, in association with Edward Bell, and the firm of

Miller, Canfield, Paddock and Stone. New York counsel for the

(more)

suit is the firm of Pryor, Braun, Cashman and Sherman.

Several months ago, Motown filed a 4-million-dollar lawsuit against Holland-Dozier-Holland, which the songwriting-producing team claims was contrived as a means to justify the total cessation of royalty payments to the plaintiffs for the purpose of applying economic pressure on them.

A main aspect of the injunction asks the court to appoint a temporary receiver to carry on and conduct the business of Motown and Jobete, and to take charge of all assets, including copyrights, and directs Motown and Jobete to make a full and complete accounting of all income and earnings. The court was asked to issue an order directing reversion from Jobete to the plaintiffs of all copyrights held by Jobete, and to ask Jobete to pay over to the court all royalties and other earnings received by Jobete including royalties from public performance rights received from BMI.

Other aspects of the suit claimed violation of federal and Michigan anti-trust and restraint of trade statutes.

AL ABRAMS ASSOCIATES

publicity – public relations
19490 greenfield, detroit, michigan 48235
phone (313) 342-8447
May 19, 1969
Client: Invictus Records

FOR IMMEDIATE RELEASE

INVICTUS/HOLLAND-DOZIER-HOLLAND–CAPITOL TIE-IN–
PRECEDENT SETTING VICTORY FOR CREATIVE TALENT

Eddie Holland has announced the details of a monumental production and distribution arrangement between Detroit based Invictus Records and Capitol Records. Invictus was represented in negotiations with Capitol by Frederick A. Patmon of Patmon, Young and Kirk Professional Corporation, a Black Detroit law firm. Holland, together with Lamont Dozier and Brian Holland, make up the phenomenal Holland-Dozier-Holland songwriting and producing team, which for the past ten years has become synonymous with the success of the Motown Sound in contemporary music.

The terms of the precedent setting deal allow Capitol to handle pressing, distribution and marketing for Invictus in the United States, Canada and Mexico on all records and tape product of the label, with Invictus retaining all administrative functions, record club and mail order distribution and foreign rights. Eddie Holland sees this is an important breakthrough for creative talent and expression. Speaking of the creative freedom afforded to him by the arrangement, Holland says: "I am in the position to create an artist, initiate a label, create songwriters and enhance the artists talents and abilities. Also, I am able to follow through administratively and creatively from one end of the company to the other. I can properly oversee the creative people and follow through with their production. All in all, I have a complete creative feeling, and it is the first time in my career that I have been able to feel this way."

Regarding his plans for working with new talent–artists, writers and producers–Holland says "many creative people are frustrated through lack of communication with the heads of the company. Most creative people have their own feelings and their own way of wanting to do and talk about things and they need someone to explain these things to. The people at the top are not patient enough with creative people to understand their feelings. In working with creative people, I can help them develop this communication and help them interpret what they are trying to say. I am interested in artists, writers and producers who are interested in doing their own thing–the thing they want to create–expressing their ideas the way they want to, a little different than they have before." Eddie Holland stresses that the victory for creative talent won by the Invictus–Capitol arrangement can be shared by all creative people.

Holland-Dozier-Holland have been acclaimed as the world's most successful songwriting and producing team by national music publications. Their compositions for the Supremes include the vocal trio's seven consecutive million-selling records beginning with "Where Did Our Love Go," as well as the string of hit records which successfully launched The Four Tops.

Commenting on the Invictus–Capitol deal, Stanley Gortikov, President of Capitol Records, said his personal goal with Invictus "is to make it as important a label as there is in the music industry. We will concentrate Capitol's marketing and distribution energies and knowhow to reach this objective. The new relationship with Invictus combines what we think to be the best independent creative production skills with marketing and distribution capabilities second to none."

When I staged the World's First Mod Wedding in Detroit (sorry London, but I beat you to it), I had the bride -- a go-go dancer -- outfitted in a specially made thigh-high mini-wedding dress (sorry Mary Quant, but I beat you too.) Pop-Artist Andy Warhol, who painted the bride's paper wedding gown, gave the bride away while Lou Reed, Nico and the Velvet Underground performed -- that's poet Gerard Malanga doing his whip dance on the right. Scott Regen, the popular Detroit DJ who was also the emcee of the Motown Mondays at the Roostertail, was best man. It looks as if he's cautioning the bride to be careful with the sword she's wielding.

This was actually an addendum to a Dick Clark (of American Bandstand fame) show at the Michigan State Fairgrounds which featured folks like Gary Lewis and the Playboys and Sam the Sham and the Pharaohs. It was a normal rock and roll show sponsored by a supermarket chain until I was asked to do the PR. When Dick Clark saw this "Happening", he hid behind a curtain until it was over. This all happened on November 20, 1966.

Pop Tunes

By
RONNIE OBERMAN
Star Staff Writer

THE EVENING STAR, Washington, D. C., Saturday, November 12, 1966

Each time the three male members of the Elgins sing their hit, "Heaven Must Have Sent You," they probably think of Sandra Edwards.

Sandra is the female voice of the group, and if it wasn't for her, the Elgins might not have a hit record.

Sandra, who phoned earlier this week from Detroit, explained that up until a couple years ago, she was a solo singer for Motown Records and the Elgins, then known as the Downbeats, also were on their own. At that time, neither she nor the group had much recording success.

She said she ran into them one night in a nightclub in Pontiac, Mich., and was asked if she knew how to sing rock-and-roll. "They said they needed a girl because the one they were using in the show was leaving," she said. "Two or three days later, we went back to the club to rehearse."

Although Sandra had not had much experience singing rock-and-roll, she said she wound up knowing almost all the songs the group rehearsed and was asked to stay.

"Heaven Must Have Sent You" is not the quartet's first hit. Their previous effort, "Put Yourself in My Place," coupled with "Darling Baby," turned out to be a two-sided hit. "Put Yourself in My Place" was big on the East coast, while the latter side did well in the West. It hit the top spot on the charts in Los Angeles.

Sandra said that working with three fellows does not present any unusual problems, except when the fellows start talking about subjects she doesn't understand, particularly baseball. Her colleagues are Johnny Dawson, 30; Norman McLean, 27, and Duke Miller, 29.

Sandra said the three got together several years ago at the same barber school. They never sang in a barbershop quartet, although they were barbers for a while, she added.

Does recording for the V.I.P. label, one of the Motown Corporation's lesser known subsidiaries, hinder the Elgins' chances at success? "Not at all," she exclaimed. "I feel that it's an advantage just being with Motown." She added that she would rather prove the group's worth on V.I.P. than on one of the bigger, more established Motown labels such as Tamla or Gordy.

On the group's name, Sandra said it was thought up by Johnny Dawson. She said he was driving with one of her girl friends one day when he looked at his watch and thought of "Elgin"—which, incidentally, was not the brand he was wearing.

Landscape View with "Hooiberg" in rear
Aruba, Neth. Antilles.

6-30-65

Dear Al,
    I retract my
comment in *Fortune*
about the girls being
Stop! seems to be unknown to adults
Number One even in
Aruba. And, by now,
your PR job has made
them as W. K. as
Lyndon J.   Best, Stanley Brown

A Abrams
Motown Records
West Grand Blvd.
Detroit, Michigan
U.S.A.

Air Mail

Post Card

90453-B

Exhibit 1

LOOKING BACK, IT IS CLEAR that some of the Motown acts who were given relatively little promotion by the company have endured as some of the best loved. The Elgins "Heaven Must Have Sent You" is now hailed as an all-time classic, especially by The Brits. When originally released, it did not create much of a stir. In fact, this article (opposite), as best as I can recall, was the only press The Elgins got in the States! And I remember that I had to beg Ronnie Oberman at the *Washington Evening Star* to even interview the group. But once I got him to really listen to their incredible sound, he quickly became a fan and it shows in his story. The reputation of the Elgins has outlasted that of the venerable newspaper which printed its final issue in 1981. I still have a copy of that issue in a box in my closet.

Exhibit 2

EXHIBIT TWO IS A POSTCARD sent from Aruba by Stanley H. Brown, an editor of *Fortune* magazine. I had read in one of the dailies that Brown was in Detroit to do a story on the city's automobile industries. I immediately reached out to Brown and convinced him to make a short jaunt down from the world headquarters of General Motors to the world headquarters of Soul. To his credit, he came to Motown and took my tour of Hitsville. The result was one short paragraph in his article in which he stated that the Supremes (and thus Motown) were unknown by most adults. But as the hits kept racking up, Brown's exposure to the Motown Sound increased. By the time he arrived in Aruba for vacation later that year, he penned this retraction of his statement in *Fortune*. Of all the compliments I ever received, Brown's statement that "By now your P.R. job has made them as w(ell) k(nown) as (then U.S. President) Lyndon J(ohnson)" will always be my favorite.

Modest Mary Sinks the Beatles

By A. L. McCLAIN

The Beatles and L o u i s (Satchmo) Armstrong were getting the musical fanfare last week, but when buyers stepped up to the record counters around the country they were asking for Mary Wells.

By selling the most records for her "My Guy," a single, the shy Detroit girl is entitled to reign No. 1 all this week. It's a nice birthday present. Mary was 21 yesterday.

She is the first female vocalist to top the Beatles in record sales since Beatlemania hit A m e r i c a. Mary also skipped merrily past a venerable institution, S a t c h m o, whose "Hello, Dolly!" had been in the top spot the previous week.

CHEERS FROM TOP

The new acclaim hasn't turned Mary's head. She's more impressed by a telegram sent by the Beatles to her record company, Motown, on their arrival in this country.

The Beatles' wire s a i d simply, "We like M a r y Wells."

The singer has several Mary Wells fan clubs in England and hopes to meet some of the members on her European tour in the fall. In July she is going to sing at West Coast nightclubs and colleges.

Although being first in the nation in record sales is something new for Mary, making the top 10 is an old refrain. Her recording of "Two Lovers" rose to No. 3, "You Beat Me to the Punch" was No. 7, and "The One Who R e a l l y Loves You" placed 10th.

Another r e c o r d i n g, "What's Easy for Two is So Hard for One," also placed among the top 10.

EXECUTIVE TOUCH

"My Guy" was written specially for M a r y by Smoky R o b i n s o n of the Miracles, a singing group, who also is a Motown vice-president.

"I liked the song right away," Mary says, "but I can't honestly say I knew it would be a big hit."

A former s t u d e n t at Northwestern High School, Mary has been singing professionally since she was 16. Her mother, Mrs. Jeneva Wells, lives on Chicago Boulevard. Her father is dead.

Her sixth album soon will be released. Its title isn't s u r p r i s i n g—"My Guy."

Mary Wells Leads the Record Parade

Exhibit 3

THE *DETROIT NEWS* INTERVIEW OF MARY WELLS was a breakthrough moment in making possible Motown's crossover to mainstream America. Why? Because it marked the first time a Motown artist was receiving the kind of attention in one of our two hometown daily newspapers that usually was reserved for sports heroes and movie stars, almost all of whom were white. Yes, it took a spectacular feat to accomplish this -- Motown's Modest Mary dethroning the Beatles from the top of the record charts, but we were on our way. Well, almost. Unfortunately, we didn't count on the newspaper strike which began two months later on July 22, 1964 and kept the presses of Detroit's two dailies silent for 134 days. Of course, those just happened to be the very days when the Supremes began racking up their string of Number One hits and becoming the world's hottest female recording artists -- a story that the Detroit dailies couldn't report until January 1965.

To Al Abrams
my first publicist
who did so much to
me in the very early
days

Happy Reading

Ben Vereen

AL ABRAMS ASSOCIATES

publicity — public relations
19490 greenfield, detroit, michigan 48235
phone (313) 342-8447

Client: Ted White Management Co.
March 10, 1969

FOR IMMEDIATE RELEASE

ONLY MACK RICE
MAKES IT HAPPEN

Detroit songwriter and vocalist Mack Rice did more to make Detroit fastbacks popular than anything before the chase sequence in "Bullitt" hit the movie screen.

Mack's pop classic, "Mustang Sally," has sold over 4 million copies internationally in over 35 recorded versions since he first penned the tune in 1965. In the first two months of 1969 alone, 5 new recordings of the song have been released. Wilson Pickett, of course, had the biggest selling version in 1966. Not many people know that Aretha Franklin and her husband and manager, Ted White, helped Mack write the song.

Now success is repeating itself for the team of Ted White and Mack Rice. Ted is Mack's personal manager, and is responsible for the success of "Coal Man," Mack's first release for the Atco label.

Mack Rice first found fame in 1958 as a member of the original Falcons, the Detroit vocal group whose recording of "You're So Fine" established R&B in the position it enjoys today. Among the other members of the original Falcons were Wilson Pickett and Eddie Floyd, both of whom have gone on to successful careers as individual vocalists. Mack and Eddie Floyd were reunited briefly during Mack's tenure as a Stax/Volt recording artist.

Mack Rice sees his potential in being both a writer and a performer. As a songwriter, Mack has written tunes that have been recorded by Sam and Dave, Ike and Tina Turner and Margie Hendrix, as well as by a sensational new Detroit group, The Lovebugs.

Mack Rice has always been ahead of his time. In a day when the multimillion dollar corporations are realizing the importance of pop music and pop recording artists to further the image and appeal of their products, it is appalling to think that Mack Rice has never even received a thank you note from the Ford Motor Company—although his "Mustang Sally" helped make the name of that automobile a household word in the black community.

With "Coal Man," Mack Rice again shows the rest of today's pop vocalists that they have a long way to go to catch up with him.

Mack Rice is again riding out in front—and this time he is on a clear track.

JAMES BROWN BROADCASTING
AUGUSTA, GEORGIA
KNOXVILLE, TENNESSEE
BALTIMORE, MARYLAND

CINCINNATI OFFICE
1540 BREWSTER AVE.
CINCINNATI, OHIO

Mr. Al Abrahms
19490 Greenfield
Detroit, Michigan 48235   Dec. 2, 1970

This letter serves as authroization for AL ABRAHMS to

represent JAMES BROWN and JAMES BROWN PRODUCTIONS as

press representative with ROLLING STONE and other

publications to be discussed at a later date.

Mr. Abrahms will report directly to James Brown Pro-

ductions in Cincinnati and his work will be co-ordi-

nated directly with Alan M. Leeds.

ALAN M. LEEDS
JAMES BROWN PRODUCTIONS

MOTOWN, INC. 18 EAST 48th STREET, NEW YORK, N. Y. 10017 · (212) 759-6677

MICHAEL ROSHKIND
VICE PRESIDENT

October 12, 1971

Mr. Al Abrams
19490 Greenfield
Detroit, Michigan   48235

Dear Al:

Just a note to let you know that effective
November 1, 1971 I will move to Los Angeles and
my office address will be:

Motown Record Corporation
6464 Sunset Boulevard
Los Angeles, California   90028

Telephone: (213) 461-3011.

Sincerely,

MR/j

246

Official State of Michigan Historical Marker Dedication

Honoring

MOTOWN

December 1, 1987
11:00 AM

Motown Historical Museum
2648 W. Grand Blvd.
Detroit, MI 48208

The Wind

REPORTER ALAN ABRAMS stands in front of the Detroit museum honoring Motown Records, where he once worked as a publicist

Star photo/Randy Moore

Motown memories a No. 1 hit

EDITOR'S NOTE: *Windsor Star* staff reporter Alan Abrams was the first employee of Detroit's Motown Records. Here he shares a few of his Motown memories after attending Tuesday's dedication of Motown's first recording studio as a Michigan historic site.

By Alan Abrams
Star Staff Reporter

Remember where you were the first time you heard the plaintive voice of Diana Ross cooing "Baby, baby, where did our love go?"

Can you remember when Marvin Gaye's I Heard it Through the Grapevine meant more to you than a cue for a raisin television commercial, or a song from The Big Chill soundtrack?

Did you ever stand in line for hours at the Fox Theatre in downtown Detroit just to get a good seat for a Motortown Revue?

Then you better be sitting down

while you're reading this. Because the Motown music you grew up with is now the theme for a museum.

But Detroit's Motown Museum, at the original Hitsville, USA recording studios and offices, is not your typical everyday stuffy museum. Take my word for it, there are no mummies at Motown.

Tuesday morning, Michigan Governor James Blanchard, Detroit Mayor Coleman Young, former Michigan governor John Swainson, Motown vice-president Esther Gordy Edwards, singer Marv Johnson, and Bill "Smokey" Robinson, the velvet-voiced former lead singer of the Miracles, unveiled a historical marker in front of the Hitsville, USA recording studio in Detroit.

Hitsville USA is my alma mater. I came there as a freshman in 1959 as the first employee of what was to become Motown Records, and for the next seven years, the converted old house at 2648 West Grand Blvd. was

my second home.

THE OLD MOTOWN recording studio, where it all began, is now a part of history, an official Michigan Historic Site. It even has a historical plaque on the front lawn, just like at those places you always drive by that mark the scenes of famous battles or where the guy who invented the beer can was born.

Hitsville, USA a historic site? That can't be. That's my old office. Look, right up there in the attic. That's where I used to sit and churn out press releases in praise of Diana Ross and the Supremes, Little Stevie Wonder, The Temptations, The Four Tops, Marvin Gaye, and all the other Motown stars that made life memorable for anyone growing up in Windsor and Detroit in the 1960s.

In those days, we were busy making music, not history. We wanted to be No. One with a bullet on next week's record charts, not a chapter in a text book on 20th century North

American popular culture.

How can my office be a landmark? See that window in the attic, the broken one in the middle? When I left Motown 21 years ago this month it was broken, and it's still broken today. I never could get anyone to fix it.

And look at the recording studio. When it wasn't being used to create the Motown Sound, it was home to a ping-pong table where Smokey Robinson and Motown's founder Berry Gordy Jr., used to spend hours playing, until Berry could finally win.

Now the studio has been recreated to look like it did in those days. The ping-pong table is long gone, but the music stands are there, holding the original sheet music, some of it with scribbled pencil notes and bars of music rewritten as the music was changed during recording sessions. The scene looks for all the world as if everyone had just stepped out into the alley to take five.

See MOTOWN, A4

Motown memories——

Continued from A1

Upstairs, where Gordy lived, and where once was a kitchen in which a big steaming pot of home-cooked chili was always simmering on the stove, is the Motown museum, a museum unlike any other you've ever seen. The music that was made here is celebrated through original photographs, newspaper clippings, songsheets and other mementos.

The Hitsville, USA studio housed the offices of those, like Esther Edwards, Berry Gordy's sister, who stayed behind after most of the company and its talent packed up and moved to Los Angeles in 1972. But Esther had a dream of turning the building into a museum to immortalize the Motown legend. And in 1980, her hard work paid off when she established the Motown Museum, a non-profit organization.

It's great, but still kind of a strange feeling, to see a full-page story from the 1965 Los Angeles Herald-American up on a wall recounting a reporter's visit to Hitsville, including "the attic where publicist Al Abrams shares space with the art department."

Suddenly I feel very old. But then I look at Smokey Robinson standing there unveiling the historical marker and remember that we share the same birthday. And he doesn't look a day over 20.

The Motown Museum is about a five-minute drive down the Lodge Expressway from the tunnel. If, like most Windsorites, Motown is in your blood, it ought to be a must for a visit. Motown is as much a part of our Border Cities heritage as the auto exhibits at the Henry Ford Museum and Greenfield Village. And it's a great place to take those out-of-town visitors during the Christmas holidays.

Impress your friends by telling them how the first Motown recording artist was actually a Windsorite, Mike Powers, and how the Supremes got their start by riding the tunnel bus to Windsor and winning first prize in the talent contest at the Emancipation Day celebration in Jackson Park.

Then mention Robin Seymour's Swingin' Time TV show, and the legendary days of CKLW radio, the Big 8. And the Elmwood Casino and the Bill Kennedy Show. Windsor always played an important part in making Motown sing.

Call the Motown Museum at (313) 875-2264 for an appointment. And tell them that the young guy who used to work in the attic sent you. And maybe you can get them to fix that window.

MOTOWN MUSEUM HISTORICAL FOUNDATION

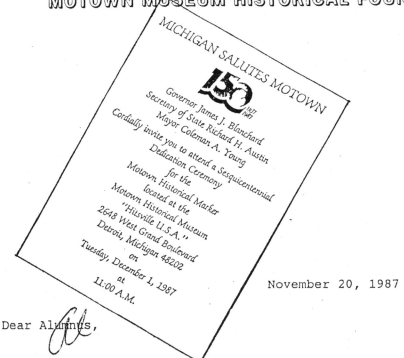

MICHIGAN SALUTES MOTOWN

150
1837
1987

Governor James J. Blanchard
Secretary of State Richard H. Austin
Mayor Coleman A. Young

Cordially invite you to attend a Sesquicentennial
Dedication Ceremony
for the
Motown Historical Marker
located at the
Motown Historical Museum
"Hitsville U.S.A."
2648 West Grand Boulevard
Detroit, Michigan 48202
on
Tuesday, December 1, 1987
at
11:00 A.M.

November 20, 1987

Dear Alumnus,

     Because you are a member of the Motown Family,
we want you to know what's happening at Hitsville USA,
"Where It All Began", in Detroit.

     The copied invitation hereon is self explanatory.
As you can see, Tuesday, December 1, 1987 is Special!
On that day, Hitsville U.S.A. will be designated a
Michigan Historic Site.

     A small reception will be held at 2654 W. Grand Blvd.
(next door-east) immediately following the ceremony. And
at 1:00 p.m. Tours of the Museum will be conducted.

     We want you to know that the Motown Museum Historical
Foundation is a Michigan tax exempt 501(c)3 non-profit
organization. We welcome your support. Any opportunity
that you may have to designate us as beneficiary of support
will be highly appreciated.

     Last, but not least, August 26-28, 1988, are the dates
scheduled for the MOTOWN FAMILY HOMECOMING REUNION in
Detroit. Mark your calendar now! Plans and details will
follow.

                and

"...no where will you find more unity than at Hitsville USA"

Sincerely yours,

Esther Edwards.

Save this letter
PLEASE PRESENT FOR ADMITTANCE
RECEPTION & TOUR

2648 West Grand Boulevard • Detroit, Michigan 48208 • (313) 875-2264 • (313) 867-0991

THE MOTOWN MUSEUM *Hitsville U.S.A.* DETROIT

MOTOWN MUSEUM HISTORICAL FOUNDATION

Feb. 5, 1988

Mr. Alan Abrams
Reporter
THE WINDSOR STAR
167 Ferry Street
Windsor, Ontario N9A4M5

Dear Mr. Abrams:

This letter is extremely belated, but the "Thank You" is very sincere.

I am truly grateful to you for helping to make Tuesday, December 1, 1987, a most memorable day in our history. The value of your coverage and participation in the Motown Historical Marker Dedication Ceremony at Hitsville U.S.A. cannot be measured. Thanks a million!

It goes without saying that your knowledge of Motown's legacy and your endorsement of Hitsville U.S.A., the birth place of the "Motown Sound" as an historic site will greatly enhance the development prospects of the Museum Project. We sent out many copies of the Windsor Star newspaper article, and got great response. Many former staffers were delighted to see you, a fellow Motown alumnus, and to know that you were doing well. Many thanks for the great surprise.

We hope you will help us make the Motown Historical Museum a major tourists attraction that will entertain, educate, motivate, unite and inspire visitors.

We look forward to an ongoing relationship with you, Al, and we want your continued support.

Thanks again, and best personal regards.

Sincerely,

Esther G. Edwards
President

Please keep in touch Al.

EGE/dh

251

February 17, 2011

Dear Mr. Al Abrams:

On behalf of Mrs. Esther Gordy Edwards and the Motown Museum, I would like to personally congratulate you upon reaching the coveted milestone of seventy years young.

Your varied and significant contributions to the development of Motown Record Corporation were remarkable and are genuinely appreciated. As an employee of Motown Records for many years, your trailblazing work truly helped to shape this world-renowned legacy.

We salute you and the indelible mark you have made on American music and how it is and will be graciously recognized as essential American popular culture and history throughout generations to come.

We wish you a wonderful 70th birthday celebration and hope you have many more birthdays! We thank you for your hard work and myriad contributions to a great music legacy.

Once again, congratulations!

Sincerely,

Mr. K. Audley Smith
CEO, Motown Museum

Happy Birthday from your Motown Museum Family!

252

CITY OF DETROIT
MAYOR'S OFFICE

COLEMAN A. YOUNG MUNICIPAL CENTER
2 WOODWARD AVE., SUITE 1126
DETROIT, MICHIGAN 48226
PHONE: 313•224•3400
FAX: 313•224•4128
WWW.DETROITMI.GOV

February 19, 2011

Mr. Al Abrams
828 Beech Avenue
Findlay, OH 45840

Dear Mr. Abrams:

It gives me great pleasure to extend congratulations as you celebrate your 70th birthday. This celebration is a milestone to be cherished.

I am always proud of the accomplishments of native Detroiters such as you who played such an intricate role in the Public Relations of Hitsville USA decades ago. I certainly look forward to your forthcoming book, Hype & Soul, detailing the long awaited story of your time at Hitsville USA, which is still one of Detroit's treasures!

Again, Mr. Abrams, congratulations on the celebration of your 70th birthday. May your special day be one of joy and an outpouring of love shared with your family and friends.

Warmest Regards,

Dave Bing
Mayor

DAVE BING, MAYOR

253

Testimonial Resolution

Al Abrams

WHEREAS   Al Abrams was born in Detroit on February 19, 1941 to Mildred and Harry Abrams. He attended Central High School and graduated at the age of 15. On May 30, 1959, he became the first employee of what was to become Berry Gordy, Jr.'s Motown Record Corporation. Working originally as National Promotion Director, he later became the company's Director of Public Relations during the glory years of 1964-66; **and**

WHEREAS   In December 1966, Abrams established his own PR firm, Al Abrams Associates. He worked with the legendary Stax-Volt Records of Memphis, where he created both the "King and Queen" album with liner notes by then US Senator Howard H. Baker, Jr., and the "Stay in School" album with liner notes by then US Vice President Hubert H. Humphey. Abrams was honored for his work in the latter campaign by received by receiving the US Department of Labor's highest civilian award, the Award of Merit, in 1969 from then-Labor secretary George P. Shultz; **and**

WHEREAS   Abrams also served as PR Director for Holland-Dozier-Holland's classic Invictus and Hot Wax Records, represented former Supreme Flo Ballard in her solo career with ABC Records, and worked for and with James Brown, Aretha Franklin and many major recording artists and performers; **and**

WHEREAS   Abrams left the music business for book publishing and became editor of the journalism department at Gale Research Company, then the third-largest reference book publisher in North America, and now a part of the global Thomson-Reuters Group. He wrote the first three of his eleven books at Gale; **and**

WHEREAS   He became an award-winning investigative reporter for the Windsor Star, where his work received the Canadian equivalent of the Pulitzer Prize. Since 1994, Abrams has been a free-lance reporter and publicist; **and**

WHEREAS   Abrams has participated in numerous Motown themed musicals, television programs, books and documentary series. Along with Motown founder Berry Gordy, Jr., Abrams received a Spirit of Detroit award at the November 2009 Motown 50 Gala. "Hype & Soul," a book honoring Abrams' legacy at Motown, is to be published in the UK in May 2011 including forewords penned by Mary Wilson of the Supremes and Lamont Dozier of Holland-Dozier-Holland. Abrams will be inducted to the Michigan Rock and Roll Legends Hall of Frame later in 2011; **and**

WHEREAS   He is married to Cecilia Abrams and has one daughter, Alannah Rose Abrams. He continually promotes the City of Detroit and its historical impact upon the music industry. **NOW, THEREFORE BE IT**

RESOLVED   The Detroit City Council congratulates AL Abrams, as he and his family celebrate 70 years of life, love and Motown.

COUNCIL PRESIDENT

COUNCIL PRESIDENT PRO TEM

COUNCIL MEMBER

COUNCIL MEMBER

COUNCIL MEMBER

COUNCIL MEMBER

COUNCIL MEMBER

COUNCIL MEMBER

February 22, 2011

DATE

Acknowledgements

At the risk of making this read like the text of one of those runaway thank you speeches at the Oscars, I recognize that this book has been decades in the making and that along the way there were a lot of people who offered and provided enormous help and encouragement. If your name is here, please know that in your own way you helped make this book possible - and I really do appreciate it. I hope the readers do too!

Of course this book wouldn't even exist had it not been for Berry Gordy Jr. taking that chance and making me a member of the Motown family on May 31, 1959, and Esther Edwards for somehow putting up with me for all those years. I will never forget our legendary Miss Ray - Raynoma Liles Gordy - or Anna, George, Fuller and all the other members of the fantastic Gordy family who adopted a stray white boy into their fold.

For starters, my thanks to Richard J. Brennan, my former colleague and desk mate at the *Windsor* (Ontario) *Star* and now the National Affairs Writer of the *Toronto Star;* Jim Phillips, Bill Hickey, Lisa Monforton, Bob Sullivan, Sandra Precop, and my other editors at the *Windsor Star* who let me cover Motown-related news events and made the *Star* the second-best place I've ever worked; William "Billy" Kingston, still my friend after more than 56 years; Sherie Rae Parker and Jayne Cutler, the REAL stars of my family, always there with greatly appreciated words of support; and the Fabulous Five: Dave and Sue Randle, the incomparable Miss Sharon Davis; Paul Nixon; and Ray Ellis - all of the UK.

I have been blessed by having had the privilege of knowing and working with some of the greatest talents and just simply all-out wonderful people in the music business: Mary Wilson; Diana Ross; Lamont Dozier (and Barbara too); my collaborator and co-star of *Memories of Motown* William "Mickey" Stevenson (and his daughters Ashley and Taylor); Martha Reeves (and Dundee Holt); Sylvester Potts and the Contours including their musical director Glen Raby; *Memories of Motown* Berlin friends and stars Melanie Burke; DeNita Asberry; Bobby Brooks Wilson; the incomparable Miss Ross Thomas (and her lovely mother); Justin Holley; Tee Turner and the Miracles; Dave Finley; The Berlin Funk Brothers; and of course Carmen Franke, moderator of the show.

Also Stevie Wonder; Brenda Holloway; Tom Good; Robert Bateman, Louvain Demps; Katherine Anderson Schaffner of the Marvelettes; Janie Bradford; Taylor Cox and Ardena Johnston of ITMI; Rebecca Jiles; Bernie Yeszin my erstwhile attic-mate; Joe Billingslea; Smokey Robinson; Claudette Robinson; Bobby Rogers; Pete Moore; Marvin Tarplin; Brian and Eddie Holland; Mike Powers; Mike McLean; and yes, even you too, Ralph Seltzer!

Then there are: Harry Weinger of Universal Music; my biggest and most loyal fan Bill Staiger; Motown historian and biographer Peter Benjaminson, whose work evokes pangs of jealousy within my psyche;

Stephanie Campbell; Mort Persky, the former Sunday Editor of the *Detroit Free Press* and creator of their groundbreaking *Detroit* magazine; Arnold S. Hirsch, formerly of the *Detroit News*; Van Gordon Sauter who went from the *Detroit Free Press* and *Chicago Daily News* to become the president of CBS News; Richard Christiansen, a living legend among Chicago newspaper critics; Andrea Fischer Newman of the Board of Regents of the University of Michigan in Ann Arbor; Professor Mark Clague of the Department of Music at the University of Michigan; Dylan Morris who interviewed me for the *Living Music* site of the University of Michigan School of Music; American Music Institute; Angela Dillard and Kevin Gaines of CAAS (The Center for Afroamerican and African Studies) at the University of Michigan; Assistant Professor Nathaniel Zeisler of Bowling Green State University in Bowling Green, Ohio; Dr. Addell Austin Anderson, Director of the University of Michigan Detroit Center; The Society for American Music, University of Pittsburgh; Professor Andrew Flory of Shenandoah University; Assistant Professor Patricia Coleman-Burns of the University of Michigan; Professor Frank Johnson of Temple University and Professor Keith Hatschek of the University of the Pacific.

But wait, there's more: Producer Extraordinaire Bernhard Kurz of *Stars in Concert* and all the talented staff at the Estrel Festival Center in Berlin - still the crown jewel of Germany — especially Miranda Meier and Mihaela Djuranovic, two of the best publicists working anywhere today; Gary "Dr. J." Johnson of the Michigan Legends Rock and Roll Hall of Fame; Audley M. Smith, Jr., CEO of the Motown Historical Museum; Christian Lerch of ORF 1 - Radio Osterreich 1; Marvin Post of Attic Books in London, Ontario, Canada; Karen Jania and the directors and staff of the Bentley Historical Museum at the University of Michigan for graciously allowing me to copy the materials in my Motown archive - I highly recommend a visit there for anyone who really wants to study the history of Motown.

Special thanks to Detroit's energized and revitalized civic leadership, Mayor Dave Bing and the members of the Detroit City Council, especially Councilman Andre' L. Spivey - who shares his birthday with Smokey Robinson, Bobby Rogers and me - for my magnificent Council Resolution.

We won't ever forget three longtime and valued friends from radio days: Chuck Daugherty; Bob Greene - "with three e's if you please"; and Bob Green; nor DeeDee and her co-workers at the GRAMMY Foundation who are living proof that MusiCares; Brian McCollum of the *Detroit Free Press* and his partner-in-crime, videographer Romain Blanquart, creators of the award-winning *Motown at 50* documentaries for the *Free Press;* Nancy Oey of El Beisbol productions, producer of the highly-acclaimed TV One *Unsung* documentary on Florence Ballard; filmmaker and San Francisco Public Defender Jeff Adachi whose *You Don't Know Jack* is a brilliant tribute to the talented Jack Soo; Richard Prince of the Maynard Institute and the *Washington Post*; Chris Stevenson; Nina Gail Sherard-Parker, the founder and executive director of the Black Heritage Library & Multicultural Center in Findlay, Ohio; Doug Ashley, who went from shooting my *Snake Walk* PR stunts to photographing the White House Rose Garden and President Bill Clinton; Laszlo Regos; Peter C. Cavanaugh; Margaret Dwiggins of the *Findlay Courier;* and Michael Punsalan of the *Toledo Free Press*.

There are so many more: John Askew, Bob Work and the wonderful clients they serve at *SunriseArc* in Orlando, Florida by promoting rather than discouraging opportunities for people with disabilities; consummate LA publicist Mike Gormley and John Smyntek, both formerly of the *Detroit Free Press;* Judy Plasky of Palm Desert, CA; David and Coco Dalton; Sandy Gardiner, former VP of British Airways; Bob Davis of Soul Patrol; the multi-talented journalist and performer J. Nadir Omowale; reporter Eric Harabadian and editor and publisher Darian Count of *Detroit Live* magazine; Laura Berman of the *Detroit News;* Ralph Terrana, Marvin Davis, Randy Russi and Tim Stantion, my *Soulful Detroit Forum* cheering section; Dick Rakovan of the Radio Hall of Fame in Chicago; Keith Hughes of Ace Records in the UK; Andy Skurow; Carl and Candy Pellegrino of motorcitymusic.com - a mecca for Northern Soul vinyl collectors; Al Bell of Stax/Volt; Robert J. and Hedwig R. Stack; Captain Ned and Anne Pahl -- a sailor and his wife; Richard and Lyda Auxier; Paul Bauer, proprietor of Archer's Books in Kent, Ohio and biographer of Jim Tully; and Jim Fracassa of Midwest Video in Detroit.

A very special thank you to my three journalism mentors: Judy Spiegelman; Regina Jones and Loraine Alterman who gave me not only tons of encouragement but my first bylines. Look what you started! And muchos gracias to Rico Neller of *La Prensa* for keeping it alive.

However, can a mere "thank you" ever suffice for the enthusiasm, talent and sheer energy of Bill Baker, Neil Rushton and Glenn Gunton and their magnificent, no, make that brilliant job of producing this incredible book? If not, please repeat this sentence until exhausted.

There are far too many who are sadly no longer with us to see this book: my parents, Mildred and Harry Abrams, for raising me to be colorblind; my cousin Bea Fogelman, founder and director of the Entertainment Network, without whom *Memories of Motown* would never have been staged in Berlin in 2009 - I only wish she had lived to see it; Ron Murphy; Marilyn Bond; radio friends Bill Williams; "Long Tall Lean, Lanky" Larry Dean; "Frantic" Ernie Durham; Larry Dixon; Ollie McLaughlin; "Joltin' Joe" Howard; Dave Shafer; Mickey Shorr; Tom Clay and Joel Sebastian; so many members of the Motown family especially Michigan State Rep. George H. Edwards; "Pops" Gordy and Mrs. Berry Gordy, Sr; Gwen Gordy Fuqua; Loucye Gordy Wakefield; Stanley Mike Ossman; Thomas "Beans" Bowles of the Funk Brothers; Ronald White of the Miracles; superstars Marv Johnson; Mary Wells; Marvin Gaye and Flo Ballard; as well as Sanford Freed; Barbara Holliday of the *Detroit Free Press;* Bob McAleer and Carl Morgan of the *Windsor Star;* and two of the all-time great record promotion men: Bob Patton and Weldon McDougall III. I miss all of you.

If I have inadvertently left anyone's name off this acknowledgement list, it was unintentional and I sincerely apologize. You see, I'm getting older every day.

Al Abrams
June 2011

Addendum ➤

EXTRA! EXTRA! READ ALL ABOUT IT

opposite: "Memories of Motown," the musical I co-wrote with William "Mickey" Stevenson, and in which we both appeared as narrators, was a critical success at Berlin's Estrel Festival Center Jan. 7 - Feb. 2, 2009. The show starred Motown legends Martha Reeves, The Contours (featuring Sylvester Potts) and the Miracles. Our show was the only global celebration commemorating Motown's 50th birthday, and so at the stroke of midnight US time, we rolled out a birthday cake. Here I am wishing I could eat a slice before we went on stage. That's Sylvester to my left.

IF READING THE PRESS RELEASES that follow and the others throughout this book whets your appetite for more, you should try and visit my Motown archive at the University of Michigan's Bentley Historical Library in Ann Arbor. Not only will you find all of my Motown press releases available for research, but also those I wrote for Stax/Volt, Invictus/Hot Wax, Florence Ballard and other artists and labels I had the pleasure of representing. Karen Jania and the entire library staff are very friendly and always helpful.

If you are flying into Detroit to make a pilgrimage to the Motown Museum, Ann Arbor is a beautiful place to spend a day. In addition to the University of Michigan, it is loaded with music venues, great places to eat and some of the best used bookstores in North America. Ann Arbor is an hour from downtown Detroit and near Detroit's Metro Airport.

So please make it a point to take in both the Motown Museum, where it all started, and the Bentley Historical Library where you can spend hours immersed in Motown's legacy. Give me a call and let me know when you are coming -- maybe I can meet you at the Bentley and give you a guided tour.

Sometimes I think I should have been paying Berry just for letting me come into work at Hitsville every day and mingle with geniuses like Smokey, The Supremes, Holland-Dozier-Holland, Marvin, Stevie, Esther Edwards, Mickey Stevenson and Berry himself. Berry, if you are reading this, please put the phone down. It is too late. The statute of limitations has passed. I am not giving you my salary back. This was just a literary metaphor.

My dream job at Motown was to get publicity for the label. "Extra! Extra! Read All About It" sums up what my press releases - some of which follow - were trying to convey to fans in the pre-historic era before the Internet, Twitter, Facebook and other social media. Here are the very words that chronicle the relentless machine that The Supremes became, the divine West Coast discovery Brenda Holloway, the gritty Sax and Soul man Junior Walker, or the myriad of other Hitsville acts I had the privilege of working with on a daily basis.

You'll even find the press release for Jack Soo, the popular Japanese-American actor who recorded Ron Miller's classic "For Once In My Life" for the company long before Stevie but never saw it released! Jack, whose story is now beautifully told in the documentary You Don't Know Jack Soo by San Francisco award-winning filmmaker Jeff Adachi, never had any of his records released by Motown. Just to show you what a small world Motown was back then, Mort Persky of the Detroit Free Press, who wrote a great forward for this book, was the first person to ever hear "For Once in My Life" when Ron sang it for Mort and his wife one night at a dinner. Maybe I should have followed up the Tommy Good "March On Hitsville" with a similar protest by Jack Soo's legions of fans of his Barney Miller TV show? Think of the coverage I could have received after a mass protest by Japanese-American Soul fans!

Sound surreal? Looking back now, the whole incredible story of the jigsaw Berry created giving us all these incredibly talented pieces to fit together to make the greatest record label the world has ever seen seems crazy. It happened though, and I hope my book gives you an authentic taste of what went on behind the scenes at that magically and manically stupendous place.

As the book was ready to go to press, news came of my induction into the Michigan Rock and Roll Legends Hall of Fame. Thinking about myself as a legend will take some doing, but I am tremendously honored to follow in the footsteps of previous inductees Berry and Holland-Dozier-Holland. Hey, maybe that's what Esther Edwards was getting at when she gave me that "Big Feet" birthday card back in 1960!

It's kind of weird sometimes now being the story - in those *Hype & Soul* days, it was never just about me or any individual, not even Berry, Smokey, Eddie, Brian, Diana or Stevie. Instead it was about what I named "The Detroit Sound". In this marketing-driven era, they would categorize me for coming up with that name as corporate branding. But in reality, we were just living our dream.

As I've tried to explain so many times, we were just a bunch of kids making music. We had no idea we were making history. It was a thrill a moment.

September 10, 1964

NEWS RELEASE

BEATLES BOOST DETROIT

During the Beatles' hectic visit to Detroit, the British foursome found time to hold a televised press conference at which they were asked what did they like about Detroit.

The Beatles' unanimous reply was "TAMLA-MOTOWN RECORDS, and their artists". Among their favorites which the Beatles singled out for mention were MARVIN GAYE, SMOKEY AND THE MIRACLES, and the SUPREMES, who recently had the Number One Record in the country with "WHERE DID OUR LOVE GO".

Berry Gordy, Jr., president of TAMLA-MOTOWN, upon hearing of the tribute paid the artists by the Beatles, announced that he planned to record an album "THE SUPREMES SING A BIT OF LIVER-POOL", which will contain many "Beatle" tunes. The SUPREMES are currently embarking upon a European tour which will include an appearance, October 11th "at the Palladium"--British television's equivalent to the Ed Sullivan Show.

The Beatles have recorded many tunes which were first made popular by TAMLA-MOTOWN artists.

FROM: Hitsville, U.S.A.
        2648 West Grand Blvd.
        Detroit 8, Michigan
        871-3340 (Al Abrams)

May 11, 1964

FOR IMMEDIATE RELEASE

THE GIRL WHO BEAT THE BEATLES

Detroiter Mary Wells' Motown recording of "My Guy" this week became the Number 1 record on the nation's list of top tunes.

By edging out Louis Armstrong for the top spot, Mary Wells becomes the first female singer to "Beat the Beatles.

February 15, 1965

FROM: Motown Record Corporation
          2648 West Grand Boulevard
          Detroit, Michigan, 48208

For additional information
contact: Al Abrams (TR 1-3340)

MARVIN GAYE REVUE
RETURNS TO 20 GRAND

    Marvin Gaye, popular Detroit recording artist, opens a ten
day engagement at Detroit's Club 20 Grand on Friday, February 19th.
Featured on the bill with Marvin are: songstress Kim Weston,
The Spinners, and the Earl Van Dyke Band. Last year a similiar
show broke all existing house records for the 20 Grand according
to owner, Bill Kabbush.

    Negotiations are currently underway for Marvin Gaye to
fulfill many of the nightclub engagements left open by the death
of Sam Cooke. These include New York's Copacabana, and major
Las Vegas and Miami Beach clubs. Tentative plans are also being
made for Marvin to sing the Academy Award best song nominee
"My Kind Of Town" on the national telecast of the Oscar presenta-
tions in April. "My Kind Of Town" is from the musical film
"Robin And The Seven Hoods" which starred Frank Sinatra. The
tune was recorded by Marvin in his best selling Tamla album
"Hello Broadway".

March 15, 1965

FROM: Motown Record Corporation
       2648 West Grand Boulevard
       Detroit, Michigan 48208

For additional information
contact Al Abrams (TR 1-3340)

<u>FOR IMMEDIATE RELEASE</u>

MORE OF THE "DETROIT
SOUND" ON NATIONAL TELEVISION

        Junior Walker and his All Stars, the group whose recording
of **"SHOTGUN"** is rated as the number ten (10) best selling recording
in the nation this week (according to Billboard Magazine), will
appear on NBC-TV's "Hullabaloo" Tuesday, March 23rd at 8:30 P.M.
E.S.T.

        "Hullabaloo" is televised locally over WWJ-TV (channel four)

        Junior Walker and his All Stars are originally from Battle
Creek, Michigan. "SHOTGUN" is on the Soul label, a subsidiary of
Motown Record Corporation.

March 18, 1965

FROM: Motown Record Corporation
       2648 West Grand Boulevard
       Detroit, Michigan 48208

For additional information
contact Al Abrams (TR 1-3340)

FOR IMMEDIATE RELEASE

POPULAR VOCALIST MARVIN GAYE
HOSPITALIZED IN DETROIT

Marvin Gaye, popular Detroit vocalist, was admitted
to Detroit's Kirwood Hospital suffering from a virus infection
and a possible case of pneumonia.

His condition is described as being serious, though
not critical.

A hospital spokesman said the young singer was also
in a very "Rundown" condition. He will be hospitalized for an
indefinite period. The hospital has placed Gaye on a "NO CALLS,
NO VISITORS" basis.

Harvey Fugua, Marvin Gaye's road manager, is being
treated elsewhere for similiar symptoms. Gaye and Fugua had
planned to leave for England last Sunday accompanying THE TAMLA-
MOTOWN REVUE on it's current tour.

March 22, 1965

From: Motown Record Corporation
       2648 West Grand Boulevard
       Detroit, Michigan 48208

For additional information
contact Al Abrams (TR 1-3340)

FOR IMMEDIATE RELEASE

Detroit;s teenagers may still be able to see the Beatles "In Person" here in Detroit this summer.

International Talent Management Incorporated (ITMI), the booking agency arm of Detroit's Motown Record Corporation (whose Supremes this week again toppled the Beatles from the top of the nations best selling record charts), will attempt to add an appearance in Detroit to the tentative schedule already announced for the British foursome's second American tour, which begins August 15th.

Berry Gordy Jr., Motown president, is currently in London, and will be meeting with the Beatles' manager Brian Epstein, in an attempt to ensure Detroit teenagers of an opportunity to again see their idols perform.

During their first visit to Detroit last September, the Beatles named many of Detroit's Motown recording artists, including the Supremes, as their own personal favorite performers. The Beatles have also recorded many of the songs which had first reached popularity as recordings by Motown artists.

A spokesman for ITMI said "If we are able to bring the Beatles to Detroit, it will be Motown's way of saying "Thank You" to Detroit; and to the teenagers of Detroit, for the constant support that they have given to Detroit's recording artists".

March 23, 1965

FROM: Motown Record Corporation
        2648 West Grand Boulevard
        Detroit, Michigan 48208

For additional information
contact AL ABRAMS (TR 1-3340)

FOR IMMEDIATE RELEASE

HITSVILLE U.S.A.
TO HITSVILLE U.K.

Detroit's Supremes, who rank number One in Billboard's
music charts with their hit "STOP IN THE NAME OF LOVE" were
lauded by the British Press for their performance on the highly
prestigious television show "Sunday Night At The London Palladium" this week.

Clifford Davis, Television Editor for the London Daily
Mirror said the Supremes "Brought the best sound the Palladium
has had from a visiting group in years. They looked good, too"
The Mirror has the greatest circulation of any newspaper in the
Western World.

"STOP IN THE NAME OF LOVE" has risen to number 29 on
the English charts and many observers think it will duplicate
it's American chart performance.

The Supremes, along with the other members of the TAMLA-
MOTOWN REVUE left London this morning, to begin the portion
of the tour that will carry them throughout England and Scot-
land and climax with a one night appearance at the Olympia
Music Hall in Paris.

<u>FOR IMMEDIATE RELEASE</u>

DETROIT PERFORMERS TO HEADLINE
"AMERICANS IN HARMONY" SHOW

Detroit's internationally renouned recording stars
The Supremes will be joined by Marvin Gaye, The Four
Tops, Martha and the Vandellas, Tommy Good and The Tabs,
Jr. Walker and The All Stars, Brenda Holloway, The
Contours, Willie Tyler and Lester and The Choker Campbell
Orchestra for the "Americans In Harmony" entertainment
festival to be held at the Belle Isle Music Shell
Thursday evening, July 1st.

The purpose of the "Americans In Harmony" show is
to raise funds for eight deserving agencies and organi-
zations including The United Negro College Fund, The
Southern Christain Leadership Conference, and such
charitable Metropolitan Detroit projects as the Building Fund for the Detroit Center for the Handicapped,
The Detroit Urban League Guild and the School Volunteer
Service of the Detroit Board of Education. All of the
artists appearing are donating their services.

Admission to the show is free. Everyone giving a
free-will donation will receive a copy of the "Americans
In Harmony" souvenir book.

The Motor City can be proud of the unique fact that
a number of the international recording stars appearing
on the program are themselves native Detroiters who
have risen to fame through the locally based Motown
Record Corporation. This Benefit Show will present one
of the greatest 'pop' music packages ever assembled for
a live show.

June 25, 1965

From: Motown Record Corporation
2648 W. Grand Boulevard
Detroit, Michigan 48208

For additional information
contact Al Abrams (TR 1-3340)

<u>FOR IMMEDIATE RELEASE</u>

MARVELETTES FLY TO LONDON FOR
START OF EUROPEAN TOUR

Tamla recording artists, The Marvelettes, arrived
in London, England March 14th for a whirlwind week of
performances on British radio and television. Subsequently the trio flew to Amsterdam, Holland on June 21st
for the filming of Dutch television spectacular entitled
"The Marvelettes' Show" featuring numbers which the group
made famous such as "Please Mr. Postman", "You're My
Remedy", "Too Many Fish In The Sea" and their latest
release, "I'll Keep Holding On".

The last stop on the current Marvelettes' tour will
be Brussels, Belgium where the international TV show,
"Face All Public", will be exclusively allotted to the
trio's performance.

The Marvelettes have been constant favorites of
the European public since the advent of their first,
million selling disc, "Please Mr. Postman", and the public
excitement generated by their current trip gives every
indication that their latest release, "I'll Keep Holding
On", will find them again riding high in the international
hit parade.

270

July 8, 1965

FROM: Motown Record Corporation
      2648 West Grand Boulevard
      Detroit, Michigan 48208
For additional information contact
      Al Abrams (TR 1-3340)

FOR IMMEDIATE RELEASE

   Detroit's singing Supremes will guest on CBS-TV's
"Fanfare" on Saturday, July 24th. Al Hirt is the host of
the hour-long variety show, which is the summer replacement for the Jackie Gleason Show. "Fanfare" is viewed
locally over WJBK-TV (channel two) at 7:30 P.M. E.D.T.
The Supremes open a three week engagement at New York's
Copacabana on July 29th.

   Junior Walker and His All Stars (of Battle Creek,
Michigan) will appear on NBC-TV's "Hullabuloo" on Tuesday,
July 13th. This show is televised locally over WWJ-TV
(channel four) at 10:00 P.M. E.D.T. At the time this show
was first televised last spring, Junior Walker's recording
of "Shotgun" was the number two best selling record in the
nation. Junior Walker and His All Stars, along with
popular songstress Kim Weston will open a week long engagement at Detroit's Club 20 Grand on Friday, July 9th.

August 16, 1965

FROM: Motown Record Corporation
2648 West Grand Boulevard
Detroit, Michigan 48208

For additional information contact
Al Abrams (TR1-3340)

FOR IMMEDIATE RELEASE

MOTOWN ARTIST BRENDA HOLLOWAY
ON BEATLES U.S. TOUR

Brenda Holloway, the 18 year old popular vocalist whose
recording of "Every Little Bit Hurts" was a hit record in
1964, is one of the featured recording artists performing with
the Beatles on their second American tour. Brenda, a native
of Los Angeles, and a Motown recording artist, is the envy of
many teenagers, as she will be flying across the country with
the Beatles during their two week visit.

The Motown or "Detroit Sound" recording artists have long
been favorites of the Beatles. During their last visit to
America, the moptop quartet singled out the Supremes, Smokey
Robinson and the Miracles, and Marvin Gaye as their personal
favorites. The Beatles have also recorded several songs which
originally achieved popularity in the form of recordings by
Motown artists.

The opening concert by the Beatles held at New York's Shea
Stadium Sunday, August 15th was taped by a crew from the Ed Sullivan CBS-TV show. Highlights of the concert will be shown by Sullivan in a special show entirely devoted to the Beatles, which will
be televised on Sunday, September 12th. Brenda Holloway may thus
very well make her debut on the Ed Sullivan Show in the very good
company of the Beatles. (The Ed Sullivan Show is carried locally
by WJBK-TV, channel two, at 8:00 P.M. E.S.T.)

Incidentally, Detroit's singing Supremes are featured in the
repeat telecast of ABC-TV's "Hollywood Palace" this Saturday,
August 21st. This show is carried locally by WXYZ-TV, channel
seven, at 9:30 P.M. E.S.T. That same night, the Supremes will be
appearing live, in concert, at the Meadow Brook Pavilion of Oakland
University at Rochester, Michigan in a program designed to raise
money for scholarships for the University.

August 19, 1965

FROM: Motown Record Corporation
       2648 West Grand Boulevard
       Detroit, Michigan 48208

For additional information contact
       Al Abrams (TR 1-3340)

FOR IMMEDIATE RELEASE

Jack Soo, the Hollywood actor who portrayed Rocky, Tony Franciosa's valet on the ABC-TV "Valentines Day" series, has signed an exclusive recording contract with Detroit's Motown Record Corporation. Soo has appeared in several motion pictures including "Flower Drum Song" and "Who's Been Sleeping In My Bed". He has an upcoming role in the 20th Century Fox film "The Oscar" in which he portrays the buddy of Stephen Boyd. Soo will also be seen in a guest appearance on the first show of NBC-TV's "Wackiest Ship In The Army" to be televised Sunday, September 19th at 10:00 P.M. E.S.T. (WWJ-TV, channel four, will carry this show locally.) Even though Soo sang - in a Rex Harrison manner - on the sound track of "Flower Drum Song", he will be making his solo singing debut for Motown.

"Beach Ball, the second motion picture to feature the Supremes will be released nationally next month by Paramount pictures. Also appearing in the film are Ed "Kookie" Byrnes, the Righteous Brothers, and Chris Noel. The Supremes sing the movie's theme song.

Two popular Motown vocal groups will be appearing at the Michigan State Fair in Detroit next month. The Supremes are headlining the stage show at the Fair from September 2nd through the 6th. The Four Tops will also be performing at the Fair as part of a troupe of popular recording artists from the NBC-TV "Hullabaloo" show.

On the Beatles front, Motown recording artist Brenda Holloway is receiving a great deal of popular acclaim as she continues her two week tour with the Beatles. Brenda was the personal choice of the Beatles as the female vocalist to accompany the moptops on their American tour.

273

FROM: Motown Record Corporation
2648 West Grand Boulevard
Detroit, Michigan 48208

For additional information contact
Al Abrams (TR 1-3340)

FOR IMMEDIATE RELEASE

Detroiter, Kim Weston, will make her network television debut on NBC-TV's "Hullabaloo" show on Monday, October 25th. ("Hullabaloo" is carried locally by WWJ-TV, channel four, at 7:30 P.M. E.S.T.) Kim's record of "Take Me In Your Arms" is currently rated as number 57 in the nation according to Billboard Magazine.

Brenda Holloway will be appearing on the "Shivaree" show on Wednesday, October 27th. (WXYZ-TV, channel seven, carries this show locally at 7:00 P.M. E.S.T.) Brenda was the Beatles' choice as the only female vocalist to perform with the group during their last North-American tour. Brenda will also be seen on ABC-TV's "Shindig" this Thursday, October 21st.

The Supremes appearance on the CBS-TV Red Skelton Show has been rescheduled for airing on Tuesday, January 25th 1966. Incidentally, the Supremes concert at New York's Lincoln Center last week was a resounding success. All tickets for the performance had been sold out for a week before the concert. In addition to the Supremes, another Detroit (and Motown) vocal group, the Spinners performed on the Philharmonic's stage.

Bob Hope has indicated that he would like the Supremes to appear with Him on his tour of American military bases in Vietnam. Hope's tour will run from December 15th through the 30th, and highlights of the tour will later be televised as an hour and a half TV special. Among the performers scheduled to accompany Hope are Carroll Baker, Les Brown, (and his orchestra), and Jack Jones. The tour would be a reunion for the Supremes and Jack Jones, as both headlined the record-breaking live stage show at the Michigan State Fair in Detroit this summer.

Two of the songs in Paramount pictures "Beach Ball" were written by a talented trio of Detroiters; Brian Holland, Eddie Holland, and Lamont Dozier. Known in the music world as the team of Holland-Dozier, these three songwriters and producers have written more songs which have climbed to the Number One position than any other team of contemporary writers, including

(cont.)

(cont.)

the Beatles' Lennon and McCartney. According to Billboard
Magazine, the Holland-Dozier team has even written more hit
songs than Rodgers and Hart! The two songs, "Surfer Boy"
and the movie's theme "Come On To The Beach Ball With Me"
are sung by the Supremes, who are featured in the film. "Beach
Ball" is the second movie to feature songs by the Holland-
Dozier team. Previously, some of their compositions were incorporated into the score for the highly acclaimed "Nothing But
A Man". Paramount pictures is releasing "Beach Ball" nationally
this month.

September 29, 1965

FROM: Motown Record Corporation
      2648 West Grand Boulevard
      Detroit, Michigan 48208
For additional information contact
      Al Abrams (TR 1-3340)

<u>FOR IMMEDIATE RELEASE</u>

Detroit's Supremes and Four Tops have been requested to headline the first show of "Pop" recording artists to entertain American soldiers in Vietnam. The Pentagon announced plans today for the 16 day tour which will run from January 6th through 22th, 1966.

The reason for the tour, according to a spokesman is that "Most of the troops over in Vietnam are about 19 or 20 years old. They would prefer to be entertained by their favorite popular recording artists such as the Supremes, and the Four Tops, rather than by performers with whom they do not identify".

The first "Pop" music show to entertain our troops will make a number of appearances in the Dominican Republic on October 8th, 9th, and 10th. The tour spokesman was quoted as saying "There are 13,000 Marines over in Santo Domingo who haven't had entertainment and they're getting mighty lonely. Detroit's Martha and The Vandellas have been requested to entertain on this tour.

Bob Parkinson (originally from Toledo, Ohio) the top-rated Washington D.C. disc jockey and Program Director of radio station W.E.A.M. will act as Master of Ceremonies for both tours.

Motown Recording Artist Brenda Holloway will make her nightclub debut at "It's Boss" (the former Ciro's) on Hollywood's famed "Sunset Strip" October 19th through 25th. Another Motown Artist, Billy Eckstine, will be appearing at the Elmwood Casino in Windsor, Ontario, Canada from October 29th through November 18th.

From: Hitsville, U.S.A.
       2648 West Grand Blvd.
       Detroit, Michigan 48208
       871-3340 (Al Abrams)

November 24, 1965

FOR IMMEDIATE RELEASE

MOTOWN SIGNS ISLEY BROTHERS;
TOP R&B GROUP; TO EXCLUSIVE CONTRACT

THE ISLEY BROTHERS, one of the most exciting Rhythm and Blues Vocal Groups in the nation, have signed an exclusive recording contract with Detroit's Motown Record Corporation.

Originally with RCA Victor, THE ISLEY BROTHERS are perhaps best known for their original version of "Shout", which is still today regarded as a classic in the field of Rhythm and Blues Recordings. "Shout" was the first of Two Million Selling Records for THE ISLEY BROTHERS, the second being "Twist and Shout" was recorded on the Scepter Label. "Twist and Shout" went on to later fame when it was recorded by The Beatles. "Shout" also attained great popularity in a later recording by Joey Dee, one of the Pioneers of the "Twist" craze of a few years back.

MOTOWN will release a single and an album by THE ISLEY BROTHERS in the next few weeks.

FROM: Hitsville, U.S.A.
        2648 West Grand Blvd.
        Detroit, Michigan 48208
        871-3340 (Al Abrams)

December 8, 1965

FOR IMMEDIATE RELEASE

     The youngest recording artist on the Motown Label, eight year old LITTLE LISA will make her national television debut on NBC-TV's "Hullabaloo" on Monday, December 20th. Jerry Lewis will be the guest master of ceremonies for the show. "Hullabaloo" is televised locally by WWJ-TV, Channel Four, at 7:30 P.M., E.S.T.

     A reporter-photographer team from Look Magazine is following THE SUPREMES to their various engagements around the country this month, in preparation for a Look feature story on the nation's Number One Female Vocal Group. The team, Jack Hamilton, Look's Entertainment Editor; and Photographer Frank Dandridge, will follow THE SUPREMES through their concert date with Judy Garland at the Houston Astrodome on December 17th. THE SUPREMES and Miss Garland are the first entertainers to perform in the Domed Stadium.

     THE SUPREMES have received the honor of being selected by the United States Information Agency to appear on the cover of the official government publication Africa. The highly prestigious publication has been highly praised as an important means of communication between the United States and the many nations of Africa.

     THE SUPREMES will tape their first appearance on the new Sammy Davis Jr. NBC-TV Variety Show in New York, February 9th through 13th, 1966. The segment will be telecast on Friday, March 4th.

FROM: Hitsville, U.S.A.
2648 West Grand Blvd.
Detroit, Michigan 48208
Al Abrams (871-3340)

November 29, 1965

FOR IMMEDIATE RELEASE

WARREN MOORE OF MIRACLES VOCAL
GROUP TO WED IN DETROIT SATURDAY

Warren "Pete" Moore will no longer be the remaining "available" bachelor among THE MIRACLES, one of the nation's most popular vocal groups. Warren will marry Miss Bonita Tyson (also of Detroit) on Saturday, December 4th in a 6:00 p.m. wedding ceremony at the New Bethel Church, 8450 Linwood, in Detroit.

THE MIRACLES have recently become an "In Group" among themselves. Lead Singer, (and Motown's Vice President) Bill "Smokey" Robinson is married to the former Claudette Rogers, who still sings with the group on their recordings. Her brother Robert is married to the former Wanda Young who is a member of THE MARVELETTES, another popular Detroit vocal group. The future Mrs. Moore and Mrs. Ronald White, are not in show business.

SMOKEY ROBINSON AND THE MIRACLES recently completed a successful engagement at The Trip on Hollywood's Sunset Strip, where they received high critical acclaim. Their current record, My Girl Has Gone, is listed among the nation's Top 20 Best Sellers, and their latest album "Going To The Go-Go" is also on the National Charts.

SMOKEY ROBINSON AND THE MIRACLES will be seen on a number of National Television Shows this week, including an appearance on ABC-TV's popular daytimer "Where The Action Is", on Wednesday, December 1st.

279

FROM: Hitsville, U.S.A.
       2648 West Grand Blvd.
       Detroit, Michigan 48208
       871-3340 (Al Abrams)

January 3, 1966

FOR IMMEDIATE RELEASE

MOTOWN NOW NUMBER ONE
IN U.S. SINGLE RECORD SALES

Detroit's Motown Record Corporation is now Number One in total single record sales for the year of 1965. (According to Billboard Magazine tabulations).

Motown came up from Fourth place in 1963 to Second in 1964 to the then leader in single sales, Capitol Records, which holds U.S. rights to all recordings by the Beatles.

Founded in 1958 by former auto assembly worker, Berry Gordy Jr., Motown has grown to become the largest independent record manufacturer in the United States. Motown has given Detroit a new worldwide fame as the home of "The Detroit Sound" group of top record artists, THE SUPREMES, MARVIN GAYE, THE FOUR TOPS, STEVIE WONDER, THE TEMPTATIONS and others.

The charts which showed the Top Ten Records of 1965 did not contain any Beatles recordings, as compared to 1964 when the Beatles dominated the charts.

The chart of 1965's Top Ten Records, show three Motown recordings among the Top Ten.

The Top Ten Records for 1965 (according to Cashbox Magazine) were:

No. 1 - "Back In My Arms Again" - The Supremes (MOTOWN)
No. 2 - "Wooly Bully" - Sam The Sham and The Pharos
No. 3 - "Mr. Lonely" - Bobby Vinton
No. 4 - "I Can't Help Myself" - The Four Tops (MOTOWN)
No. 5 - "Satisfaction" - The Rolling Stones
No. 6 - "Downtown" - Petula Clark
No. 7 - "You've Lost That Lovin' Feeling" - Righteous Brothers
No. 8 - "Come See About Me" - The Supremes (MOTOWN)
No. 9 - "The In Crowd" - Ramsey Lewis
No. 10　"You Were On My Mind" - The We Five

1965 was a bad year for the Beatles.

A closer relationship between the Beatles and Motown is in the works. The Beatles have already requested that the team of Holland-Dozier-Holland, who have written and produced all of THE SUPREMES and FOUR TOPS' Number One Records, to write two songs especially for the Beatles.

The Beatles special 1965 Christmas and New Years record, which is sent only to their fans and is not available for airplay or for sale, features the Beatles singing Holland-Dozier-Holland's "It's The Same Old Song" popularized by Motown's FOUR TOPS.

THE SUPREMES' upcoming album "I Hear A Symphony" features a song entitled "Yesterday", as written by the Beatles' Lennon and McCartney. THE SUPREMES' new single, "My World is Empty Without You" (by Holland-Dozier-Holland) is also featured in the album.

Highlighting THE SUPREMES' engagement at Miami's Eden Roc Hotel last week, was their appearance in Miami's Orange Bowl Parade on New Year's Eve. THE SUPREMES rode in the "Life In Gay Paree" float (three floats behind the Orange Bowl Queen) and were seen by millions as NBC-TV televised the

Parade on New Year's Eve and again on New Year's Day.

Detroiters last week had the opportunity to see
SMOKEY ROBINSON AND THE MIRACLES perform for the first time
since their spectacular success at the Trip on Hollywood's
Sunset Strip. The group was called in to headline the 1965
edition of the Motortown Revue at Detroit's Fox Theatre when
headliner MARVIN GAYE suddenly became ill. GAYE was KO'D with
an attack of Tracheo-Bronchitis, the same illiness that plagued
President Johnson earlier in 1965. This was the second time
in nine months that GAYE had been forced to cancel engagements
due to illness.

A television crew from Canada's top-rated "This
Hour Has Seven Days" show will arrive in Detroit on January
18th to film THE SUPREMES during their engagement at The
Roostertail Club in Detroit. CBC-TV will televise the segment
as a portion of a special program entirely devoted to THE
SUPREMES during their hometown engagement, filming THE SUPREMES
at their homes, at work, and at Detroit's Motown Record Studios.
Fortunately, Detroiters will be able to see the show over
CKLW-TV, Channel 9, in Windsor, Ontario. CBC-TV was inspired to
do the show after reading a two-part interview by Toronto Star
Writer, Gerry Barker, with THE SUPREMES and Berry Gordy, Jr.

FROM: Hitsville, U.S.A.
2648 West Grand Blvd.
Detroit, Michigan 48208
871-3340 (Al Abrams)

June 21, 1966

FOR IMMEDIATE RELEASE

TEMPTATIONS TO RECORD RADIO SPOT
FOR DOMESTIC PEACE CORPS

THE TEMPTATIONS, popular exponents of
the Motown Sound, who have recently lined up
two plum engagements - an appearance with Adam
West, TV's Batman, at New York's Shea Stadium
on June 25th, and a concert with THE SUPREMES
at the Forest Hills (New York) Stadium on August 20th - will soon be heard over the nation's
air waves in a special radio campaign in connection with the Federal Government for the
Domestic Peace Corps.

The message asking youngsters to
pitch in with the Peace Corps Program to help
their country and themselves, will be coupled

-more-

283

with a portion of THE TEMPTATIONS' hit recording
of "Ain't Too Proud To Beg" and distributed by
the Federal Government to every radio station
across the U.S.A. and broadcast for several
weeks this summer as a spot announcement for
the Domestic Peace Corps.

THE TEMPTATIONS will tape the message
when they arrive in New York on June 23rd
(Thursday) preceding their appearance at Shea
Stadium.

THE TEMPTATIONS are again following
in the footsteps of their Motown stable-mates
THE SUPREMES, who last year recorded the successful "Things Are Changing" radio jingle for the
President's committee on Equal Employment Opportunity.

"Ain't Too Proud To Beg" is listed by
Billboard Magazine as the Number 20 best
selling record in the nation this week.

-more-

THE TEMPTATIONS, THE FOUR TOPS, and
CHRIS CLARK have been added to the line-up of
Motown recording artists to be appearing in the
"A Tribute to Detroit" special presentation of
ABC-TV's "Where The Action Is," which is to be
filmed at Detroit's Roostertail Nightclub.
The taping date has been changed from Friday,
July 1st to Thursday, June 30th, so that these
additional artist could be available for the
show.

FROM: Hitsville, U.S.A.
         2648 West Grand Blvd.
         Detroit, Michigan   48208
         871-3340 (Al Abrams)

July 7, 1966

FOR IMMEDIATE RELEASE

SUPREMES' DIANA ROSS
EMERGES AS AUTHOR

Diana Ross, the lead singer of The Supremes, America's Number One Vocal Group, and Ringo Starr of The Beatles have both written forewords for the upcoming autobiography of Murray "The K" Kaufman. The tome, titled "Murray The K Tells It Like It Is, Baby" will be published by Harcourt, Brace and World in October.

Kaufman is an ex-New York disc jockey best remembered for hosting the controversial "It's What Happening Baby" special on CBS-TV last year, which received criticism from Senator Everett Dirksen and other T.V. critics.

Additional forewords to Kaufman's book are contributed by Willie Mays, Sybil Burton and Bob Dylan.

Michigan Rock and Roll Legends
www.michiganrockandrolllegends.com

MICHIGAN ROCK AND ROLL LEGENDS is an online hall of fame dedicated to the artists and songs that are part of the state's rich and diverse musical legacy. MRRL was created in 2005 to help preserve this vital aspect of Michigan's cultural history. It is hoped that the site will not only give recognition to those important contributors to the rock and roll movement in the state, but will also keep the spirit of Michigan music burning bright.

Honorary Inductions to MRRL were started in 2008 to give credit to the people behind-the-scenes who were significant contributors to the history of Michigan rock and roll. These would include artists, photographers, label owners, publicity directors, music promoters, session musicians, songwriters, and record producers – important people who may not be household names to most Michigan music fans.

Al Abrams was Michigan Rock and Roll Legends' Honorary Inductee in 2011. Al's work as the national promotion director for Tamla Records and Jobete Music, and later as director of advertising and public relations for Motown was instrumental in helping the company become one of the most successful record labels in the history of popular music. Past Honorary Inductees from the Motown family include label owner Berry Gordy Jr. in 2009, and the songwriting/production team of Holland-Dozier-Holland in 2010.

Abrams' efforts also benefitted almost all the stellar list of Motown artists who have been inducted into MRRL from 2005 through 2011 via email vote. These Artist Inductees are: The Four Tops, Marvin Gaye, Martha & The Vandellas, Rare Earth, Smokey Robinson (solo), Stevie Wonder, The Supremes, The Temptations, Mary Wells, The Miracles, Jr. Walker & The All Stars, The Marvelettes, The Funk Brothers, and Diana Ross (solo). Al Abrams also promoted or did publicity for many of the Motown recordings that have been voted Legendary Michigan Songs from 2007 through 2011: My Girl – The Temptations; Do You Love Me – The Contours; I Heard It Through The Grapevine – Marvin Gaye; The Tracks Of My Tears – The Miracles; Dancing In The Street – Martha & The Vandellas; What's Going On – Marvin Gaye; Money – Barrett Strong; My Guy – Mary Wells; War – Edwin Starr; Baby I Need Your Loving – The Four Tops; Ain't No Mountain High Enough – Diana Ross and also by Marvin Gaye & Tammi Terrell; Shotgun – Jr. Walker & The All Stars; Superstition – Stevie Wonder; Please Mr. Postman – The Marvelettes; Heat Wave – Martha & The Vandellas; Baby Love – The Supremes; and I Can't Help Myself – The Four Tops.

Gary (Dr. J) Johnson
"Rock and Roll Historian and Teacher"

A PARTING WORD...

Looking back, perhaps it was fate that the publication of this book has been so delayed. During the final round of proof reading before going to the printers, press stories began to emerge that the Motown record label was to be shuttered.

Thus, it is both ironic and appropriate that *Hype & Soul* should be published now, giving an insight as to how I became Motown's first employee in 1959 and helped Berry Gordy establish his fledgling company as a household name, ultimately becoming arguably the greatest record label of all. As proof that we were doing something right, consider this: Motown will endure forever as the only record label in history whose trademark became a noun -- even in the venerable Oxford Dictionary -- lending its name to an entire genre of music.

I sincerely hope this book will be a fitting and lasting tribute to everyone who made the dream become a reality.

Motown R.I.P. - Long live Motown.